OUR LIFE OF GRACE

The just shall flourish like the palm tree:
he shall grow up like the cedar of Libanus.

(Ps. 91:13)

OUR
LIFE
OF
GRACE

By CANON F. CUTTAZ

Translated by ANGELINE BOUCHARD

FIDES PUBLISHERS ASSOCIATION
CHICAGO, ILLINOIS

Manufactured by American Book–Stratford Press
75 Varick St., New York, New York

55

Contents

PART TWO / THE EFFECTS OF GRACE
DISTINCT FROM IT

Foreword

ADVANTAGES OF UNDERSTANDING THE EFFECTS OF GRACE

Upon entering the château of Thorens, the first thing a pilgrim sees as he crosses the threshold is the pictorial genealogical table of the de Sales family, which proudly traces its ancestry as far back as the days of Charlemagne. Obviously members of the family placed this table there to remind themselves, whenever they entered their home, of the nobility of character and life that their noble lineage demanded of them.

The Christian must also be shown the picture of the spiritual grandeur conferred upon him by grace, so that he may be constantly inspired to elevate his sentiments, his ideas, and his acts to the height of his supernatural dignity. According to the Apostle St. John, there is no better stimulus: "Whoever is born of God [if he knows and understands the price of such a benefit] does not commit sin, because His seed abides in him and he cannot sin, because he is born of God" (I Jn. 3:9; cf. also 3:6).

There is no question here, of course, of an absolute impossibility, inasmuch as the state of grace does not remove the freedom to do wrong. Rather is it a moral impossibility,

1

a great sense of fittingness, a supreme and very efficacious motive. The Beloved Apostle means that the child of God should not sin any more, and that in fact he would not sin if he realized the value of the benefits grace procures for him and that his sin would destroy.[1] If he had a practical knowledge of the splendor of his state, the just man could no longer agree to give this state up. He would do everything to remain in it and to make it more permanent.

Why, then, do so many Christians have such a low opinion of grace? Why do they so easily resign themselves to losing it, and why do they experience no anxiety and almost no regret when they are deprived of it for months? Do they think sin is a mere trifle? Do they think so little of the sacraments, good works, merit, the priesthood, and of their Redemption by Christ? Do they have so little understanding of dogma and do they practice Christian morality so badly because they are ignorant of the value of grace and its benefits? Do they even suspect that grace exists? How could they measure what they lose in losing grace and failing to regain it, and what they gain by preserving it and by striving to increase it? The answer to all these questions is this: *They do not know the gift of God!*

Even the better educated Christians think that to sin is "to fall out of favor with God," [2] and to merit His punishments in this world and in the next. That seems to be all they know about it. Granted such feeble motives, how would they be adequately armed to conquer temptations, to accomplish the sacrifices of duty, to demand of themselves the efforts implicit in all spiritual progress? No one will renounce the present, concrete, and tangible goods that sin offers if the benefits of virtue do not exert a greater attraction upon the

---

[1] Pointing out the benefits we receive through grace also points to the ills sin brings in its wake. The benefits of grace are a measure of the evils of sin. Thus, when we consider the effects of grace we are also dealing with the effects of sin.

[2] We have approached a number of persons in various walks of life and asked them this question: "What is the state of grace?" In almost every instance the answer was: "It is being free from sin." The implication of this answer is that grace is wholly a negative thing, as if the soul in the state of grace were empty, whereas in reality it overflows with riches!

will. No one will remain in the state of grace or return to it through penance unless he sees great advantages in it.

But the advantages and benefits of grace must be known. *We do not desire what we do not know.* If we are to strive to preserve grace and to increase it, we must have a high esteem for it. We must know what it is, what it accomplishes in a soul, what it is worth to the one who possesses it both for the present life and for the life to come.

It would seem that too often a negative approach is taken to the spiritual life, rather than a positive one. There seems to be too much emphasis on the sin that destroys it and not enough on the riches that constitute it. And yet how much more fruitful a positive approach would be!

St. Paul compares faith to a great shield (Eph. 6:16) that protects us against even the most violent temptations by furnishing the will, by means of the truths it teaches, with motives and resources of strength to resist and triumph. And among these teachings, the most efficacious are those that concern grace and its effects.

If Christians were better informed, they would measure the ravages of sin with greater exactitude. They would avoid sin not only for fear of future punishment, but for fear of present sufferings which have a far greater impact upon the will. They would tell themselves that to commit sin would not only be to expose themselves to hell in the next life but also to deprive themselves in this life of immense spiritual riches. They would push themselves to acts of virtue with the conviction that while these acts give a right to eternal rewards, they also have wonderful effects here and now.

Having a better understanding of the price of grace, they would better understand the price of all that produces it. First, they would realize the value of baptism, which is the primary source of grace, and look upon their baptism as one of the most important events in their life; they would also be less inclined to delay the baptism of their children for some trifling reason. Besides, they would understand the value of penance, and have prompter recourse to it after sin so as to heal the wounds of sin at once. They would understand the value of Communion, which is such an easy and fruitful means of preserving and increasing grace. And the value of Holy Orders, whose principal purpose is to communicate the power to give grace. Indeed, they would better understand the worth of all the sacraments, all of which procure or increase it; the worth of everything that is a means of obtaining, preserving, and intensifying grace; the great price of actual grace, of prayer, effort, sacrifice, and good works.

Given an understanding of grace, Christians would have deeper appreciation for the benefit of the Redemption which merited grace for us, and for the Church which distributes grace to us. They would have a deeper and more exact understanding of Christianity. For everything in Christianity is a function of grace. Grace is the center from which radiates the light that makes Christianity luminous and the beauty that is its greatest attraction. The synthesis of Christianity is centered upon grace; and it is through grace that Christianity is explained.

As long as we are ignorant of the meaning of grace, we are ignorant of the elevation, transformation, and wonderful enrichment it works within men. For grace is the best source of the Christian's pride, happiness, and moral power, of his courage in trials and his zeal in striving for virtue. Ignorance of grace is ignorance of what is most fruitful for our devotion; of the dogmas best suited to stir the heart and will to good; of the most consoling, and inspiring truths of our religion. It is ignorance of the most touching manifestations of God's love for man, of the intimate and affectionate relationship grace establishes between God and us, and remembrance of which so greatly facilitates recollection, prayer, and the interior life.

*   *   *

May a more complete and suitable teaching of grace dissipate these paralyzing shadows and enable the Christians of our time to know as much about grace as did the faithful during the first centuries of Christianity. The Apostles, whose Epistles were full of this subject, and the Fathers, who alluded to this doctrine as accepted by all without question, established other truths and drew practical conclusions from

the doctrine of grace. In many prayers and rites of the primitive Church, the liturgy assumed grace was understood, for
example in the ceremonies of baptism and the choice of
baptismal names.

Why should the doctrine of grace be less accessible to our
contemporaries? Are they less receptive than the newly-con-
verted dockers and fishermen of Corinth and Salonica, who
were still unfamiliar with the sublime truths of Christianity?
Do they not, on the contrary, have the advantage of a long
Christian heritage? Is not the enlightening action of the Holy
Spirit on the baptized as powerful as ever? Does He not continue to make them say: "Father! Father!" and teach them
to grasp, appreciate, and understand their sonship? Does He
not continue to form within them the mind of the children
of God, to give them understanding and the taste for the
mysteries and marvels of grace, to sow within them a hidden
attraction to these supernatural realities?

What priest has not discovered for himself the remarkable
facility of certain souls of good will, even without training,
to penetrate these matters, to learn and to meditate about
them with holy eagerness? These souls are constantly increasing in number. They take an interest in these questions,
read works about them, and nourish their spiritual life with
them. (The success of the present work, in its fifth printing
in France almost without benefit of publicity, is proof of it.)

The reason is that these are difficult times for Christians.
Anyone who wants to live his faith with sincerity and logic
must demand of himself struggle, sacrifice, and great effort.
Irreligion and the corruption of naturalism or secularism
are broadcast everywhere. Many environments have become
hostile to religion. No one can preserve his religious convictions, his virtue, his piety, and even less conquer them, without the most fortifying spiritual food which the faithful,
under the impulsion of the Spirit, instinctively seek in the
theology of grace.

If this movement continues to grow, one need not be a
prophet to foresee a magnificent renewal of Christian life ·
and a beautiful harvest of saints.

It was to contribute, according to our capacities, to this

flowering of holiness that we published this work. The experience of the ministry has shown us that there are many
practicing Catholics who would need very little to remain
in the state of justice and to demand of themselves the extra
energy necessary to observe all the major Commandments.
They would certainly find this extra spurt of energy in a
more enlightened conviction concerning the *effects of grace,*
inasmuch as each of these effects is a precious good and consequently a powerful incentive to avoid sin.

We should like to help our colleagues, overburdened with
the work of their ministry, to teach these effects. Is it not
our Savior's mission, by His own avowal (Jn. 10:10) to give
grace, supernatural life, to men and make it grow in them,
to bring it to those who do not have it and to increase it in
those who do? Did He not become man and dwell among
us in order to provide those who receive Him with the means
of becoming the children of God and to make them share
in the fullness of His divine life?

This is also the mission of the priest, who takes Christ's
place. His work is to pour grace into souls and to intensify
it. Grace is the reason for the priest's ministry, the goal of
his powers, the object of his actions, the reason for his vast
beneficence.

The peoples of the world will value his priesthood only if
they value grace. They will appreciate the worth of his services only if they realize the spiritual treasure they receive
from him. They will be grateful to him only if they understand the benefits they receive through his intervention.

Priests of Christ, my dear brothers, if you want to restore
to your functions the aureole with which the centuries of
faith surrounded them, instruct your faithful on the value
of the heavenly gifts that you are bringing them. Make the
supernatural riches they receive through you shine forth in
all their splendor. Show them the price of divine life.

It must be your desire to lead to and preserve in the state
of grace all or at least most of the souls under your care. It
is your duty to work at it with all your strength, so that when
you leave them you can confidently repeat the Master's

words: *"Those whom Thou hast given Me, I guarded"* (Jn. 17:12).

How beautiful would be the parish where this dream came true! With what pleasure heaven could look down upon it, what a reward for the apostle, the devoted artisan of this marvel! Thank God, this dream is a reality in certain regions.

In France and in all Christian nations, there are souls scattered all over the land that live in God's friendship, some of them having never lost this friendship since their baptism and others having returned to it after varying intervals of time. For example there are French villages—in Anjou, Vendée, Brittany, Normandy, Flanders, Provence (and we could add villages in Italy, Ireland, Spain, and Canada) where the majority of the population may well be in the state of grace.

Even though "the masses have become materialistic and think only of financial gain and selfish pleasures, . . . one cannot associate with groups of young people without noticing the stirrings of souls that aspire only to rise. An elite exists. . . . It is characterized by a true sense of Christianity, a desire to strive for perfection and to live in grace. Those who make up this elite sense that their Christianity will be complete only when the state of grace has become the normal state for them" (M. Barrault, *La sainte France contemporaine*).

The state of grace should be the normal state of all baptized persons, as it was for the first Christians, whom the Apostles called *"saints."*

Our young Catholics are understanding this more and more.

It is up to you priests to multiply this elite, not only among your young people but in all groups of your faithful (cf. an exhortation by Cardinal Mercier to his priests on this subject, *Note* on p. 13 below).

It is our view that most theology books give too little space to sanctifying grace. They devote only a few pages to it, while filling many pages with controversies on actual grace.[3]

Controversies are useful. They must be studied. But there

---

[3] Cf. *Note* containing a passage by Father d'Herbigny, p. 14 below.

is something else in theology which is still more useful. That
is the substantial food of the soul, the source of light and
strength. Such, we feel, is the study and meditation upon
sanctifying grace and its effects.

That is why we have relegated to *Notes* most of the discussions that have come across our path. We felt it would
be more fruitful to insist on the moral and mystical consequences of the effects of grace, to inspire a solid conviction
of their reality, and to dispel the too frequently held view
that these are pious imaginings of Christian devotion.[4]

Dear reader, the purpose of this work is to strengthen
within you the conviction that these are magnificent, sublime, and concrete realities, with which you must nourish
your soul and illumine as with a radiant sun the days of
your earthly pilgrimage. And by giving you a more complete
knowledge of these superabundant riches of grace, of which
St. Paul speaks (Eph. 1:7, 2:7), by helping you to explore
the wonders and the vision of the divine splendors that are
within you, we hope to help you to free yourselves from the
clutch of external things and to live with a more intense
interior life. For it is even truer of the just man than of the
daughter of the king extolled by the Psalmist, that " all his
glory is within" (Ps. 44:14).

Only the heavenly Bridegroom of the soul can see all its
ravishing beauty. But He has deigned to draw back a corner
of the veil that hides this beauty from us, and through
Revelation to give us glimpses of it that fill our astonished
hearts with grateful admiration.

May the "Mother of divine grace" bless these pages, and
obtain that they may lead us to a greater esteem for the state
of grace.

---

4 Father de Ramière, in his work *La divinisation du chrétien,* remarks that
"Many Christians, while believing in the divine promises, cannot decide to
accept them in their magnificence. They probably fear to attribute too much
goodness to the One whom they call 'the good God.' They convince themselves that His promises are somewhat exaggerated when they hear they
have been called to be the associates of the divine nature, the adopted
brothers of Jesus Christ, the sons of the Heavenly Father, to live even now
by God's life and to enjoy His happiness eternally. Most of them see only
figures of speech and pious hyberboles in such words." Indeed, for some,
the terms "mystical" and "mythical" are synonymous.

LOGICAL ORDER OF PRESENTATION

Chapter 1. Grace confers upon the just man the capacity to possess God in glory.

Chapter 2. This capacity is a participation in the divine nature; whence the soul's resemblance with God and its supernatural beauty.

Chapters 3 and 4. Whoever participates in the nature of God has become his adopted child, the brother of Christ and of the other just, and the object of God's love.

Chapter 5. But so much love and favors are the sign of God's complete forgiveness: grace justifies, quickens, rectifies, and sanctifies.

Chapter 6. This love induces the Father to unite Himself with His child, to live with him, and to dwell in him.

Chapter 7. In deifying the "to be" of the just man, grace also deifies his "to act"; and this it does through the infused virtues.

Chapter 8. The exercise of these virtues, the presence and and love of the Father involve actual graces.

Chapter 9. To make a filial response to grace, the gifts are necessary.

Chapter 10. Deified in his "to be" and in his "to act," the just man possesses a supernatural power of glorification and impetration.

Chapters 11 and 12. He also possesses the power to merit.

Chapter 13. And the power to make satisfaction.

Chapter 14. All this constitutes an intense and very precious supernatural life. In short: 1) the deification of the just man in his essence and in his powers of action; 2) the supernatural fruitfulness of his activity.

THE DIVISIONS OF THIS STUDY OF GRACE

These effects of grace could be grouped into three categories, constituting as it were three sections of the work.

The first would include those that are so closely related to grace that they seem to be identified with it. The theologians call them *"formal"* effects: aptitude for glory, participation in the nature of God, supernatural sonship, justification.

In the second group are those effects which, although they necessarily derive from grace, are absolutely distinct from it: the dwelling of God in the soul, the infused virtues, the actual graces, and the gifts of the Holy Spirit.

The third category includes those effects whose effective realization is conditioned upon the subject's cooperation. Anyone who has grace is necessarily a child of God, necessarily endowed with the infused virtues, the gifts. But he does not necessarily glorify God, he does not necessarily obtain favors, he does not necessarily make satisfaction and gain merit. To accomplish these things, he must put into act the capacities that he has received through grace. Hence, these last-named effects apply only to adults.

In his treatise on grace, St. Thomas reduces the first two groups of effects to a single category, and uses only two categories which constitute two functions of grace.[5]

1. Inasmuch as grace justifies the soul, heals it, and makes it agreeable to God, deifies our "to be" and our "to act," it is called *operating grace.*

2. Inasmuch as grace acts with us, concurs in our operation, it is called *cooperating grace.*

"If grace [actual grace and also habitual grace] is taken for God's gratuitous motion whereby He moves us to meritorious good, it is fittingly divided into operating and cooperating grace. But if grace is taken for the habitual gift, then again there is a double effect of grace. . . . The first of which is *being,* and the second, *operation.* . . . And thus habitual grace, inasmuch as it heals and justifies the soul, or makes it pleasing to God, is called operating grace. But inasmuch as it is the principle of meritorious works, which spring from the free-will, it is called cooperating grace" (*Summa,* Ia IIae, q. 111, a. 2, c.).   *   *   *

Depending on the needs of the souls to whom they addressed themselves, and above all on their background and

5 Cf. the *Note* on St. Thomas' views on grace, p. 14 below.

their intellectual propensities, even divinely inspired authors stressed one or the other group of effects. It seems that these writers can be divided into two rather distinct schools, whose divergencies we should not exaggerate; far from being contradictory, they complement one another and are in perfect accord.

One school would be that represented by St. John and the Greek Fathers; the other would be the school represented by St. Paul and St. Augustine.

"St. John is absorbed in the contemplation of the divine life communicated to men by Jesus Christ. He presents grace as a new nature that dwells in us and, raising us above our earthly condition, makes us sons of God. St. Paul, at least the St. Paul of the Epistle to the Romans, insists on the redemption and conversion of sinful man. He seems to conceive of grace above all as a divine help given from heaven purely out of mercy, that heals the wounded will, changes it, brings it back to the good with gentleness and above all with wonderful power.

"These two conceptions of grace might readily be called the 'physical' and the 'moral' conceptions of grace. . . . St. John is principally concerned with man's *elevation* through the life of grace, and St. Paul's concern is with *healing*. The Johannic conception was developed chiefly by the Greek Fathers, and the Pauline conception by St. Augustine. The former view was admirably systematized by the Scholastics; the latter was exaggerated and distorted by Luther and the Jansenists" (Rousselot, in *Recherches de science religieuse,* Vol. XVIII, 1928, pp. 87 and 103). But there is no opposition between these theories of grace, for a careful and intelligent reading of the texts shows:

1. That St. John constantly presupposes the medicinal aspect of grace, that the nature elevated and deified is first of all a wounded, sick, and lost nature, and that birth according to the Spirit is a rebirth.

2. That St. Paul's theology cannot be limited to a single chapter from one of his Epistles; that justifying faith is not the whole of his religion; that beneath it lies a fund of ideas concerning grace and salvation which can be summed up quite

accurately in these three words: divinization, communion, mysteries.

3. That with St. John as with St. Paul, the implicit doctrine is very readily harmonized with the doctrine that is explicitly set forth.

Throughout the Old Testament and even more in the New, the word "just" is opposed to the word "sinner" and signifies the soul that is faithful to divine law and a friend of God. "Justice" is synonymous with holiness. To "justify" is to make someone pass from the state of sin to the state of grace.

Abraham asked God: "Wilt Thou destroy the just with the wicked?" And God answered: "If I find in Sodom fifty just within the city, I will spare the whole place for their sake" (Gen. 18:23, 26). Here the word *just* is opposed to *wicked*.

Through the lips of the prophet Ezechiel, the Holy Spirit Himself has defined the just man:

> If a man be just, and do judgment and justice, and have not eaten upon the mountains, nor lifted up his eyes to the idols of the house of Israel: and hath not defiled his neighbour's wife, . . . and hath not wronged any man: but hath restored the pledge to the debtor, hath taken nothing away by violence: hath given his bread to the hungry, and hath covered the naked with a garment: . . . Hath withdrawn his hand from iniquity, and hath executed true judgment between man and man: Hath walked in My commandments, and kept My judgments, to do truth: he is just, he shall surely live, saith the Lord God (Ez. 18:5-9).

The word "just" likewise signifies purity and holiness for the Psalmist. "Do not enter into judgment with thy servant: for in thy sight no man living shall be justified" (Ps. 142:2).

The sacred books find no greater praise to give Noe and Joseph than to call them "just." Joseph was "a just man" (Mt. 1:19). "Noe was a just and perfect man" (Gen. 6:9).

The word "just" recurs very often, especially in the Psalms, Proverbs, Wisdom, Ecclesiastes, and also in the Gospels and Epistles. It is the title that even Pilate and his wife gave to Christ (Mt. 27:24), as did the Acts of the Apostles (3:14), and St. John (I Jn. 2:1).

Our Lord uses the word "just" to designate the saints and the elect (Mt. 5:45; 9:13; 10:41; 13:43; 25:37,46; Lk. 14:14; 15:7).

Likewise, St. Peter (I 3:18), St. Paul (Rom. 5:19). This Apostle often uses the substantive "justice" as a synonym of holiness, of the state of grace: (Rom. 1:17; 6:21,22; 4:11; 5:17; 10:6; II Cor. 3:9; 5:21; 9:10; Gal. 2:21; 3:21; 5:5; Phil. 1:11; 3:6,9; Eph. 4:24; 5:9; I Tim. 6:11).

I Pet. 2:24; II Pet. 1:1.

I Jn. 2:29; 3:7; Jas. 3:18; Heb. 11:33.

According to the inspired author of the Epistle to the Hebrews, "Now my just one lives by faith" (Heb. 10:38) and God is pleased with him.

The proper name of the soul in the state of grace is therefore "just." It is a name that should be dear to Christian devotion and known by all.

The word "just" in its rich terseness encompasses the whole of this work.

Our title is "Our Life of Grace," and not "the State of Grace," to stress the fact that grace in itself is not only a permanent but also a dynamic reality, a principle of intense activity and not simply a "static" condition as might be suggested by the word "state."

May we live this Life in all its intensity.

*   *   *

Note on Cardinal Mercier's views on grace (see p. 7 above):

Cardinal Mercier said to his priests during an ecclesiastical retreat (*La vie intérieure*, 6th Conference):

"I beg of you during your mental prayer to draw from the inexhaustible sources of this treasure that we are accustomed to condense into a single word: grace, sanctifying grace. Assimilate this doctrinal substance of Catholic teaching, for it is the only one that it is absolutely necessary to know and to make part of one's life, the only one that must be given as food to nourish what is best, healthiest, and purest in the baptized souls of your flock. Oh! Say to yourselves and to your faithful that only the riches of grace matter; for without sanctifying grace there is no salvation.

"Therefore, preach this truth instantly, lovingly, to the children in your catechism classes. Tell them that grace is the precious pearl of which the Gospel speaks, and that in order to buy it we must give little thought to all the rest. Teach the sinner that mortal sin is called "mortal" because it kills within us this life of grace that is the only true life. You are not forbidden to influence them through the motive of fear of death and of hell. You must at certain moments have recourse to this extreme means. But in the habitual course of your sermons and your spiritual direction, you must lay greatest stress on the immensity of the divine love that reveals to us the immeasurable extent of God's munificence, and the unparalleled disaster that is visited upon the Christian soul by the frightful crumbling of the edifice of grace, at the moment when the will has the misfortune to commit mortal sin cold-bloodedly, with deliberation and full consent."

Note on the Controversies over Actual Grace (see p. 7 above):

To quote Father d'Herbigny, *Recherches de S. R.*, 1920, p. 138: "In the treatise on grace, does it not often happen that the polemics of the systems usurp class-time and leave little time for an appreciative study of sanctifying grace? Certain manuals scarcely mention the presence of the Holy Spirit in the soul in the state of grace, that divine gift that is God Himself, as St. Thomas loved to repeat; they pass over the prodigious love that edifies us. And yet the Fathers contemplated and commented upon these truths with rapture; and Peter Lombard, after St. Bernard, and the Victorians, stressed them to the point of exaggeration. The soul's whole effort and time are exhausted by discussions on the nature of the facts that prepare this state of grace. In this marvelous treatise on God's union with men and with their activity, certain professors find a way of speaking above all of human divisions, rivalries, and oppositions! And does it not happen that the heat of the conflict sometimes grieves the Holy Spirit and hampers His action? Although He is the soul's Guest and divine Helper, toward whom the whole treatise should converge, He is passed over almost in silence."

Note on the Divisions of Grace, according to St. Thomas (see p. 10 above):

St. Thomas discusses grace at the end of his *Prima Secundae,* to complete his general study of morals, and to lay the foundations of his detailed study of morals in his *Secunda Secundae.*

After having shown that God is our supreme end, the end that must assure our beatitude, and that our acts must all be directed toward Him, he specifies the conditions for the efficacy of our acts; their internal and external principles: the law and grace. Then he concerns himself with the particular virtues and gifts that flow from grace. Of all the conditions required if our acts are to lead us to God, grace is the most important.

The *Tertia Pars* and a part of the *Supplement* are devoted to the sacraments as sources of grace. And the work is rounded out by a study of the last ends, the eternal flowering or privation of grace.

The holy Doctor speaks of the virtues and gifts in the *Secunda Pars,* after he has already discussed the adoption of the just man with regard to the sonship of the Son, and the indwelling of the Holy Spirit with regard to His missions.

In his treatise on grace, St. Thomas deals with five questions: Question 109 shows the necessity of grace; Question 110 studies the nature of grace; Question 111 discusses its species; Question 112, its efficient cause; Question 113, one of its effects: justifica-tion; and Question 114, another of its effects: merit.

THE
FORMAL EFFECTS
OF GRACE
INSEPARABLE
FROM IT

1 The Seed of Glory and of Resurrection

THE *fundamental effect* of grace, the reason and principle of all the others, the first link in the golden chain that unites the just man to God, the first root of the luxuriant vegetation of divine gifts that grace suddenly brings forth in the soul where it is planted, is the capacity, the *aptitude it gives for glory or the happiness of heaven*. Is not the beatific vision the strictly supernatural good of creatures, to the point that all other goods, even grace, are goods only as means to attain the beatific vision? [1]

Chronologically, it is true that the full development of this effect—the vision and possession of God—will come only after death, in heaven, i.e. it will be the last effect. But in its principle—a radical aptitude for this glory—this effect is received even here on earth together with grace.

---

[1] M. E. Neveut writes in *Divus Thomas*, 1929, p. 589: "Above all, grace is the principle of glory for the soul, and Father Cuttaz is right to begin with this effect which comes first logically. The theologians all recognize it, since they see in grace the seed of glory. Billot clearly proves that in creatures there is only one strictly supernatural good, and this good is the intuitive vision. Grace is eminently supernatural through its necessary relationship with glory. The author makes a very apt distinction between the right to glory and the principle or capacity for it: grace is a proximate and immediate power, or a capacity for 'the light of glory'."

Logically, this effect is the first, because it is the reason for and the root of the others, which all flow from it and are explained by it: we understand why and how grace makes us children of God only if we know that it makes us participate in His nature. And we know this only after having understood that it confers a right to and an aptitude for the beatific vision. The vision is the end; the rest is only a means. And the means are known only by the end.

This effect is also the first because of its importance and value, since it assures man of what is most essential and necessary for him: salvation, a supernatural end, the possession of God which will complete his being and beatify it.

It is not our purpose to explain the marvels of this beatifying possession of God—vision, love, delight—since we assume they are already known to our readers. We shall limit ourselves to a discussion of the effects of grace *in this life*.

For the one who possesses it, grace is the seed of glory and of resurrection: 1) the seed of glory for the soul; 2) the seed of resurrection for the body.

These are the truths we should like to establish in this chapter.

1. The Seed of Glory for the Soul

By the word *seed* we here mean that grace confers the right to and an aptitude for glory.[2] We say: right and aptitude. For in human affairs, the one does not necessarily accompany the other. There are many who have no right to what they may have a capacity for. Many would be excellent rulers but cannot legally claim the scepter of power. Many, too, could fulfil certain lucrative or honorific functions to which they have no access.

Conversely, a person may have a right to certain goods without having the capacity to utilize them or to benefit from them. A man can inherit an automobile without knowing how to drive it, a musical instrument without knowing how to play it, a mine without knowing how to exploit it, an in-

---

[2] See *Note* at the end of this chapter, p. 44 below.

dustry without knowing how to direct it. Usually, such persons still retain the faculty of selling these goods and exchanging them for other things which they are able to use.

But when it comes to heaven, such exchanges are impossible. It would be absolutely illusory and vain to have the right to go to heaven without the necessary capacity. Here the right implies the capacity, and the capacity presupposes the right. The one is inseparable from the other.

Grace is not only the condition for glory.[3] It is its principle and its cause as well—its necessary principle and cause. Without grace, no one can go to heaven or be admitted to the kingdom of heaven. But all who possess grace have the right to and an aptitude for heaven.

Let us demonstrate this *fact,* give a cursory *explanation* of it, and look into its *consequences.*

A. *The Fact*

This fact can be known only through divine revelation, since it relates to realities that are absolutely supernatural, freely given by God, and exceeding the demands and powers of all created nature. We can know it only because God has said it.

Now, God has revealed this fact explicitly and clearly. He said it Himself; He said it through His Apostles; and He said it through His Church.

He said it Himself, for example in His discourse with Nicodemus (Jn. 3:21). This eminent member of the Sanhedrin came to see Jesus one evening. He probably chose the cover of darkness so as not to be seen by his colleagues, who were hostile to Jesus, but more probably because in warm climates the cool of evening was more favorable to prolonged discussions and also because it was easier to be alone with Jesus at night. Nicodemus came to question our Lord on the conditions for admission into the Kingdom He was announcing. The Master declared with an insistence and solemnity that

---

[3] The beatific vision is called *glory* because it is in fact an incomparable honor for a creature to be united so intimately to God and to participate in His own happiness. Our Lord also calls it the *Kingdom of God,* and Christian terminology calls it *heaven.*

showed the importance of His answer: "Amen, amen, I say to
thee, unless a man be born again he cannot see the kingdom
of God" (Jn. 3:3).[4]

The Jewish doctor expressed his amazement, not without
irony, at a condition that was apparently impossible and even
ridiculous, because he understood Christ's words in their physical sense: "How can a man be born when he is old? Can he
enter a second time into his mother's womb and be born
again?" (Jn. 3:4). Jesus answered by repeating His first affirmation, without diminishing it in any way but by specifying
that He was speaking of a spiritual rebirth, symbolized by the
ablution of the water of baptism and worked by the Holy
Spirit: "Amen, amen, I say to thee, unless a man be born again
of water and the Spirit [by baptism], he cannot enter into the
kingdom of God. That which is born of the flesh is flesh; and
that which is born of the Spirit is spirit" (Jn. 3:5-6). We must
be born again of the Holy Spirit, and this spiritual life can
come only from Him: the flesh is incapable of giving this life,
for it can only produce the life of the flesh.

It is a mysterious birth and life that is not perceptible to
the senses, that reason cannot by its own resources demonstrate, that can be known only through faith, through a divine
revelation. That is what Christ wants His questioner to understand: "Do not wonder that I said to thee, 'You must be
born again.' The wind blows where it will, and thou hearest
its sound but dost not know where it comes from or where it
goes" (Jn. 3:7-8). The same is true of this spiritual birth. The
Jewish doctor again referred to this regeneration by the Spirit
and by water. He wanted to know how these things could be.

Jesus answered: "Thou art a teacher in Israel and dost not
know these things?" [5] Then, appealing to His divine authority He solemnly continued, going from the singular to the

---

[4] The "kingdom of God" is the heaven that Christ came to make more
easily accessible to men.

[5] Let us note in passing that if the masters of Israel did not know the
sublime realities of the supernatural life, this lack is partially excusable.
The Old Testament had spoken of it only in vague terms. Christians have
a greater responsibility for their ignorance, coming as they do after the
repeated and illuminating revelations of Christ and His Apostles, especially
the one we are studying here.

plural: "Amen, amen, I say to thee, we speak of what we know, and we bear witness to what we have seen; and our witness you do not receive" (Jn. 3:11).

He affirmed it because He knew it. To be admitted into the kingdom of God, we must be born again, and born of the Holy Spirit, that is, we must receive a new and divine life, aptitudes with which our natural birth has not provided us. In the words of St. John, we must be born "not of the will of the flesh, nor of the will of man, but of God" (Jn. 1:13), and become His children. This supernatural birth is not common to all men, as is all that stems from their nature, but the privilege of those who cleave to Christ, the divine Word who became man to merit this favor for them. It is a new and supernatural life that consists in sanctifying grace. Only through this life can we enter the Kingdom of God, heaven. And it is because baptism is the normal means of acquiring this life that it is indispensable to salvation, according to our Savior's categorical teaching (Mt. 16:19).

We find the same explicit doctrine taught by the Apostles. That grace is the principle of salvation, that when we are justified by grace we can expect to go to heaven, is one of the truths that St. Paul insists upon especially in his Epistle to the Romans. In fact, the entire second portion of this Epistle (from Chapter 5 through Chapter 8) is devoted to demonstrating this truth: ". . . through our Lord Jesus Christ . . . we also have access by faith unto that grace in which we stand, and exult in the hope of the glory of the sons of God. . . . And hope does not disappoint" (Rom. 5:1-5). For the Apostle, the gift of glory is included in the gift of grace as a conclusion is included in its premises. The former calls for and implies the latter; it "bears" it as a flower bears fruit or as seed bears the plant, providing—according to the sacred writer—we remain steadfast and do not lose it through sin.[6]

---

[6] "The purpose of Chapters 5 to 8 is simply to establish these two things: although initial justice and final salvation are separated by time and space, they are united by a bond of causality. They are the two links at opposite ends of an indissoluble chain in the mind and plans of God, although it is the sad privilege of our free will to be able to break it. Grace is the seed of glory, faith is the pledge of vision, the gifts of the Holy Ghost

Paul gives a certain number of proofs for his affirmations, the principal ones being the following:

1. The intensity of God's love for us that the gift of grace manifests on the part of God and of Christ (Rom. 5:6-11).

If God delivered up His only-begotten Son to the worst of deaths in order to justify us, when we were still in sin and hence the most wretched of creatures, when we were His enemies, unworthy of His favors, why would He not save us from eternal damnation now that we have been justified in the blood of this Son, have been restored to His friendship, and become His children, the objects of His paternal tenderness? How could He fail to give us the normal culmination of what He has already given us, namely, glory, salvation?

In the Apostle's thought, to confer grace on the sinner is a greater work than to give glory to the just man (and we shall explain why). Hence when God endowed us with grace when we were still sinners, He did more than He will do for us when He admits us to heaven now that we have been justified. How, then, could He fail to complete what He has begun? The logic of His love postulates that glory will some day be the crowning of grace: "For if when we were enemies we were reconciled to God by the death of His Son, much more, having been reconciled, shall we be saved by His life" (Rom. 5:10).

2. The superabundance of the Redemption (Rom. ch. 5). Because the God-Man is more powerful than the first man, He has done more to give us life than the first man did to kill us. Our Redemption is superabundant. Now, the result of Adam's sin was death of the body and of the soul in this world through the privation of supernatural life and grace, and eternal damnation in the next world.

Our Savior thus restores the life of the body by the glorious resurrection, and the life of the soul by justification here on earth and glory in heaven. He does this so that "as sin has reigned unto death, so also grace may reign by justice unto life everlasting through Jesus Christ our Lord" (Rom. 5:21).

---

are the earnest of beatitude, and the beatific state of the elect is the delayed but spontaneous flowering of charity, which is a particular aspect of justice" (Prat, *The Theology of St. Paul,* Vol. I, Chapter II, Section 2).

The purpose, the fulfillment of the grace we receive in this life, therefore, is glory for all eternity.

3. The effects of baptism. Chapter 6 of Romans is devoted to a presentation of a third proof drawn from the effects of baptism.

This sacrament incorporates us into and identifies us with Christ; it "implants" us in His death and in His life. In a certain respect He makes us die and rise again with Him, like Him, and in Him:

"For if we have been united with Him in the likeness of His death, we shall be so in the likeness of His Resurrection also. . . . But if we have died with Christ, we believe that we shall also live together with Christ" (Rom. 6:5,8).

Having participated in His death, we shall also participate in His life. Having imitated Him, and been reborn in His death, we shall imitate Him and reproduce Him in His life. The process has already begun by our justification (the reception of sanctifying grace). But it must be continued, and some day completed by our admission, body and soul, into His eternal felicity. And the Apostle concludes: "For the wages of sin is death, but the gift of God is life everlasting in Christ Jesus our Lord" (Rom. 6:23).

4. Our divine adoption (Chapter 8 of Romans). One of the essential effects of grace is to make us children of God, adopted brothers of Christ (who is the Son by nature). St. Paul assumes that this dogma is well known to his correspondents.

But every son is destined to possess the property of his father. He is his heir, a coheir with his brothers: "But if we are sons, we are heirs also: heirs indeed of God and joint heirs with Christ" (Rom. 8:17). What is God's property, that which brings Him happiness and in which Christ participates, if not the vision of His own infinite perfections, the contemplation of the wonders that are within Himself?

Such is the good to which our adoption, that is, grace, confers a right and an aptitude. Such is the heritage to which our divine sonship prepares us and to which, under the impulse of the Holy Spirit, our whole being and all of creation aspire (Rom. 8:9-22).

5. The divine decree. The Apostle affirms categorically that

God has decreed to call to glory those whom He has called to grace (on condition that they do not place any obstacle to it by sin): "For those whom He has foreknown He has also pre-destined to be conformed to the image of His Son. . . . And those whom He has predestined, . . . He has also justified [He gave them grace], and those whom He has justified, them He has also glorified" (Rom. 8:29-30).

And by the unceasing and powerful action of His Provi-dence, He helps them to attain this glorious goal and makes everything converge upon this end: "We know that for those who love God all things work together unto good" (Rom. 8:28). For those who love God are God's children. In the plans of the Father, the gift of grace must culminate in the gift of glory, of which it is the prelude, the condition—better still— the seed, and the principle. All who are justified will be glorified.

St. Paul was obliged to affirm, in opposition to the Judaizers who attributed salvation to works, that is, to the observation of the prescriptions of the Mosaic Law, that salvation is abso-lutely gratuitous, supernatural, that it comes from grace and grace alone, that salvation can only be obtained through grace and never without it. We might cite, among his many affirma-tions, the following: "There is a remnant left, selected out of grace. And if out of grace, then not in virtue of works [of the Law]; otherwise grace is no longer grace" (Rom. 11:6). Salva-tion is heaven: grace is the means to it.

We find the identical teaching in Paul's Epistle to the Ephe-sians: "But God, who is rich in mercy, by reason of His very great love wherewith He has loved us even when we were dead by reason of our sins, brought us to life together with Christ (by grace you have been saved); and raised us up together, and seated us together in heaven in Christ Jesus, that He might show in the ages to come the overflowing riches of His grace. . . . For by grace you have been saved through faith; and that not from yourselves, for it is the gift of God; not as the out-come of works, lest anyone may boast. For His workmanship we are, created in Christ Jesus in good works. . . . (Eph. 2:4-10).

The Apostle considers our salvation—our admission to heaven with Christ—as something already accomplished, from the fact that Christ, our head, whom we must follow, into whom we are incorporated, already enjoys it and that the joys of heaven are the normal complement of grace implanted in us by baptism. It is impossible to state the matter more clearly: salvation comes from grace, and from grace alone. Grace is the seed of glory.

The following passage from St. Peter's First Epistle is explicit, and deserves detailed analysis: *"Blessed be the God and Father of our Lord Jesus Christ, who according to His great mercy has begotten us again, through the Resurrection of Jesus Christ* [bringing us forth to the life of grace by baptism: an absolutely gratuitous and supernatural gift, since it is the effect and sign of great mercy, great love, on God's part and the source of a great obligation of gratitude on ours] . . . *unto a living hope* [for a good that we do not yet possess in itself but in hope: a life without end], *unto an incorruptible inheritance* [because it is wholly spiritual] *undefiled* [by sin], *and unfading* [because it is eternal], *reserved for you in heaven* [that is the glory of heaven]. *By the power of God you are guarded through faith for salvation, which is ready to be revealed in the last time* [salvation, the fullness of eternal happiness, which is not remote, for death is near for each of us]" (I Pet. 1:3-5). Let us carefully note the preposition *unto*: Our rebirth is unto an inheritance, grace is unto glory. Grace is the means, the principle of glory.

As for the Apostle St. John, we need only recall the first two verses, known to all, of his First Epistle: "Behold what manner of love the Father has bestowed upon us, that we should be called children of God; and such we are . . . and it has not yet appeared what we shall be. We know that, when He appears, we shall be like to Him, for we shall see Him just as He is" (I Jn. 3:1-2). Who will see Him as He is? Who will enjoy this beatific vision? Those who have been His children through grace here on earth. Heaven is reserved for them. It is the heritage of the children. Heaven, the heritage of the children, is reserved for them.

The Church has faithfully transmitted to her children of each age this clear teaching of her divine Founder and of the Apostles. For example, in the Council of Trent, she defines

that the person justified by the good works that he performs
... truly merits ... "eternal life, and in case he dies in grace,
the attainment of eternal life itself" (Session VI, Can. 32).

This, then, is the *fact* (that grace is the seed of glory) in-
contestably included in revealed doctrine.

But why is grace the necessary principle of glory? What
explanation can we offer for it?

We shall try to explain this, thus providing the theological
reason for the fact and offering a few interesting consequences.

B. *The Explanation*

This explanation is suggested by our Lord in the parable
of the ten virgins (Mt. 25:1-13).

Having been invited to a wedding, these young girls—ten
was the customary number for "bridesmaids"—came with their
lamps in hand, because weddings were usually held at night,
to the home of the bride, their friend, to wait with her for
the bridegroom who was to come and lead her with joyful
pomp to their future dwelling. Five of them, being wise, prudent, and clear-headed, took the precaution of bringing a pro-
vision of oil in a vessel. The others, giddy, thoughtless, devoid
of practical wisdom, "foolish" in the words of the Gospel, did
not think of taking this precaution.

For an unspecified reason, the bridegroom delayed, and one
after another the young girls fell asleep while their lamps continued to burn. All of a sudden, toward midnight, a cry was
heard: "Here is the bridegroom. He is coming. Quick! Let
us go and meet him!" They all awoke and tried to revive the
flame in their lamps. But the improvident virgins had no oil.
They then turned to their more prudent companions: "Give
us some of your oil, for our lamps are going out." The wise
virgins answered, saying, "Lest there may not be enough for
us and for you, go rather to those who sell it, and buy some
for yourselves" (Mt. 25:9).

While the foolish virgins ran to buy oil, the bridegroom
arrived. Only those who were ready joined the procession and
entered with him into the banquet hall, and after that the
door was closed. When the others came back, they knocked
suppliantly: "Sir, sir, open the door for us!" But he answered:

THE SEED OF GLORY AND OF RESURRECTION

"Amen I say to you, I do not know you." It was too late. They should have been there when he arrived.

The allegory is transparent: The Bridegroom is God. The lamp is our soul. The oil is sanctifying grace and the charity that accompanies it; the wedding banquet is the beatific vision, heavenly and eternal felicity. Only those are admitted who possess the precious and necessary oil at the moment the Bridegroom arrives.

Why? Because while our intellect can know something about God through creatures (His existence and a few of His attributes, especially His power),[7] it cannot through its own resources [8] perceive Him intuitively, face to face, and apprehend Him directly in His Being. This requires the help of a supernatural instrument: a divine light must make God visible.

In the darkness of a starless night, the splendors of nature, the grandeur of mountains, the graceful poetry of lakes, the rich colors of woods, fields, and flowers, the impressive stretch of plains and oceans are not visible. We must wait until the sun rises, to see them. True, the sun does not create these things, for they existed before its appearance. But the sun makes them perceptible. So is it with God in relation to us. He is present to us with all His infinite beauty since He is everywhere, and especially in the souls of the just. But during this life, it is night. He is not visible. We know something about Him by His actions, but we do not see Him. We do not have the necessary light, we have no instrument of supernatural vision. In heaven, grace will furnish us this "light of glory." It will not produce the splendors of the divine Essence and its incomparable perfections, but simply make them visible to us. Grace

---

[7] "For since the creation of the world His invisible attributes are clearly seen—His everlasting power also and divinity—being understood through the things that are made" (Rom. 1:19-20).

[8] We know that the beatific vision is absolutely supernatural, exceeding the powers and demands of all created nature. Thus no one can enjoy it unless he has received from God a faculty of the same order. The Ecumenical Council of Vienne defined this truth against the Beghards in 1312, by condemning the following proposition: "The soul does not need the light of glory to raise it to the power to see God and to enjoy Him in beatitude. Every intellectual nature is capable of this by its own powers." (Denz. 475, Enchir., Symbol. et definit.) This was also the error of Ontologism, condemned by the Church in the 19th century.

is like the lamps by which the "wise virgins" could contemplate the features and charms of the Bridegroom and the lavishness of the nuptial banquet.

This direct view of God will fill our hearts with such delight, love, and passion (if I dare say so) for Him that we shall never again be able to turn our gaze away from Him, never again stop admiring Him, never again be separated from Him (and hence never again offend Him). Since the marvels of His Being are without limit, we shall never have done contemplating new facets of His perfections; we shall never exhaust this immeasurable wealth. We shall go from discovery to discovery, from amazement to amazement, without weariness or boredom. We shall remain in love with Him eternally, to a point which is utterly beyond us here on earth.

This vision will stimulate and put to use all the virtualities of our minds and hearts, all our faculties for knowing, loving, possessing, all our natural and supernatural aptitudes and powers, in a plenitude of delirious joy. It will be an intense participation in the life of God who is unceasing and infinite activity. We shall have all the happiness which we are capable of enjoying, because we shall perceive God to the maximum limits of our powers. In the words of the Psalmist, it will be a "torrent of pleasure" (Ps. 35:9).

Grace might therefore be compared to a powerful projector placed within the soul, through which, from the moment of our entrance into heaven, we shall see God intuitively, in the splendor of His beauty. As St. John wrote to the Christians of Palestine: "Beloved, . . . it has not yet appeared what we shall be. We know that, when He appears, we shall be like to Him, for we shall see Him just as He is" (I Jn. 3:2). And St. Paul told the Corinthians: "We see [God] now through a mirror in an obscure manner, but then face to face" (I Cor. 13:12)— that is, we shall see Him in Himself and no longer through created reflections. Through grace, we possess the principle of light that will make God visible to us; but this grace is still locked up, so to speak, in the sheath of our flesh, and, like a covered beacon, it cannot shed its rays to light the road.

It may be objected: "Of what use are a hidden light, latent virtualities, dormant power, causes without effects?" We answer: Then of what use are the acorn that is not yet an oak, planted fields that are not ready for harvest, flowers that have not yet been replaced by beautiful ripe fruit, seeds that have not yet attained their full development, and the human soul of an infant that cannot yet use all its faculties?[9]

The newborn infant can neither think, nor judge, nor reason, nor abstract an idea from the objects that come before its senses, nor can he apprehend the universal. How, then, can he rise above the purely animal life? He has received a mind by which he belongs to the human race. He has an intellect, but he cannot yet use it, nor the faculties which depend upon it—the will, for example—because the organs of his interior senses, especially the imagination, have not yet been sufficiently developed. He has reason, but he cannot make use of it as long as these physiological conditions are not realized. He possesses the power to think and to will; but he cannot yet use this power and make it bear fruit in acts. The exercise of this power is for the time being inhibited.

The difference between what the child is now and what he will be later is simply a difference in act. He already possesses the radical and basic power to perceive the immaterial, but not the proximate power that culminates in action.

Generally speaking, that is the difference between the just man on earth and the blessed in heaven. The latter perceives the divine Essence intuitively, *in actu;* whereas the former perceives it only in potency. Through grace, the just man has the radical aptitude [10] for seeing God, but this aptitude is latent

---

[9] It is St. Paul himself (cf. I Cor. 13:11-12) who compares what we shall be in heaven with what we are here and now through grace in terms of the difference between an adult man and an infant.

[10] "The proper function [of sanctifying grace] consists in ordering the very essence of the soul to its supernatural end; in other words, it makes the soul radically apt for the intuitive vision of God and for the love that results from this vision" (J. Van der Meersch, *Dict. Théol.*, article on Grace, col. 611).

"The life of God consists principally in the contemplation and perfect enjoyment of His infinite essence. . . . Sanctifying grace, . . . because it has an immediate influx on our being and not on our act, makes our *to be* divine, but is not the immediate principle of our *acting* divinely. Grace does not confer actuality, but only the root of divine life. . . . This life, of

and tied down, as it were, as long as the conditions for its exercise are not fulfilled. St. Thomas teaches that: "the grace . . .
which we have at present, although unequal to glory in act,
is equal to it virtually as the seed of a tree, wherein the whole
tree is virtually [in potency]. So likewise by grace the Holy
Spirit dwells in man; and He is a sufficient cause of life everlasting; hence according to St. Paul (II Cor. 1:22) He is called
the pledge of our inheritance" (Ia IIae, q. 114, a. 3, ad 3).

A "pledge" is given to seal a bargain, to sanction a contract, to guarantee a promise. It is a partial payment on the
total that one promises to pay off. Grace is the pledge of
glory. It is the guarantee of the whole heavenly heritage. It
confers the Holy Spirit who, at the proper moment, will
render the divine Essence luminous and perceptible to our
souls.[11]

It is said that the Christian is a man who waits. The *Credo*
declares: *"Et exspecto. . . ."* True, but he is also a man who
possesses. While he does not yet possess the fullness of the first
effect of grace, he bears within himself even now the principle
of this effect.

C. *The Consequences*

We shall point out six principal consequences of sanctifying
grace.

1. *"Grace is the beginning of glory"*

Grace possesses everything necessary to produce glory when
the time comes, just as the grain of wheat contains all that is
necessary to bear a golden sheaf when the external conditions
are verified. Grace contains glory germinally. So true is this
that we can assert with the Angelic Doctor: "Grace is nothing
else than a beginning of glory in us" (IIa IIae, q. 24, a. 3, ad 2).
Grace is heaven in its principle; it is perfect felicity in its root;

---

the divine and not the created order, truly exists at least germinally in the
soul of the just man inasmuch as he is just and lives by faith, even though
it is still "hidden with Christ in God" (Keller-Lavaud, *Revue Thomiste,*
Vol. XII, p. 466).

[11] Cf. quotations from Cardinal Mercier and Father Plus in the *Notes* at
the end of this chapter, pp. 45-46 below.

it is eternal life in its cause; it is the river of divine "pleasure" in its source; it is the fruit of infinite delights in its flower.

Thus, the just man is already one of the blessed in the same sense that the sinner is one of the damned and that the child is a man. As the sinner bears within the depths of his being the principle of the unending tortures that await him and that will automatically descend upon him forever if he dies without repenting (inasmuch as he has refused God, he will be deprived of Him for all eternity); so the just man already possesses here and now within his soul the source of the divine happiness that is reserved for him, "the fountain springing up unto life everlasting," to feed his enjoyment without end.

Between the just man and the sinner, therefore, there is a capital difference that will place them at opposite extremes for all eternity and will become a limitless, impassable abyss (Lk. 16:25). While it is true that the just man does not enjoy the beatific vision here on earth any more than the sinner, it is no less certain that the sinner is unworthy of this vision and must be shut out from it, whereas the soul in the state of grace possesses the right and the aptitude for it, can and must lay claim to it, and is marked and equipped to attain it. It is a matter of days or years of waiting, as long as the conditions for admission into heaven have not been fulfilled. These conditions are two in number: one is absolute and general; the other does not necessarily apply to everyone.

The first condition is that the time of trial (*status viae*) fixed by God for each one be at an end. As long as this time continues, the soul is free to choose its supreme end, to accept or refuse God as the ultimate term of its being, to cleave to Him or turn away from Him (that is the very definition of the time of trial).

Now, if the soul were allowed to contemplate God's divine Beauty or to intuitively perceive His infinite perfections, it would be so powerfully enraptured that it could not tear itself away from them (as we have said on p. 30 above). It would not have the freedom *not* to want God as its end, and *not* to love Him more than everything else. Such a soul could neither commit sin nor merit, and this would be contrary to the nature of "trials." Now the end of this time of trial coincides

for each one of us with death, because such is God's decree.[12]
We come into this world to freely determine our eternal destiny, by choosing our end and determining the degree of our
union with God and consequently of our felicity.

Moreover, the soul must be completely purified of all venial
sins that might remain on its conscience and all remnants of
sins. It must have fully paid the temporal debt of punishment
it still owes, for it cannot be united to the thrice-holy God as
long as it retains any blemish of sin. This purification is accomplished in purgatory by those who have not been wise
enough to accomplish it here on earth.[13]

Once these conditions have been realized, the just man can
knock at the portal of his Father's heavenly palace and ask
admission, just as any son can claim his share of the paternal
heritage when the time comes. He is among the chosen ones
"whose names are written in heaven" (Lk. 10:20), and for
whom a place has been reserved in the abode of eternal happiness. He is among the fortunate guests who have come clothed
in their wedding garment and are allowed to sit at the royal
banquet (cf. Mt. 22:11). If he perseveres in this state, heaven
is open to him. He can confidently count on it. The sinner,
on the other hand, if he persists in his sinful dispositions, has
nothing to look forward to but hell, the prolongation of his
sin. Those of us who have been justified are already saved—in
hope (cf. Rom. 5:1-2).

Let us immediately draw a practical conclusion from this:
since grace is the beginning of glory—*inchoatio gloriae*—our
life in grace (here on earth) must begin here and now what
our life in glory will be—as St. Paul says: "But our citizenship
is in heaven" (Phil. 3:20). In other words, it is our vocation
here on earth to live the life of heaven. Even now we must
keep our minds, hearts, and wills fixed, concentrated on God.

---

[12] Such was not the case for our Lord, who enjoyed the beatific vision from
the first moment of His human life, by virtue of the hypostatic union of His
humanity with His divine Person. The grace within Him thus produced its
total effect immediately, and attained its fullest development without delay.
From the start, therefore, He was *in statu termini*. And that is one of the
reasons why He could not merit for Himself increases in grace or (essential)
glory.

[13] Cf. the *Note* at the end of the chapter, p. 46 below.

Even now we must live in the closest, most loving, and continual intimacy with Him. Even now, we must find our happiness near Him and in Him.

2. The Excellence of the Just Man

There is an infinitely greater distance between the sinner and the just man, in the sense of inferiority, than there is between the just man and the blessed in heaven; just as there is a far greater gap between the animal devoid of reason and the child, than there is between the child and the adult. Between man and child the difference is simply one of degree, development. Between the animal and the child, however, the difference is one of nature. The just man and the blessed are both in the supernatural order, hence on the same level; whereas an abyss separates them both from the sinner. We should even say that the man in the state of grace surpasses the man in the state of sin far more than the latter surpasses the animal. For the divine life of the former is much more elevated, more perfect and more precious than the intellectual life through which the sinner surpasses the being devoid of reason. In any event, the just man surpasses the sinner far more than the greatest worldly personage surpasses the lowliest of humans.

3. The Excellence of Justification

Another consequence of grace is that the glorification of the just man is a far less remarkable work than the justification of the sinner (Ia IIae, q. 113, a. 9). The distance between sin and grace is infinitely greater than that between grace and glory. The change that is worked in the soul of the child through baptism or of the sinner through absolution is far more momentous than what happens to the soul of the just upon entering heaven.

St. Thomas asks whether the justification of the ungodly man (the sinner) is the greatest of God's works, and he answers in the affirmative: "A work may be called great in two ways: first, on the part of the mode of action, and thus the work of creation is the greatest work, wherein something is made from nothing; secondly, a work may be called great on account of what is made, and thus the justification of the ungodly, which terminates at the eternal good of a share in the Godhead, is greater than the creation of heaven and earth, which terminates at the good of the mutable nature" (Ia IIae, q. 113, a. 9). Grace is a super-creation.

The production of a single degree of grace in a single soul is a work superior to the creation of the worlds and of the entire universe.

Then our Doctor compares justification to glorification: "In absolute quantity, . . . the gift of glory is greater than the gift of grace that sanctifies the ungodly. . . . [But] . . . in proportionate quantity . . . the gift of grace that justifies the ungodly is greater than the gift of glory that beatifies the just, for the gift of grace exceeds the worthiness of the ungodly, who are worthy of punishment, more than the gift of glory exceeds the worthiness of the just, who by the fact of their justification are worthy of glory" (*ibid.*).

He had already said: "There is a greater distance between nature and grace, than between grace and glory, which is merely the perfecting of grace" (q. 95, a. 1).

St. Thomas quotes St. Augustine: "Let him that can, judge whether it is greater to create the angels just, than to justify the ungodly. Certainly, if they both betoken equal power, one betokens greater mercy" (Ia IIae, q. 113, a. 9). Hence, the justification of the sinner is the most important, the most wonderful, and the most touching of God's works, the one that demands and reveals the greatest power and above all the greatest love.

4. *The Duration of Grace*

If grace is the principle of the beatific vision, it follows that it subsists in heaven. Far from ceasing to be the principle of the beatific vision in heaven, grace then attains its fullest efficacy, its maximum effect, and all its virtualities enter into play in the most intense, extensive, and complete, the richest and most perfect act that is most like the pure act of God: the vision, love, and possession of the divine Essence.

Grace subsists in heaven. Nay more, in heaven it can no longer be lost (or increased).[14]

5. Its Necessity

As the principle of the beatific vision, grace is absolutely necessary, as a necessary means. Nothing can take its place. No one can be admitted to heaven unless he possesses grace, even though it may not be his fault that he is without grace. Grace is the wedding garment without which no one is admitted to the feast of the Bridegroom (Mt. 22:11-12). Thus, we have a grave moral obligation to acquire grace—an obligation that is nothing else but the obligation of saving our souls.

And since baptism of water or of desire—*in re vel in voto*—is the absolutely indispensable means of obtaining grace, it is just as necessary to the soul as is grace.

6. The Proportion between Grace and Glory

The beatific vision will be the same for all the blessed, in the sense that it will have the same object for all, and will be of the same nature (intuitive, face-to-face), and that it will satisfy all the possibilities of happiness in each one. But this vision will not necessarily be of the same degree for all. It may be more or less perfect, according to the power of that which is its instrument and confers the aptitude for it, namely, sanctifying grace. Those who possess more grace will have a more perfect vision of the wonders and beauties of God, and will have greater love and joy in Him. Glory will be proportionate to grace, and there will be an inequality in glory to the extent that there is inequality in grace.

To increase our grace is by the same token to increase our glory, that is, our eternal felicity. Whatever raises the level of grace also raises the level of glory. Every meritorious act, every sacrament validly received, every confession, and above all every Communion [15] thus has this twofold effect: the one for

---

[14] Other consequences relate to its nature: 1) grace has to be a spiritual reality; 2) but also an intrinsic and physical (which is not to say material) reality, inherent in the soul; 3) it is incompatible with sin, as we shall prove later on.

[15] Cf. the work by the present author, *Pain Vivant*, Chapter 3.

grace, the other for glory; the one temporal and immediate, the other for the future and eternity.

Reciprocally, all that confers new degrees of glory gives, by that very fact, the right to new corresponding degrees of grace. Otherwise—since grace is the instrument of glory—the first degrees of grace would be unobtainable. Whoever has a right to the end, also has a right to the necessary means. That is why our good works, which merit an eternal reward, also merit the grace that confers the capacity for this reward. (Cf. Chapter 12, below.)

How precious, therefore, are the few hours of our earthly pilgrimage, for during these hours we have the faculty, by intensifying our sanctifying grace, to intensify our eternal happiness! With a view to attaining this goal, we should use with the greatest care every instant and every means placed at our disposal. Time is a sacred thing, not to be wasted!

2. Grace, the Principle of Resurrection for the Body

We have just shown that grace gives our soul the capacity to possess God.

But since we are composed of matter and spirit, we have a body as well as a soul. In truth, we can live without the body and outside the body through the life of the soul, and that is how we shall live from the time we die until our resurrection. However, this state of separation is somewhat contrary to human nature, and it is meant to be temporary. At the end of the world, body and soul will be permanently reunited. Then will be produced a final effect of grace: the extension to the body of the soul's glory, and the transformation of the body by glorious attributes.

Before Adam's sin, grace in man was like a precious diamond mounted on a jewel-box of magnificent gifts. These gifts have been called "preternatural" because, although they did not dispose man to his supernatural end or of themselves lead man into the divine order, they exceeded the powers and demands of man's nature, but not that of the angels, who by their very essence are subject neither to concupiscence, death, nor physical suffering.

"This rich endowment was a sort of connecting link between human nature and elevating grace. It proceeded from grace as its cause and served as its ornament and bulwark. Although it was separable in the strict sense of the term, it always accompanied the grace granted to the first man and disappeared only when grace was destroyed through sin" (Thouvenin, *D.T.C.*, art., "Innocence," col. 1939).

Thanks to the gift of *integrity* or innocence, all the inferior powers, the sensitive appetite and the passions, perfectly obedient to reason, never turned to their object before or against its judgment, or before or against the command of the will.

The gift of *knowledge* would have consisted, for the descendants of the first man, in a special facility resulting in part from the other gifts, to retain the knowledge learned from their first father and to penetrate more easily into religious truths.

By virtue of the privilege of *immortality*, men were to enter glory without passing through death (after spending a period of time, varied in length, undergoing trials in the theological sense of the word and gaining merit).

Finally, by the gift of *impassibility* or exemption from suffering, God by a special providence would have exempted them from all internal or external causes of physical or moral suffering, and that is why nature was meant to be perfectly subject to them and work was to be a pleasure.

The Father had willed to treat man like a beloved child, and to provide a varied and normal [10] framework for the wonderful image of His own divine nature that He had placed in man. It is because of sin that these gifts no longer are adjuncts to human nature. For anyone in the state of grace not to have these gifts—i.e., for anyone in the state of grace to die, to suffer, to learn slowly, and to maintain mastery of the will over the lower appetites only with difficulty—is a "violent" state, a privation in the philosophical sense, the continuing

---

[16] Normal, not in the sense that these gifts were absolutely required by the very essence of grace, even less by the essence of man, but because it was fitting that they should be added to man's essence together with the gift of grace.

punishment for original sin. God had revealed these gifts to our first parents to help them not to violate His command.

In His mercy, God restored His grace and love to repentant man, but He did not restore the preternatural gifts. This effect of grace has been deferred until the moment of entrance into heaven.[17]

The Father does not love man any less, but His tenderness does not find expression in exactly the same way as in the beginning. Even after you have made your peace with a friend who has insulted you, can you love him in the same way you did before he offended you? Can a husband even after forgiving his wife's infidelity, have the same spontaneous, fresh, and trusting love for her that he had before? Does not the very ardor of his affection command him to take measures to prevent his wayward wife from falling again and to delicately remind her where new imprudences could lead her? He who has already fallen can fall again. Does not the emotional persistence of past sins induce the avoidance of future sins? Does not experimental proof of the evil effects of sin act as a vaccine against it? The reason these gifts no longer form the framework of grace here on earth is that sin had to be punished and prevented. But grace by itself, abstracting from sin, continues to postulate these gifts. That is why in heaven, when it will no longer be possible to sin, they will be reunited to grace, greater and more perfect than before. And in this way, the whole being of man, even his body, will benefit from the Father's heritage.

We say the preternatural gifts will be magnified because their perfection will be far greater than in Adam.

Their duration will no longer be provisional, as it was then, but certain and eternal.

They will no longer have their source merely in an external act of God, but in the very glory of the soul.

Finally, precious properties will be added to our bodies, which our first parents did not yet enjoy. In his famous chap-

---

[17] Cf. *The Effects of Baptism*, Chapter 6, concerning the fact that baptism does not restore the preternatural gifts of which original sin despoiled our race, but makes up for them by the graces it brings to the soul.

ter of First Corinthians, St. Paul describes them with lyrical joy (cf. I Cor. 15:42-57).

Immortality. "What is sown in corruption [the body buried in the earth through death] rises in incorruption" (42). The mortal body will be clothed in immortality.

Impassibility. Being immortal, the body will be exempt from everything that can provoke death: suffering, sickness, accidents, fatigue, old age, weakness, hunger and thirst. There will be an absence of sufferings, but not of pleasures. On the contrary, the body will enjoy all the legitimate pleasures of which it is capable. It will be impassible but not insensible.

Agility. "What is sown in weakness rises in power" (43). The body will be able to move about as the will directs, instantaneously and with ease.

Clarity. "What is sown in dishonor rises in glory" (42). Some of the light of the soul will be reflected in the body, as in Jesus' body on Tabor.

Subtlety. "What is sown a natural body rises a spiritual body" (44). The body will be capable of passing through other bodies without resistance, penetrating everywhere after the manner of spirits, just as Jesus' body emerged from the Blessed Virgin's womb and later from the grave, and arrived at the Cenacle after the Resurrection without displacing or moving anything, somewhat the way X-rays or air waves pass through certain bodies.

In a word, the body will be liberated from the chains of matter and from its miseries. It will be perfectly adapted to the life of heaven, and, as it were, spiritualized.

Through grace, the Holy Spirit makes our bodies His temples. He consecrates them to Himself for all eternity and reserves them for Himself. He marks them with the seal of divine ownership, so as to set them, like living stones, in the luminous walls of the heavenly Jerusalem.

Our bodies participate in the love of the Father, and even though, according to the plans of His wisdom, this love does not produce its effects in them at this time, these effects are merely deferred until the eternal resurrection.

Christ has redeemed our bodies, too, by His sacrifice. By

His death He merited a glorious immortality for them, and "we ourselves groan within ourselves, waiting for the adoption as sons, the redemption of our body" (Rom. 8:23).

Touched by grace, a participation in the eternal life of God, they keep the seed of glory within them. Their burial after death resembles the sowing of seed (to use St. Paul's metaphor). It is in order to preserve this magnificent symbolism, so full of teaching and of hope, that the Church wants us to "bury" the bodies of the faithful and forbids their incineration (or cremation) under pain of refusing to give them religious burial (Codex, C. 1240[5] and 2339).

Thus even the rite of inhumation, according to the liturgy, is a prelude to the resurrection, radiant with consoling promises. The Church deposits the bodies of her children into the tomb as a ploughman throws his grain into the furrow with a view to the wonderful transformations of the coming spring. Some day these bodies will rise up again with a new life, just as a seed corrupted in the soil rises up a vigorous stalk, heavy with grain. Because they were sanctified by grace at the moment death struck, they have been marked for a glorious eternity. A participation in the blessed life of the soul is their destiny. Elevated by grace, they, too, will be regenerated by glory. Having been honored by a supernatural union and presence of God, they will share in the ineffable and beatifying union of vision. Glory, the maturation of grace, will also shine upon them. God does not separate what He has united. Just as the hypostatic union makes the humanity of Christ share the dignity and (possible) prerogatives of the Godhead, so the substantial union of soul and body will make the body share the happiness and splendors of the soul.

As Bishop Gay writes: "It is true that the redemptive grace deposited by God in the soul [of the just] does not exempt from death the body that is substantially united to it and that must atone in the grave for the dishonor of having served as a refuge, an arsenal, alas, as an accomplice of so many evil desires. And yet so great are the plenitude and power of this grace that it impresses upon the body a divine mark, so that when the soul departs it leaves within the body an indefinable perfume of the Holy Spirit which becomes a seed of resurrection unto eternal life" (*La Vie Chrétienne*).

True, because of orignal sin we bear in our bodies the principle of the dissolution of their elements. And yet through grace we also possess the principle of the permanent reunion of these elements, the all-powerful seed of a glorious resurrection. St. Paul considered this resurrection as certain as Christ's, and in his triumphant enthusiasm confidently taunted death with Osee's scornful apostrophe: "O death, where is thy victory? O death, where is thy sting?" (I Cor. 15:55).

Grace implants within us the Author of life Himself, the life-giving Spirit who has already resurrected Christ unto glory, "the first-fruits of those who have fallen asleep" (I Cor. 15:20), whose death and resurrection we are to reproduce in our own lives.

The Consequence. Since this is the glorious destiny grace prepares for our bodies, we must respect and honor them as God Himself will honor them, as the Church honors them even after they are corpses: as dedicated temples.

There are irreverent uses of the body that we must not allow ourselves, sacrilegious contacts that are forbidden, according to St. Paul's warning (I Cor. 6:15-16). We must make of our bodies instruments of life and light, and not instruments of death. Grace not only confers upon the body precious prerogatives for the next life, but also imposes rigorous duties upon it in this life. We must esteem the prerogatives and fulfill the duties.

Above all, we must express our gratitude to God for having implanted in us the principle of such great blessings.

The Preface of the Mass for the dead gives admirable expression to these acts of thanksgiving: "It is truly meet and just . . . that we should . . . give thanks unto Thee, O Lord, . . . through Christ our Lord. In whom the hope of a blessed resurrection hath shone upon us, that those whom the certainty of dying afflicteth, may be consoled by the promise of future immortality. For unto Thy faithful, O Lord, life is changed, not taken away: and the abode of this earthly sojourn being dissolved, an eternal dwelling is prepared in heaven." Our hearts should be stirred to gratitude when we repeat this hymn to our future glories, so consoling in our bereavements.

The material world will also participate in some way in the glorious destiny of the children of God. Because it is at their service, because it is both a framework and a means, and because it is a part of their earthly life, it will have its place in their heavenly life and for their sake will be embellished and transfigured. To quote St. Paul: "For the eager longing of creation awaits the revelation of the sons of God. . . . because creation itself also will be delivered from its slavery to corruption into the freedom of the glory of the sons of God" (Rom. 8:19-21).[18] And in his Apocalypse, St. John writes: "And I saw a new heaven and a new earth" (Apoc. 21:1), that is to say, a transfigured heaven and earth.

Such is the prodigious efficacy of grace for the world to come.

But its effects do not belong entirely to the future. Grace produces effects, and magnificent ones, here and now. The remainder of this work will be a study of these effects.

The most important of these, the principle of all the others, is *participation in the nature of God*.

*   *   *

Note on Grace, the Seed of Glory (see p. 20 above):

Father Terrien (*La grace et la gloire*) sees our adopted sonship as the foundation of the effects of grace, which are the infused virtues, the gifts of the Holy Spirit, the indwelling of God in the soul.

According to Father Froget, the foundation of the effects of grace is the indwelling of the Holy Spirit in the soul of the just man.

According to Father de Smedt (*Notre vie surnaturelle,* Chapter 2), "all the effects [of grace] are explained by this fundamental property, namely, that grace forms the bond that really unites divine nature to the substance of our soul; and as a result of this bond, the soul in the state of grace possesses a character, a perfection of the divine order."

---

[18] Cf. also Is. 65:17; 66:22; II Pet. 3:13: "But we look for new heavens and a new earth, according to His promises. . . ."

And he indicates five formal effects of grace in the following order:

1. Sanctifying grace results in our being loved by God with a love of friendship.
2. It makes us truly children of God.
3. It gives us a strict right to heavenly beatitude.
4. It makes us temples of the Holy Spirit.
5. It brings with it an infusion of the supernatural virtues and gifts. (Two-thirds of his book is devoted to this last-named effect: the virtues and the gifts.)

Inasmuch as the effects of grace do not follow one or another mutually exclusive order, we can, without forming a vicious circle, prove one effect by another. The theological reason for some of them, drawn from the reason for others, is not their only or their principal foundation. They are founded on Revelation (Scripture and Tradition). Aptitude for glory, participation in the divine nature, adoption, the special indwelling, etc., can each be established solely on the authority of God and of the Church. Theological arguments merely confirm the divine testimony. When we demonstrate God's supernatural love for the just by His special indwelling in their souls, and reciprocally when we demonstrate His indwelling by His love, we are considering both of them as affirmed by the Holy Spirit. Thus we are not proving a point by itself.

Hence it should not be surprising that the reality of one effect is confirmed by the reality of effects that come after it. It is a legitimate procedure, conformable to the rules of logic.

Note on Grace as the Pledge of Glory (see p. 32 above):
Cardinal Mercier writes: "Grace and glory are essentially of the same order. The latter is simply the development of the former. Intelligible union with the divine substance in the mind of the blessed realizes the beatific vision in glory. It realizes even here on earth the immediate possession of God by sanctifying grace and charity, in the obscurity of faith and with the help of hope. . . .

"Grace is the seed, glory is the harvest. The former reaches fulfillment in the splendid fruits of the latter. Sanctifying grace and charity, its first effect, are already substantially heaven. The measure of charity (and of grace) determines the measure of glory. The reason the blessed differ among themselves in glory,

like the stars in the heavens, *sicut stella differt a stella,* is that
the divine essence is united to their intellects in varying degrees. Now this degree of union corresponds exactly to the degree of charity (and grace) that the soul possesses at the moment
it appears before the tribunal of God" (*Retraite sacerdotale,* "La
vie intérieure," 6ᵉ Entretien).

Father Plus writes: "Believing is closer to seeing than is generally thought, if believing is given its fullest sense (living faith
accompanied by grace). To expect something is already to possess it, when there is question of a good that has been promised
with certainty. To love, whether on earth or in heaven, is still
to love.

"Here on earth, the seed; in heaven, the fully blooming
flower. Here on earth, possession in darkness; in heaven, possession in the light. Here on earth, a turning toward God; in
heaven, God seen face to face. We are already saved, but our
salvation must be consummated. . . . St. John mingles the past
and the future: 'This is the promise he has given us, the life
everlasting' (I Jn. 2:25). 'God has given us eternal life' (I Jn.
5:11).

"The fire is lighted, but it is covered with a few ashes.

"When the wind of the last trumpets blows over these few
ashes, the fires will blaze up brightly. . . . The life of heaven must
not only be considered as a future to hope for. It must also be
visualized as a present to be lived here-and-now" (*In Christ
Jesus,* Chapter 3).

Note on Purgatory (see p. 34 above):

Purgatory is not the *"status termini"* in the strict sense of the
word, but an intermediary state in some way resembling the
"status viae" since in purgatory we prepare ourselves—without
freedom or merit, of course—for the possession of our last end.

Formerly, a third condition was required, namely, the Redeemer's entrance into heaven. But since the Ascension, this condition no longer holds. It was fitting that no one be admitted to
heaven before our Lord Himself entered in body and soul, to
demonstrate that all men owe this blessing to His merits. It was
fitting that the Head should precede His members.

That is why it is the Church's common doctrine that the just
who died before the Ascension ascended into heaven only after
Christ. It is believed that they had enjoyed a certain happiness
(in limbo), but not the beatific vision. This effect of grace re-

mained in abeyance just as it does in purgatory. Grace produces the *"lumen gloriae,"* the principle of vision, at the proper moment.

We now know that this moment is the end of purgatory (when the just man is obliged to pass through it) or the very instant of his death if he has no further expiation to make.

2 Partaking of the Nature of God

THE aptitude for the beatific vision conferred by grace is a veritable participation in the nature of God. In a certain respect it deifies the soul that possesses it. In this Chapter we shall discuss: 1. *the fact* of our participation; 2. *the explanation* of our participation; and 3. a few *consequences* of our participation.

1. The Fact

The infallible Church teaches this truth in her liturgy and through her most authentic doctors.

At Mass, when the priest pours a few drops of water into the wine to be consecrated, He asks for himself and for those present that they "may be made partakers of His divinity who vouchsafed to become partaker of our humanity." The mixture of the water and the wine calls to mind and symbolizes this twofold participation, the drop of water representing humanity, and the wine, the divinity.

The Preface of the Ascension proclaims that "Christ . . . was lifted up unto heaven, so that He might make us partakers of His Godhead."

48

The Secret for the Fourth Sunday after Easter reads: "O God, who by the sacred intercourse of this sacrifice hast made us partakers of the one supreme divine nature. . . ." And the Postcommunion for the Mass of St. Cyril (March 18) asks: "May the sacrament of Thine own Body and Blood which we have received, sanctify our minds and hearts, . . . and thereby make us worthy to become partakers of the divine nature."

The Fathers have relied upon this dogma, as upon a principle admitted by all, even heretics, in order to establish the divinity of Jesus Christ and of the Holy Spirit. We have many examples of this, especially among the Greeks. St. Cyril of Alexandria (†444) declares: "The Spirit is God by nature, since it is by participating in Him that we participate in the divine nature, that we can be called children of God and hence gods ourselves" (*In Joan. comment.* P.G., 73; p. 157, I, I, 1-13). And in his work on the Blessed Trinity, he says: "The Spirit is God and transforms into God . . . those who are worthy of it, by communicating the divine nature to them Himself."

We find the same doctrine taught by St. Athanasius (295–373): "The Son is He through whom the Father deifies. . . . Whence it follows that if He were God only by participation and not consubstantially, He could not deify others. . . . The true Son became man in order to make us gods" (*Epistula de Synodis.* P.G., 26; p. 784, 5,1).

St. Basil declares: "Souls that bear the Spirit within them (*animae quae spiritum ferunt*) attain a resemblance with God; and this results in the most sublime thing possible, your deification (*hinc est ut deus fias*)" (*De Spiritu Sancto,* 375; P.G., 32, p. 116; Ch. 19:23).

St. Ambrose asks: "Who would dare maintain that the Holy Spirit is by nature different from the Father and Christ, since it is through Him that we receive the image and likeness of God and that we become partakers of the nature of God, according to the words of St. Peter?" (*De Spiritu Sancto,* P.L., 16, p. 723; 1.I, Ch. 6:80).

Pseudo-Dionysius declares: "Salvation is reserved for those who have been deified. This deification is, insofar as is possible, an assimilation to, an identification with God" (*De Eccl. hierarchia,* P.G., 3, p. 373, Ch. 1:3).

St. Augustine remarks: "It is evident that since God calls men gods, He must deify them by His grace. . . . He alone deifies who is God of Himself and not by participation in another. It is He, too, who justifies, because in justifying men He makes them sons of God. If we become children of God, we become God" (*In Psalmum* 49:2, P.L., 36, p. 565).

These excerpts, and many more that we could cite, show how familiar this magnificent doctrine of the deification of the just man through grace was to the great minds of the first centuries, with what vigor they affirmed it, and with what fervent insistence they presented it. In doing this, they were merely imitating the Apostles and reproducing their very explicit teachings on this subject.

Grace, according to St. Peter and St. John, is the seed of God in us: "For you have been reborn, not from corruptible seed but from incorruptible" (I Pet. 1:23).

And St. John affirms: "Whoever is born of God does not commit sin, because his seed abides in him" (I Jn. 3:9).

Material seeds are cells that become detached from living bodies by division and become the embryos of new living bodies of like nature. Since God is absolutely indivisible and simple, He can detach nothing from Himself that would produce beings like to Himself. But He can create and introduce in creatures a principle that is a reproduction of His nature. Regardless of whether the planting of seed is produced by division of living matter or by creation, the essential elements of the concept of sowing seed are: 1) the seed must communicate to another being the nature and the traits of the one from which it comes; 2) it must be produced by the being that communicates. Hence, if the Holy Spirit calls grace "the seed of God," grace must at least come from Him and reproduce His nature in the one who receives it.

Other expressions used by the sacred writers lead to the same conclusion.

For example, they declare and repeat that the just man is "born of God, begotten, regenerated by God, that he is the son of God. . . ."

But how can we say that a man is another's son, begotten by him, born of him, that he received life from him, unless he participates in the nature of this other, and belongs to the same species as he? Neither plants nor animals can be born (in the strict sense of the word) of a man. Birth, generation, sonship all imply a similitude of species, of nature. The classical definition is well known: "*Origo viventis a vivente in similitudinem naturae*—the transmission by a living being to another of a life like its own." That is the purpose of generation: to preserve the species by transmitting it unchanged. All that is necessary for generation is that a living being communicate to another living being a share in its nature or "the transmission of like life to a like being." The mode of transmission is not unique or essential. Thus, if we are to rightly claim we are born of God, begotten of God, sons of God, it is necessary and it suffices that God make us share in His own nature.

St. Peter seems to affirm this participation explicitly in his Second Epistle: "He [Jesus Christ] has granted us the very great and precious promises, so that through them you may become partakers of the divine nature, having escaped from the corruption of that lust which is in the world" (II Pet. 1:4).[1]

2. Explanation of the Nature of This Participation

The reality of our participation in the divine nature through grace is incontestable, inasmuch as this point has been explicitly revealed. We have yet to try to explain the nature of this participation.

By participation do we mean that the just possess the divine nature in common with and like the Three Persons of the Blessed Trinity?

Evidently not. For then there would be as many divine persons as there are just ones, all of them infinite, uncreated, eternal, immutable, and enjoying the beatific vision. But that is not the case.

---

[1] Cf. *Note* giving an opinion on this text, p. 63 below.

Well, then, in the just, perhaps divine nature and human nature are united while remaining distinct, as in the case of Christ? That is equally false. In Christ there is only one divine Person, the Second Person of the Blessed Trinity, who possesses in His own right and perfectly both human and divine nature, and through the latter all the attributes and perfections of God. Now, the case of our Lord Jesus Christ is unique. The hypostatic union is His inalienable privilege. And daily experience teaches us that we are only human persons, far removed from the perfections of the divine nature.

Hence grace does not communicate to us divine nature in itself, as it is possessed by the Persons of the Blessed Trinity.

Would participation be a part, like a living cell that separates from a living being to produce another like itself? Does participation signify a "sharing," a division, as implied in the current expressions: to participate in benefits, to share in dividends, to participate in an enterprise or an inheritance? In other words, does participating in the divine nature mean having a part of it that others do not have? It is not that, either. Divine nature is absolutely simple and indivisible. No part of this nature can be separated from the rest. Hence, to participate in it cannot mean to "share" a part of it.

Could divine nature "inhere in," be united to our human nature, be implanted in it as a new faculty (while our human personality remains intact) by means of a union that is not "hypostatic" but "accidental" in the Scholastic sense of the term? Grace is indeed an "accident" (as we shall explain later), something that is added to our being after it has already been constituted and something that belongs to it, that depends upon our human personality. It is a new principle of our already-existing aptitudes. But divine nature cannot be an "accident," something that belongs to a human, finite, created, imperfect person essentially subject to change. For that would be a contradiction. It is true that grace gives God—as we shall see later—, that it is the principle of a special indwelling of the Three Persons of the Blessed Trinity in the soul, of a special and supernatural union with the divine nature. But it cannot make this nature ours, in whole or in part.

Thus the participation to which grace gives rise can only be an imitation, a replica, a reproduction, a created and finite miniature of the divine nature, something like the small clay model of an immense cathedral. Grace is God's clay model within us.

But then, exactly what does grace produce in us? Does not every creature (even the sinner) possess a few replicas or reflections of the divine attributes through which it participates in some way in the perfections of God? Yes, and that is why our reason can rise by its own efforts to a certain knowledge of the Creator (cf. Rom. 1:20). However, these perfections do not constitute the nature of God in the strict sense, that is, according to the Scholastic definition: i.e., His essence considered as the principle of His own operations. For the nature or essence of a being is that which distinguishes it from other beings of a different species, it is the thing that specifies it. For example, a being that possesses what is necessary to constitute a man—a body and a soul—and thus verifies the definition of a man (a rational animal), possesses a human nature.

To live is natural to plant and animal life, but it is above the nature of minerals. It is natural for animals to know through their senses, but it is above the nature of plant life. It is natural for man to reason and make free choices, but it is above the nature of unreasoning animals. In the strict sense of the word, nature thus includes whatever distinguishes a being from those inferior to it; whatever is natural to the former and above the nature of the latter.

It is clear, therefore, that whatever perfections created beings possess, similar to the perfection of God, cannot constitute their nature in the strict sense. For the perfections of God's nature are absolutely above the nature and powers of all created or "possible" beings.

Such is the intuitive, direct vision of God (without the benefit of any intermediary). Being natural to Him alone, this vision exceeds the natural capacities and exigencies of all creatures. For creatures possess a natural aptitude for knowing the perfection of beings only by means of created images or ideas "inherent" in the intellect but distinct from it and from the object these images or ideas represent.

We can therefore affirm in all truth that when God makes us participate in the intuitive vision of His Essence through grace, He makes us participate in His nature; that when He endows us here on earth with at least a radical aptitude for this vision, He communicates to us at least germinally a participation in His own action. Evidently He does not make us participate in all the properties or perfections of His Essence (for some of them are incommunicable, such as His "aseity," His infinity), but He makes us participate in the principle of His own action: the vision of Himself.

Such a participation does not abolish the distinction between God and ourselves; it does not produce a pantheistic fusion.

It is only a created, limited, supernatural, "accidental" reproduction added to our souls. God's nature, on the other hand, the principle of His vision, is uncreated, infinite, like His Essence with which it is fused in perfect simplicity.

Within us, this participation in the divine nature is not necessary or immutable (here on earth it can either be lost or intensified). In God, it is eternal and without any possibility of change.

In God, vision is infinite, adequate to its object, which is infinite. In us, it is not comprehensive. It allows us to see Him in the same manner as He sees Himself, by the same procedure: intuitively, but not with the same degree of perfection. We cannot exhaust the object, which is infinite. We cannot grasp it in its entirety by our intellect, and yet we grasp it directly in itself. That is what we mean when we say that this participation is formal, according to the same form, the same mode and species as the vision which God has of Himself; and yet it is only analogous, i.e., not in the same degree or of equal intensity.

All these differences suffice in great part to establish a fundamental distinction between God and ourselves. Grace does not metamorphose us into God. It does not fuse us with Him. And yet it assimilates us to Him in a very real way.

Grace communicates to us as much of God as a creature, that inevitably remains personally distinct from Him, can receive. It makes us participate in His divinity to the maximum (not as to degree but as to mode of acting). Grace raises us up in a certain respect to His level. To use an expression taken from the art of music, grace transposes us to a superior order, the divine order, from the natural to the supernatural order.

Grace takes nothing away from the perfections proper to our nature, but adds on new perfections that are superior to it. It destroys none of our human properties, but adds divine properties to them that are natural and proper only to God. Grace does not make us stop being men, but makes us become in a very lofty sense supermen, divinized men. It "engrafts" us upon God, so to speak.[2] Just as the wild stock participates in the perfection of the species upon which it is engrafted, receives its properties, and bears its leaves and fruit; so the just man receives a communication of the nature and life of God (by acquiring the capacity for God's own operation, namely vision) and a communication likewise of His divine dignity.

But the plant graft and the "wild stock" are of the same order and differ only in species. God on the other hand belongs to an order that is infinitely superior and supernatural to man. This gives us some faint notion of the incomparable elevation that this union brings about in man.

Let us consider an animal, a swallow for instance. It cannot speak or express ideas, understand language, study, perform intelligent and free acts, or perfect itself. It builds its nest today the way it did in Assyria in the days of Tobias.[3] Let us suppose that suddenly, this little swallow—while retaining its bird's body, wings, feathers, beak, and feet, acquired the capacity to speak, reason, learn, change and improve its manner of living and acting, and gave evidence of intelligence and freedom like a human person. How sur-

---

[2] There is no need to remark that God does not become a single individual with us (as is the case of a graft and its subject): that would be pantheism. Instead, the created image of His nature, namely grace, enters our being and elevates our personality.

[3] 7th century before Christ. Cf. Tobias 2:11.

prised we would be! The story would spread all over the
world, and people would flock to see this wonder. And it
would be a wonder, a real miracle. For it is not of the nature
of an animal to produce such acts. In this case, God would
have endowed an animal nature with an added human nature.

This is a description of what grace produces in us. We
acquire the capacity to perform acts that exceed our nature
and are natural only to God. The distance between these
divine acts and our human nature is even much greater than
the distance between human acts and animal nature. The
former are above the nature of all existing or possible creatures, and hence absolutely supernatural. The latter are only
relatively supernatural, i.e., for creatures devoid of reason
and not for angels or men. Divine nature, in which grace
makes us share, surpasses our human nature to an infinitely
greater degree than the latter surpasses animal nature.

Through grace, something happens within us that is analogous to what happened in the Divine Word through the Incarnation (but in reverse order). Through the hypostatic
union, the Word humbled Himself to the point of associating a human nature to His divine Nature, thus making it
possible for Him to accomplish human acts. Through grace,
a created reproduction of divine Nature inheres in a created
person (i.e., a man) the way an accident is united to a substance, thus bringing to this person new energies that make
him capable of performing the act proper to God, namely,
vision. The Word descended; the just man ascends. The
Word humbled Himself in order to raise us up. To repeat
the words of St. Athanasius, "the true Son of God became
man in order to make us gods" (cf. p. 77 above).

Whereas the hypostatic union "humanized" the Word,
grace divinizes man. And it is in order to divinize us that
the Word "humanized" Himself. "The Word was made flesh
to give us the power to be born of God and to become the
children of God." Grace is thus, as it were, the prolongation
of the Incarnation, and the union that it makes us contract
with God constitutes the flowering of the hypostatic union in
us. The Church has good reason, therefore, to sing with

enthusiastic gratitude: "A wondrous fellowship: the Creator of the human race, taking unto Himself a living body, . . . hath bestowed upon us His divinity" (Ant. 1, Second Vespers for the Circumcision).

3. The Consequences

From this marvelous effect of sanctifying grace there result for the soul other very precious effects that we shall study in the remainder of this work. For the present, we shall point out three of these effects: 1) resemblance with God; 2) supernatural beauty; and 3) supernatural grandeur.

Resemblance with God. God sees Himself intuitively. Through grace, the just man will see God in the same manner. This is the act that is most fitting and essential to God, the most distinctive and characteristic act of His divinity. Hence it is the act that brings us closest to Him, that makes us commune most abundantly in His divine nature, that assimilates us to Him most perfectly; the act that makes us most like Him. Evidently, this likeness will be more perfect when we actually enjoy the Vision in heaven, but it already exists in our soul germinally since, through grace, we possess the aptitude for it. In all truth, therefore, we can transpose St. John's words to the present tense: *"Similes ei erimus. . . .*" (I Jn. 3:2). We shall be to Him, and we are like to Him even now.

The *"character"* that certain sacraments produce impresses upon our souls the resemblance, the image of Christ the Priest. Grace impresses the likeness, the image of God Himself. It impresses upon the soul like a seal one of His most personal traits. In a certain respect it produces God within us; it marks us with His sign. We are stamped with His seal, as St. Paul wrote to the Ephesians and the Corinthians (Eph. 1:13; II Cor. 1:22). Through grace we resemble God more closely than children do their earthly fathers. Our resemblance with Him is much deeper, more extensive, and more perfect. It assimilates us to God more perfectly than our natural birth assimilates us to the man who has begotten us in the flesh.

All creatures resemble God in a certain degree. All of them bear within them something of Him and participate more or less in His perfection. Some resemble Him only insofar as they exist, others inasmuch as they are living beings, and still others by reason of their intellect and free will. Being effects of His power, all creatures are more or less perfect reflections of His divinity. But no creature (not even the angels solely through their essence) participates in His nature. This is the sublime privilege of souls in the state of grace. Lofty as the natural similitude of creatures with God may be, it is still infinitely inferior to the similitude of the just, for theirs is a supernatural likeness. St. Cyril of Alexandria says: "The Holy Spirit has made us participate in God; He has impressed upon us a resemblance with God and has elevated us to His own image" (*In Joannis Evang.,* P.G., 73; P.L. 9:1-13).

The devil well deserved the name "father of lies" (Jn. 8:44) when he promised our first parents that by transgressing God's command they would become like to Him. That is exactly the opposite of the truth. Actually, they lost this glorious likeness when they lost grace through their sin. "Grace," says Father Monsabré, "is God impressing His likeness upon us, just as a seal impresses its likeness upon wax, or better still as a man impresses the character of his ideas upon the material objects that he fashions. There is this difference, however, that the divine character communicated to us is living and makes of us living images of the very substance of God."

Supernatural Beauty. God is infinite beauty, and all created beauty is but His pale reflection. To resemble Him, to participate in His nature is to have beauty proportionally. The soul of the just man has more beauty than all the rest of the universe. It is more limpid than tranquil lake waters and a cloudless sky; more immaculately white than the freshest lilies and the most virginal snows; it has more harmony and proportion, more splendor and light, more restful variety, power and grace than the rarest flowers, the most perfectly formed bodies, the most admired landscapes, and the most famous masterpieces. After God, nothing is as beautiful as grace. Grace wears its name well. For, according to one of its meanings, it makes the soul gracious.

In heaven the sight of God plunges the elect into ecstasies of admiration and fixes their minds upon Him, filling them with love for His beauty. Likewise, making all due allowances, if we could contemplate a soul in the state of grace in this life we would want to embrace it forever in our enthusiasm, and only the sight of God could separate us from it.

So great is this invisible beauty that the body sometimes receives invisible reflections of it which, as has been noticed in the saints,[4] transforms even the physical features. It is the dawn of the glory that will be reflected from the soul upon the body after the resurrection.

The Fathers and the saints have sung with delight about the beauty of the just soul. St. Clement of Alexandria teaches: "The man in whom the Word dwells (through grace) participates in the 'form' of the Word; he resembles God. His is not a sham beauty but a real beauty, for he is God" (P.G., 8, 1, III, Ch. 1). St. Cyril of Alexandria explains: "It is the ancient beauty of our nature that reappears."

Why is the nuptial garment, the symbol of grace, required for admittance to the wedding of the Bridegroom? Is it not because it adorns the "guest," enhances his beauty, confers upon him a splendor, a charm, and a beauty that liken him to the Bridegroom?

St. John Chrysostom proclaims: "It is as if God had taken a young man disfigured by illness and suddenly made him a marvel of beauty exceeding all others. Thus has He adorned our soul [through grace] with a beauty that makes it attractive and lovable" (P.G., 62, p. 13; ad Eph., hom. 1, Ch. 1,3).

St. Thomas says that the beauty grace gives the soul comes from the shining forth of God's splendor. And the *Catechism of the Council of Trent* teaches that grace makes souls resplendent with beauty. The soul adorned with grace is a true marvel. "Lord!" St. Teresa of Avila used to cry out, "if

---

[4] The Curé of Ars, for example.

sinners saw what I see, it seems to me they would never want to lose the splendor of grace that sin takes from them."

Even though this beauty is interior, *"omnis gloria filiae regis ab intus,"* it is none the less a sublime reality that the elect, the angels, and God Himself contemplate with love and delight. This is one of the secondary joys of heaven. How incomparable is the beauty of this multitude of beings reflecting, like living gems, the rays of God's beauty!

The reason the Blessed Virgin is "altogether beautiful— *tota pulchra,"* the most beautiful of creatures, is that she possesses grace in the highest possible degree, *gratia plena.* Wearing this garment of justice with which the Lord has clothed her, she says in the words of the Introit of the Mass of the Immaculate Conception: "I will greatly rejoice in the Lord, . . . for He hath clothed me with the garments of salvation, and with the robe of justice He hath covered me, as a bride adorned with her jewels."

Do we value this beauty of grace more than beauty of body? It is far from perfect in every way!

The beauty of grace does not dread the wrinkles of old age, the abuse of time, or even death. This beauty does not fade. It is preserved for all eternity. Far from being the capricious privilege of birth or nature, it is within reach of all and can easily be increased. It never confuses the heart or the senses, but on the contrary inspires them to goodness. It does not bring death to the soul through the eyes, but edifies and sanctifies.

It is not miserable and sometimes vicious creatures that find delight in grace, but the angels, the elect, and God Himself, whose love is the only thing that matters.

Those of us who believe in grace, who are Christians, must look farther and higher than the flesh, and be concerned not so much with the color and form of a person's hands, eyes, and face, as with the ravishing beauty of the soul. And beauty of body must never be cultivated at the expense of the soul's beauty. We must esteem souls as God does, placing the beauty of grace infinitely above every other.

We are familiar with the famous words of St. Gregory the Great. When he was still only a monk he noticed some young slaves of great beauty being sold in the market place in Rome. He asked about their country of origin and their religion and was told they were pagans from Brittany. "What a pity," he answered, "that the grace of these foreheads reflects souls devoid of interior grace!" And he resolved to work for the conversion of the Bretons. In his eyes, the soul's grace was far more precious than grace of body.

May it be the same for us! Let us take at least as much interest in the beauty of our souls as in that of our bodies. Respecting the logic of our faith, let us give each of them the esteem and rank that is its due. Let us spread the cult of beauty wherever it is to be found and with an appreciation of true values.

The Grandeur of a Soul in the State of Grace. God is the greatest, the most beautiful, and the most perfect of all beings. Hence creatures are all the greater, the more beautiful and perfect, in the measure that they more closely resemble and participate more intensely in God's divine attributes.

Now nothing brings souls closer to God, impresses upon them a more exact likeness of Him, or confers upon them such a lofty share of His Being as does grace, for it makes them participate in His own Nature. Not one of His reflected perfections in the created world, magnificent as it may be, not all the wonders and riches of the universe is worth a single ray of grace—not even genius, or the poetry of spring, the grandeur of snowy peaks, the most charming landscapes, the expanse of oceans, or the infinitude of stars and worlds. The reason for this is that grace belongs to a superior order and brings man a greater share in the Godhead than can be found in all the worlds taken together. By means of a single degree of grace, God communicates Himself infinitely more than He does through all of created nature. This reflection of His divinity is more intense than all the others in the universe. There is more splendor, beauty, and perfection in the just man than in all other creatures (devoid of grace) taken together. His dignity exceeds that of the greatest personages of this earth. He is above kings and emperors.

"The heavens are magnificent, the universe is a masterpiece, the human intellect produces wonders. But the splendor of the heavens, the harmony of the universe, the glory of genius and of great fame are thrown into shadow before the soul of an idiot, of a beggar, of a man in rags who can say with the Apostle: 'By the grace of God I am what I am— *Gratia Dei sum id quod sum*' (I Cor. 15:10)" (Monsabré, 1875, 18th Conference).

"There is a vast distance between a worm and a man; and yet it is not so great as the distance between a man in his original state and a man who has been divinely transformed" (Beaudenon, 33rd Meditation).

St. Augustine affirms: "The grace of God surpasses the stars and the heavens in dignity. Far more, it leaves the most sublime angelic natures far below it." He even goes so far as to place elevation through grace above Mary's privilege as the Mother of God; and he offers as proof of this our Lord's answer to the woman who proclaimed blessed the womb that had borne Him (cf. Lk. 11:28). By this he meant that Mary's divine maternity in itself does not give a participation in the divine nature, as does grace.

"It is more glorious for Mary to be the daughter of God through grace than His mother by nature" (Nieremberg, *Le prix de la grâce*).

We must acquire a more exact knowledge of this sublime grandeur that grace confers upon us, so as to thank God more fervently for it and to make our conduct harmonize more perfectly with it.

Should not our whole life be a hymn of thanksgiving for such a blessing, and should we not, like the Virgin Mary, sing our *Magnificat* every day to the Almighty who has done such great things in us, and has raised us from our lowliness to such heights: *Et exaltavit humiles?*

But the very foundation of our dignity also points to our obligations. It is our duty to respect ourselves and to respect other just men and women, to revere the divine in them and in ourselves, to refuse to allow ourselves any vulgarity in thoughts, words, or actions, to acquire distinction in our sentiments, language, and manners, to elevate our ideas and our tastes. *Noblesse oblige.*

While we have a right to be proud of our supernatural grandeur, we must above all else be worthy of it. Hence, we must strive to make our conduct harmonize with our spiritual state, what we do with what we are. We must not allow this resemblance with God to remain hidden in the secret depths of our soul but on the contrary express it outwardly, manifest it in practice, make it blossom and bear fruit in acts, ensconce it in a framework of divine virtues and works, encase it in holiness. For likeness in nature calls for likeness in thoughts, will, love, and operations. Since we are divine in our being, let us be divine in our acts. The moral beauty of our life must rise to the level of the divine beauty that grace has implanted in us.

At least, and above all, let us avoid sin that would destroy these incomparable privileges. Sin would cast us down from ineffable heights and strip us of untold riches.

"Every tree bears fruit in keeping with its nature: since your nature is divine, your actions must be divine as well. That is the reason why, immediately after telling us that we participate in the divine nature, St. Peter immediately adds that we must flee 'from the corruption of that lust which is in the world' (II Pet. 1:4)" (Pesch, *De Gratia*, No. 344).

St. Leo counsels: "Let us become aware of our dignity, and having become partakers of the divine nature let us not fall back into our former lowliness" (P.L., 54, Sermon 213).

Note on II Pet. 1:4 (see p. 51 above):

A few authors wonder whether this text must be understood to mean present participation or future participation in heaven. The answer does not seem clear to them.

"Does the author present this communion of divine life to us as an end already obtained in this life or as a goal to be attained in the life to come? The *consortium divinae naturae* would then be a formula equivalent to the eternal reign of our Lord and Savior Jesus Christ, set forth in II Pet. 1:2 as the term and reward of our moral life." (Cf. Tobac, D. A., art. "Grace.")

The word "promises" in II Pet. 1:4 might seem to indicate a reality as yet unfulfilled.

But many of Christ's promises are realized even during this life, and the Fathers and most of the exegetes have interpreted

St. Peter's words to be in the *present* tense: for example, St. Ambrose, St. Cyril of Alexandria, and St. Leo. The Church alludes to them in her prayers as a participation here and now. Thus in the Offertory of the Mass, she says: *"Da nobis . . . ejus divinitatis esse consortes*—grant that . . . we may be made partakers of His divinity. . . ."

In the preceding chapter we have shown that the beatific vision calls into being even in this life a proportionate aptitude that is itself already a participation in the divine life. While the act of vision will make us *consortes divinae naturae,* the thing that confers upon us a capacity for it, even if it is only rudimentary, the thing that is its fundamental source, already produces this effect. For does a son participate in the human nature of his father only when he is accomplishing intellectual operations like those of his father?

3 Divine Adoption

PARTICIPATION in the divine nature, whose source is grace, acquires for the just man another prerogative that is quite as precious and magnificent: elevation to the dignity of being a child of God, *supernatural adoption*.

We shall approach this subject as follows: 1) we shall establish the reality of this adoption; 2) we shall set forth its nature and its excellence; 3) we shall point out a few consequences of our divine adoption.

1. The Reality

BECOMING CHILDREN OF GOD!

We should never have dared hope for such a favor or aspire to such an honor if God Himself had not clearly revealed it to us as a surprising, stirring, and sublime reality.

But His affirmations are so categorical, so insistent, that we must unhesitatingly accept them with hearts full of gratitude and joy. As the Church sings in the prologue to the Our Father during Mass: *"Taught by our Savior's command and following His divine instruction we make bold to say: Our Father. . . ."*

True, there is little mention of it in the Old Testament. When the Fatherhood of God is referred to it, it usually ap-

plies to common and natural fatherhood in the broad sense.
Or when there is mention of a special fatherhood, an adopted
fatherhood, this concerns not individuals but the Hebrew
people that Yahweh has chosen in order to preserve the purity
of faith and morality amid the corruption and errors of nations, just as the ark preserved Noe's family on the waters
of the flood. This adoption refers to the chosen people with
whom God has made a covenant, whom He cares for, protects, reprimands, and surrounds with special attentions, as
a father does his child. All this presupposes a truly paternal
affection on God's part.

Evidently, this people is composed of individuals, each of
whom is the beneficiary of Yahweh's paternal affection and
protection. But this paternity does not relate directly to
interior grace, since it persists, as does the covenant, even
during periods of prevarication among the people. At such
times God's Fatherhood finds expression in chastisements,
just as a father's sincere love sometimes manifests itself by
the punishments he inflicts upon a delinquent child. Nevertheless, God's fatherly love remains even in this case, which
would not be the case for adoption through grace.[1]

It was left to Jesus Christ the Son to reveal this Fatherhood
to men. For it was He who merited for them this incomparable benefit, gave them the means of becoming His
brothers, raised them to the full stature of this sonship,
brought them the consequences of God's tenderness and liberation, and united them all into a single family, into a single
Mystical Body, whose Head He is: the Church.

And it was by the anticipated virtue of His merits that the
just who lived before Him were able to share in them, even
though imperfectly.

The Fatherhood of God is the principal object of His
teachings. This is the good news—the Gospel—He came to
announce to men, the great innovation of His religion, the
source of the uniqueness of the kingdom that He came to
found. His disciples were to adore God as a Father, and their

---

[1] Cf. Lebreton, *History of the Dogma of the Trinity*, New York, Benziger,
1939.

worship was to be penetrated with tenderness, trust, self-sacrifice, and filial sincerity.

In the one prayer He taught them, the first words He placed on their lips and the only title He asked them to give God was the title of Father, *Pater noster*—a name that inspires and is the keynote of all Christian devotion. That is the characteristic of the new worship He came to establish, the summing up of the religion He came to teach.

The Sermon on the Mount, the charter of His kingdom, can be rightly understood only in the light of this dogma. "You therefore are to be perfect even as your heavenly Father is perfect. . . . Thy Father, who sees in secret, will reward thee. . . . For if you forgive men their offenses, your heavenly Father will also forgive you your offenses. . . . Therefore I say to you, do not be anxious for your life, ... for after all these things the Gentiles seek . . . . your Father knows that you need all these things" (Mt. 5:48; 6:4,14,25).

The whole argument presupposes sonship. Pagans live in anxiety, because they do not know of God's Fatherhood. To know and to believe in it are the privilege and the mark of Christians. For Christians God is not merely, as He was for the Jews, the all-powerful Master whose authority and rights are forcibly obeyed through fear, the Lawgiver of Sinai hidden in clouds of thunder, the terrible Judge ready to punish those who despise His Law, the Sovereign whose anger is dreaded and who is addressed only with fear and trembling. He is also and above all the loving Father who surrounds His children with paternal tenderness and solicitude, the Father to be imitated, for whose sake we must do all things and in whom we must place our trust.

While the Synoptics do bear witness to our supernatural sonship, the Fourth Gospel contains many more and much more explicit references to it, especially the famous passage of the Prologue: "But to as many as received Him [Christ] He gave the power of becoming sons of God; to those who believe in His name: who were born not of blood, nor of the will of the flesh, nor of the will of man, but of God" (Jn. 1:12-13).

Does this passage refer to the sonship common to all men

who (because they receive life and all else from God) can call themselves children of God in a broad sense? On the contrary, it refers to a special sonship, the privilege of those who receive Christ and cleave to Him through faith, a sonship whose foundation is not birth from a man but birth from God. It is a sonship that is a special and signal favor, a favor that many fail to profit by because they do not posit the necessary condition for receiving grace, namely, receiving Christ. None of these marks of divine sonship applies to man's natural, common, and necessary sonship.

The discourse after the Last Supper is full of this idea of God's Fatherhood. Throughout, Jesus refers to God as a Father.

Jesus spoke of the Father with affectionate insistence. It is through Him that we go to the Father. Who sees Jesus has also seen the Father. And He promised to speak plainly of the Father (cf. Jn. 14:6,9; 16:26).

The sonship that Jesus has revealed to us is the reason for His New Commandment: the command of fraternal charity, the mark of His disciples, on which the Beloved Apostle laid so much stress in His teaching because He seems to have understood the dogma of our divine adoption and its admirable consequences in a particularly luminous way. He often came back to it in his Epistles, and referred to it to inculcate his lessons in spirituality.

In his first Epistle to the Christians of Palestine, St. John had already expressed the same doctrine: "Behold what manner of love the Father has bestowed upon us, that we should be called children of God; and such we are" (I Jn. 3:1). This is an effect of God's love, a completely gratuitous favor that is not implicit in our nature; a prerogative that He is willing to freely add to our nature: the gift of His benevolence that makes Him our Father—"*dedit Pater*"—and makes us His children—"*ut filii Dei nominemur et simus.*" He is our Father, and not the Father of others, He is the Father of Christians and not of pagans. Consequently it is a special sonship, not open to all.

Could this effect of grace in our souls have been expressed more categorically? (Cf. I Jn. 31:1,2,9; 5:1,4). "Whoever is born of God does not commit sin, because His seed abides in him and he cannot sin. In this the children of God . . . are made known" (I Jn. 3:9-10). (The Gospel often uses the word *semen* to mean child.) "Whoever is not just is not of God" (I Jn. 3:11). Whoever does good "is born of God—*ex Deo est.*" Whoever believes that Jesus is the Christ is born of God.

The other Apostles taught the same thing, and drew practical conclusions from it for their Christians. St. Peter wrote: "As obedient children, do not conform to the lusts of former days when you were ignorant. . . . And if you invoke as Father Him who without respect of persons judges according to each one's work, conduct yourselves with fear . . . . love one another heartily and intensely. For you have been reborn, not from corruptible seed but from incorruptible, ... Crave as newborn babes, pure spiritual milk" (I Pet. 1:14-2:2).

To turn the Romans and the Galatians away from slavery to Jewish practices to which the Judaizers were trying to lead them, St. Paul reminded them that henceforth they were to emancipate themselves from such practices since they were sons: "Now you have not received a spirit of bondage so as to be again in fear, but you have received a spirit of adoption as sons, by virtue of which we cry, 'Abba! Father!' The Spirit Himself gives testimony to our spirit that we are sons of God. But if we are sons, we are heirs also" (Rom. 8:14-15).

And to the Galatians: "But when the fullness of time came, God sent His Son . . . . that He might redeem those who were under the Law, that we might receive the adoption of sons. And because you are sons, God has sent the Spirit of His Son into our hearts, crying, 'Abba, Father.' So that he is no longer a slave, but a son. . . ." (Gal. 4:5-7).

The Apostle almost always speaks of God as "our Father" (cf. I Thess. 1:1; 3:11). Bellamy writes: "The dogma of natural adoption is among those that have been taught most clearly and frequently in Scripture. Not only is the fact of adoption affirmed, but in a certain degree its nature and the privileges that it brings with it are also affirmed" (D.T.C., "Adoption," col. 426).

And in the Epistle to the Hebrews, St. Paul shows the admirable condescension of Christ, who "is not ashamed to call them brethren" (Heb. 2:11).

Tradition is just as positive in its affirmations. Like the Apostles, the Fathers refer to this dogma as an indisputable basis used even by heretics in arguments against errors and in support of spiritual doctrine. The Greek Fathers, in particular, stressed this dogma with loving insistence.[2]

We have such an abundance of source material on divine adoption that we must limit ourselves. We shall therefore choose St. Athanasius (†373) among the controversialists, and St. John Chrysostom (†470) among the preachers.

Writing against the Arians, St. Athanasius said: "So great is God's goodness that He has made Himself the Father, through grace, of those whom He created. . . . They are the ones who, because they receive the Word, also receive from Him the capacity to become the sons of God. There was no other means of becoming His sons . . . than to receive the Spirit of the One who is truly the Son by nature" (P.G., 26; *Adversus Arianos,* 59).

Likewise: "The Son of God became the son of man so that the sons of man, that is, of Adam, might become the sons of God. In fact, the Word, who is eternally begotten by the Father in an ineffable and incomprehensible way, was born in time of the Virgin Mary so that those who had been born in an inferior way might have another and superior birth from God. Thus He has a mother upon earth; and we have a Father in heaven. Moreover, He calls Himself the Son of man so that men may call God their Father" (P.G., 26; *De Incarnatione,* 8).

In explaining to his people the genealogy of our Lord according to St. Matthew, St. John Chrysostom, the eloquent Bishop of Constantinople, cried out in a transport of love: "Let us be filled with boundless admiration: the Son of God

---

[2] Rousselot says: "The Johannic doctrine of divine adoption or generation has been exploited with enthusiastic predilection by the Greek Fathers. It is really the heart of their theology, and while it has never been the object of an explicit Conciliar decision, the reason may well be that it constituted the common foundation of the religious thought of the 4th century" (*Recherches de Sciences relig.,* 1928, Vol. 18, p. 90).

according to nature humbled Himself to the point of calling Himself the son of David, to make you the son of God. He endured having a slave as His father, so that you, slave, might have the Lord as your Father. . . . It is much harder, as far as the human intellect can judge, for God to become man, than for Him to make man a son of God. . . . He was born according to the flesh so that you might be born according to the spirit; born of woman so that you might cease being [merely] the son of woman" (P.G., 57, 2; *in Matth., Hom.* 2, written about 390).

But the Greek Fathers were not the only ones to extol our divine adoption. The Latin Fathers, and the greatest among them, have spoken about it with delight. Among the hundred passages we could cite as proof of this, we shall quote the following letter written by St. Augustine to Honoratus:

"Such is the grace of the New Testament, hidden within the Old and constantly foretold in figures, that through it the soul may understand its God and be reborn to Him. It is a spiritual birth, not of blood . . . but of God. It is called an adoption. We were something before becoming children of God and we have received the favor of becoming what we were not; just as the adopted son, before his adoption, was not yet the son of the one who adopted him, but already existed. And this generation by grace distinguishes the Son of God who came to become the Son of man in order to enable us, who were the sons of man, to become the sons of God" (Letters written between the years 354 and 430: *ad Honoratum cat. Epist.*, 140, ch. 9:9)

The Church could not fail to remind her faithful of this truth and to introduce into her liturgy a doctrine that is so important, so consoling, and so fruitful for devotion. And it was particularly fitting that she remind the faithful of it especially on those blessed days when new children are born to God through baptism: Easter and Pentecost.

The Paschal liturgy from Holy Saturday to the Sunday *in Albis* (inclusively) is full of this idea that illumines all its rites and prayers. Let us cite a few examples:

The Collect after the Third Prophecy on Holy Saturday: "O God, . . . who throughout the world dost multiply the children of Thy promise by diffusing the grace of Thy adoption. . . ."

The Collect after the Fifth Prophecy on Holy Saturday: "increase by Thy sacred adoption the children of that promise. . . ."

The Second Prayer of the blessing of the font: ". . . to regenerate the new people, whom the font of baptism brings forth. . . ."

The Preface: "May He by a secret mixture of His divine power render this water fruitful for the regeneration of men, to the end that a heavenly offspring, conceived in holiness and born again a new creature, may emerge from the stainless womb of the divine font: and that all, however distingiushed either by sex in body or by age in time, may be brought forth to the same infancy by grace, their spiritual mother."

The Collect of the Mass: "O God, . . . preserve in the new children of Thy family the spirit of sonship. . . ."

The following passage from the Canon: "This oblation of our servitude . . . which we offer also for those whom Thou hast deigned to regenerate in the water of the Holy Spirit. . . ."

The Preface of Pentecost: "Who . . . sent forth the Holy Spirit, as He had promised, on the children of adoption. . . ."

Let us add the Collect of the Transfiguration (August 6): "O God, who . . . didst in wondrous manner foreshow the perfect adoption of sons. . . ."

From Apostolic times onward and throughout the ages this dogma of our divine sonship through grace has been explicitly taught and believed in the Church. It did not pass through the three ordinary phases of progress, as have other dogmas: the period of implicit and peaceful faith, the period of controversy, and the period of definition and explicit faith. There was no development in the strict sense, since the dogma was completely clear from the start. Consequently, it has very little history. Heresy never attacked it in itself, for it had been categorically affirmed by Revelation.

In the absence of contradiction, the Scholastics did not feel the need to treat it *ex professo*. They spoke of it in dealing with the sonship of Christ.

St. Thomas devoted only three articles in his *Tertia Pars* to divine adoption, although we must agree they are packed with meaning. In the first of these, he shows the fittingness of this adoption on God's part, and its superiority over human adoptions. In the second, he shows its relationship with the three divine Persons. In the third, he discusses the subject who is capable of being adopted, that is, the likeness to God that divine adoption presupposes in the subject.

In the 14th and 15th centuries, the Nominalists raised a controversy. They did not deny the reality of our adoption through grace, but taught that this adoption is neither the effect, nor the grace, nor the charity of God, but purely a decision of God who has chosen to consider the just as His children. Hence it would be simply a "forensic" adoption, like those of men. The Council of Trent condemned this view at least implicitly by declaring that our sonship derives from the same principle as do justification, grace, and physical and intrinsic reality (Session VI, Ch. 4, Denz. 736).

From that time on there has been no divergence among Catholic theologians on this subject, and sonship has been inserted in the treatise on grace where it logically belongs.

The only arguments that have arisen since then have concerned two very secondary points.

a. The point as to whether grace and adoption are related to the point of being absolutely inseparable and of each requiring the presence of the other.

The partisans of the negative have been rare: to the extent that grace makes us participate in the nature of God, it makes us His children.

A few authors have held that an exception should be made for the just of the Old Law, in view of St. Paul's words: "God sent His Son, . . . that He might redeem those who were under the Law, that we might receive the adoption of sons. . . . So that he is no longer a slave, but a son" (Gal. 4:4-7). Well, then, if under the Old Law men were slaves, they must not have been sons.

But the Apostle explained what he meant and answered

this question himself: "But before the faith came we were kept imprisoned under the Law. . . . Therefore the Law has been our tutor unto Christ. . . . Now as long as the heir is a child, he differs in no way from a slave, though he is the master of all; but he is under guardians and stewards until the time set by his father. So we too, when we were children, were enslaved under the elements of the world" (Gal. 3:23-4:3). He was referring to the many detailed prescriptions of the Law concerning rites, and especially circumcision, to which certain converted Jews, the Judaizers, wanted to subject Christians. And St. Paul continued: "But now, . . . how is it that you turn again to the weak and beggarly elements, which you desire to serve again? You are observing days and months and seasons and years" (Gal. 4:9-10), i.e., the Jewish practices regarding religious feasts.

Through Christ, the children of God are henceforth liberated, like the son who, according to civil law, is released from the authority of his tutor when he comes of age, and can dispose as he pleases of himself and his possessions. But he was no less son, heir, and master, during his minority. Thus, the just under the Old Law were sons of God quite as much as those under the New, but they were so to speak under a guardian.

Besides, they were children of God not, according to Bellamy, "in virtue of the Mosaic law, powerless in itself to raise them so high, but in virtue of the anticipated influence of the New Testament to which they belonged radically through their faith in the Messias-Redeemer and through charity. . . .

"Moreover, the coming of the heavenly heritage being subordinate to the coming of Christ, the just of the Old Testament were in a far inferior situation to the just in the New Testament, with regard to the privileges of supernatural adoption. God manifested His fatherly affection less openly, He revealed Himself to them more as an all-powerful master than as a Father, His supernatural helps were less abundant, the means of obtaining and increasing sonship were less fruitful and fewer in number. The law was more one of fear than of love. Adoption was to have its eternal fulfillment [the beatific vision] only after the Savior's death, so that it might be more apparent to the world that all salvation comes from His Redemption, that all divine adoption is a derivation of His own ineffable sonship, and that no one comes to the Father but through Him [cf. Jn. 14:6] (D.T.C., art., "Adoption," col. 434).

b. The second controversial question is this: even if grace and adoption are inseparable, is grace or is the indwelling of the Holy Spirit in the soul the foundation or formal cause of adoption?

Lessius in the 17th century and Peteau in the 18th, as well as a few modern thinkers, have held the view that the indwelling of the Holy Spirit is the foundation of adoption.

However the opinion that considers grace itself as the foundation is much more common. This seems to have been at least the implicit view of the Council of Trent, and we can say it possesses theological certitude. According to the Council, to be justified, to be reborn in Christ, to become the adopted son of God, and to receive grace are one and the same thing under different aspects: "Unless they were reborn in Christ, they would never be justified." It defines justification as "the state of grace and of adoption of the children of God." Hence justification and adoption are brought about by the same cause, namely, grace.

That is the explicit teaching of the Catechism of the Council of Trent, when it says that baptism fills our souls with grace, whereby we become just and children of God (cf. No. 50). It seems very clear.

The foundation of our adoption is what makes us participate in the nature of God Himself, what brings us forth in God and causes us to be regenerated by Him. And this foundation is grace.[3]

Grace makes us children of God: this is a truth of faith. No truth has been more clearly affirmed in Scripture and Tradition, none is dearer to the heart of the Church, and there is none on which the Fathers, especially the Greek Fathers, have insisted with greater fervor. And this emphasis

---

[3] Cf. *Note* containing other opinions at the end of this chapter, pp. 84-85 below.

is well justified, for grace is one of the principal foundation stones, one of the most abundant sources of Christian devotion.

It is most fortunate that the theologians and ascetic writers of our own day are striving to give grace the importance it deserves. In view of its significance, we shall go into further detail as to the nature and excellence of our divine adoption through grace.

2. The Nature and Excellence of Our Adoption

Our sonship is something very special. Strictly speaking, it is neither a natural nor purely an adopted sonship.

a. It is not natural, but a matter of adoption. St. Paul specifically uses the word "adoption" (Gal. 4:5; Rom. 8:15; Eph. 1:5). True, he is the only one to use it. But other passages of Scripture use equivalent terms, for instance, those that call Christ *Unigenitus*—only-begotten, or that teach the gratuitousness of our sonship through grace.

Natural sonship is founded on the communication of the substance of the one who begets to the one begotten. First, in the generation of plant and animal bodies, a part of the father passes on to the son, becomes the son. This is the less perfect of the two modes of natural sonship.

Secondly, generation may occur through total communication, in such a way that father and son have but one substance, involving a relationship of fatherhood for the one and of sonship for the other. This is true only of the Blessed Trinity. The Son receives from the Father His own substance (*numero eadem*), and possesses it in common with Him. This is the most perfect Sonship possible, and the humanity of Christ participates in it since sonship derives from the person. But divine Nature cannot be passed on to creatures either by division (for it is simple, spiritual, and indivisible), or by total communication, for that is the privilege of Christ alone. Thus our supernatural sonship could not have its source in a division or in a total communication of the divine Nature. That is what we mean when we say that it is not *"natural."* The only other thing it can be is an adopted sonship.

Moreover, natural sonship is necessary. The Sonship of the Word through the Father is absolutely necessary. The sonship of man through man is also necessary in the sense that if a man performs a generative act (something that he is physically free to abstain from), and if a child is born, this child cannot *not* be his son. The son receives and keeps this relationship of sonship throughout his life.

Now a son "can . . . demerit. He can be driven from his father's house for his bad conduct. . . . He can even, in certain exceptional circumstances, be legitimately disinherited. But when, repentant and taught by misfortune, this new prodigal son returns to his father's house, he resumes his place in the family and is not an adopted son." [4] Whatever he may do or wherever he may go, he continues to carry his father's blood in his veins. From the moment he begins to live and as long as he lives, he is the son of the man who begot him. His sonship is inseparable from his existence.

It is otherwise with regard to adoption. It does not always, or even ordinarily, begin with life. It may never take place at all. Nothing makes it obligatory. It is free and gratuitous. We are not sons of God by the fact of our corporeal birth. We become His sons only after we are born and after waiting a certain length of time for our baptism. Since original sin, only the Blessed Virgin Mary received grace at the moment of her conception. As Pope Pius IX tells us, this is the "unique" privilege of her Immaculate Conception. There is also the exceptional case of St. John the Baptist who received grace three months before his birth.

But even if we received grace with life, as did Adam and Eve, we could still lose it through sin, just as they did. Grace is not bound up with human nature. It is not due to human nature. It is supernatural. It is called for neither by our nature nor by God's. In this sense we must say it comes by *adoption,* that is, through the free and gratuitous gift of God.

---

[4] P. Froget, *op. cit.,* Chapter 8.

b. Our grace comes to us by adoption, but it has several marks of superiority over human adoptions.

1. *A superiority of effect.* It is not purely exterior and "forensic," as claimed by the 14th and 15th century Nominalists (Occam, G. Biel, P. d'Ailly, and others). According to them, it would be the result of a decree by God deciding to consider the just man as his child and heir, while remaining perfectly free, if He so willed, not to do so. Thus adoption would have only an accidental relationship of coincidence with grace, not a relationship of essential causality.

Our divine adoption is something more and better than that. In a certain respect it imitates natural sonship. Its foundation is within the soul. According to St. John, Christ merited for us "the power of becoming sons of God: *filios Dei fieri*" (Jn. 1:12). And not only does God call us His children, but such we really are: *Ut filii Dei nominemur et simus*" (I Jn. 3:1).

Now someone who has merely been adopted bears the name of son, but he is not really, inwardly, a son.

The Apostle adds that through grace we are "born" of God, that we are His "seed," that we are "like to Him." And St. Paul says we were "begotten" by Him. But has it ever been said that an adopted son was born of his adopted father, that he is his seed, begotten by him, that there is a community of blood between them? To be exact, such expressions presuppose the communication of God's substance, a participation in His nature.

Moreover, even if a man can be content with fiction and appearances, even if he can consider as his son someone who really is not, God cannot do that. Penetrating the innermost reality of all beings with His all-seeing eye, He could not consider them as anything but what they really are. For Him, the interior must always correspond with the exterior, the invisible with the visible, the thing with the name, the ontological point of view with the logical point of view. With God, no abstraction or fiction is possible. He does not call anyone His child unless He has made him His child. He does not love anyone with a Father's love unless he is really His son. Hence our divine sonship is not merely a legal fiction. It is interior, it is better than sonship by adoption.

It can be said that our divine sonship is midway between truly natural sonship (through the communication of substance) and merely external adoption as realized by men. It is related to both. It resembles and differs from each of them. It is less perfect than natural sonship, but more perfect than adopted sonship. Like the former, it rests on a certain communication of nature, but this communication is not substantial and is made neither through a gift nor a division of substance. Moreover, divine sonship does not possess the mark of necessity which characterizes adopted sonship.

Actually Scripture sometimes calls divine sonship "generation," and sometimes "adoption." It is not precisely one or the other in the ordinary sense. It is less than a generation in the strict sense, and yet more than an adoption. There is no human term that can express it adequately, because the words are taken from what exists in the sensible world, and because there are no examples of generation or adoption like it in creation.

Divine adoption is a unique case: God alone can make it a reality. Without Revelation we would never even have surmised it, just as without the revelation of the mystery of the Blessed Trinity we would never have known the mode of natural generation, through the total communication of nature, which permits two Persons to possess one Nature in common—one as the Father and the other as the Son.

Thus our supernatural adoption is superior to human adoptions by reason of what it produces in the soul. St. Thomas says: "God, by bestowing His grace, makes man whom He adopts worthy to receive the heavenly inheritance; whereas man does not make him worthy whom he adopts; but rather in adopting him he chooses one who is already worthy" (IIIa, q. 23, a. 1).[5]

Moreover, adopted parents consider their adopted child as their own and may even have parental sentiments toward him. But it is not within their power to endow him with

[5] "Legal adoption is a fiction. The adopted child is considered by his adopted parents as if he were their child and receives from them the heritage

filial sentiments. While it is possible that the adopted child
will come to love and help them with filial devotion, as is
his duty, it is not they who will directly produce such dispositions in his heart.

But our heavenly Father does communicate to us, together
with His nature, the spirit of adoption that makes us cry
"Abba, Father" (Gal. 4:6). That is to say, He infuses in us,
together with grace, a filial mentality that makes us look to
Him as a Father: through the supernatural virtues, faith
(filial obedience to His word), hope (the desire to possess
Him, trust in His love and in His promises), and above all
charity (tenderness, and filial devotion toward Him); through
the gifts also—docility to His action, chiefly the gift of piety
that helps us to behave toward Him like real sons.

Hence, our divine adoption is superior to human adoption
in its *effects*.

2. *Superiority of its motive*. Human adoption is born of a
need. A couple generally decide upon it because they have
no children of their own or because they have too few. It is
very rare that the sole reason for adoption is the desire to
do good to the adopted child and for his good alone.

But what essential advantage can our adoption give God,
who is infinitely rich and sufficient unto Himself? The Angelic Doctor says that God adopts us only "in order to communicate to others the abundance of His perfection. Where-
fore, as by the work of creation the Divine goodness is
communicated to all creatures in a certain likeness, so by
the work of adoption the likeness of natural sonship is communicated to men" (IIIa, q. 23, ad 2). Our adoption is absolutely gratuitous on God's part, absolutely free, absolutely
supernatural. He had no need whatever of it. We had no
right to it. *"Voluntarie genuit nos*—of His own will he has
begotten us" (Jas. 1:18). It has no other motive than His
love, or other purpose than our well-being.

---

to which their natural child would have had a right. Society recognizes this
fiction and sanctions its effects. Nevertheless, the object of this fiction is not
transformed into a reality. The fact remains that the adopted child does not
possess the blood of those who declare he is theirs by adoption.

"The grace of divine adoption is not a fiction, it is not a convention, it
is a reality." (Mercier, *op. cit.*)

When a couple have an only son, they refrain from giving him adopted brothers who will share in his inheritance and in their affection. God has acted more generously in our regard. He had an only-begotten Son. He did not want Him to remain alone, but sent Him into our world to acquire a multitude of brothers (cf. Rom. 8:29).

3. *Superiority of the heritage* this adoption assures us. This inheritance is worth more, infinitely more, than all the riches in the world. It is God Himself, the unlimited Good. It is eternal and eternally possessed. It brings perfect happiness.

Human sonships have the serious disadvantage that the inheritance to which they give a right cannot be received until after and through the death of the father. The father must be lost in order to enjoy the use of his goods. Truly a sad necessity! We become heirs only by becoming orphans.

Besides, if there are several children the inheritance is divided, parcelled up. One does not receive the same share as another; what is given to one is taken away from another. Each child cannot possess the whole.

Our heavenly heritage is free of these defects. No one is excluded, because the heritage is possessed indivisibly. It consists precisely in the intimate and supernatural possession of the Father Himself, everliving and giving Himself to all His children, without detriment to any and without any exceptions.

True, we cannot go to heaven without dying to this world and to the creatures that are dear to us. But in heaven we shall find our Father who is worth infinitely more than everything we leave behind, and we shall be reunited to the multitude of souls waiting for us there. In heaven we shall have perfect peace possessed in ineffable delight.

4. But the great superiority of our supernatural sonship comes from *the dignity of the Father* that it gives us and from the manner in which it gives Him to us.

To be adopted by a powerful emperor, with the right of succession to the throne, is quite a different thing from being adopted by a penniless and worthless beggar. Adoption is worth as much as the father, as much as his heart and his goods.

The Father that grace gives us is not a creature, not a man: *"Neque ex voluntate carnis, neque ex voluntate viri, sed ex Deo nati sunt—*Who were born not . . . of the will of the flesh, nor of the will of man, but of God" (Jn. 1:13). This Father is God, the Creator and Master of all, the Infinite, the Eternal.

What is His heart worth? He has defined Himself as *Love* (I Jn. 4:16).

What is His love worth? We shall explain that later on.

And what are His possessions worth? We have just called that to mind.

And our divine sonship makes this Father present to us. Human fathers communicate a part of their substance, but not their whole selves. They do not become present in their children. They cannot compenetrate and dwell in them as God does in His children. The human cell, the seed of the son, becomes detached from the father. It lives apart from the father. Grace on the contrary, while distinct from God, does not leave Him. It draws Him, carries Him along toward itself. God follows grace. Wherever grace is, there God is by a special presence; and He is there forever if His son wills it.

Death will not steal from us either the Father or our brothers. They belong to us for all eternity. When death has ruthlessly deprived us of those whom we love, we shall still have the best of fathers and the best of brothers: Jesus. Even though our earthly family is decimated, we shall always have our family of grace. What a consolation for us in our bereavements!

In the words of our Lord, our divine sonship is superior not only to human adoptions but even to natural sonships in the strict sense, to the point that human fatherhood is as nothing compared with the Fatherhood of God through grace (cf. Mt. 23:9).

3. The Consequences of Divine Adoption

In the following chapter we shall study some of the dogmatic consequences of this divine adoption.

For the present, we shall merely mention two of its practical consequences.

a. *Pride.* Let others take pride in their princely power, their titles of nobility, or their illustrious genealogy. We Christians have something more and something better. We are descendants in the direct line and in the first degree of God Himself. In our veins flows His blood, so to speak, and His likeness is impressed upon our souls. Ours is something more than a noble or royal lineage. Ours is a divine race. We can and should be proud of it.[6]

Christian parents, why do you put off making your newborn child a son of God through baptism?[7] Why do you sometimes make him wait so long for this blessing? If he were to be adopted by a king or one of the world's great, how eager you would be! In the case of baptism the adopted Father is the only great One, God Himself. Is it not an honor for you to be the father or the mother of a son of God and thus to share God's own fatherhood?

In a human adoption you might fear that this child would belong less completely to you, that his affection for you would be lessened. There is no such danger here. Once your child has become the son of God, he will be required to love you even more tenderly. Your parenthood and that of God are not on the same level, and cannot be in competition with one another.

b. *Filial spirit.*[8] As children of God, we must have a truly filial spirit toward Him, with all the sentiments and dispositions that this word implies. This means we must make special efforts to honor Him by the holiness of our lives, as our Lord has counseled us: "Even so let your light shine

---

[6] Cf. at the end of this chapter, passages by Bishop Pichenot and Father Beaudenom in *Note* on p. 85 below.

[7] Without mentioning the other advantages of this for your child. Cf. *Les Effets du Baptême* by the author of the present work.

[8] Filial spirit, or spirit of adoption, which implies: filial tenderness for the Father, fervent curiosity, close friendship, docility, fraternal charity, trust, imitation, loyalty and joy . . . , as we have already tried to show in our work *L'Enfant de Dieu: ou L'Amour du Père.*

The present work is meant to indicate what God does for His children; whereas *L'Enfant de Dieu* sets forth what we must do for our Father, how we must answer His love. These two works are complementary.

before men, in order that they may see your good works and give glory to your Father in heaven" (Mt. 5:16). And the Church asks God: "Grant . . . that we may faithfully keep the spirit of adoption, whereby we are . . . Thy children" (Collect for the Feast of St. Jerome Emilian, July 20).

He has given us this filial spirit together with grace, pouring the infused virtues into our hearts, especially the virtue of charity, and the gifts, above all the gift of piety. But it is up to us to put this filial spirit into practice and to conform our behavior to it. It is up to us to act, think, will, and love in a filial spirit. It is not enough for us to be sons of God; we must also act like His sons.

A filial attitude is also called for toward those who have served as instruments of the Father to beget us to the supernatural life, or who are intermediaries in increasing this life in us. They truly share in His divine Fatherhood: they are the fathers of our souls. It is with good reason that the penitent addresses his confessor as "Father."

The baptized person is really the child of the person who has poured the sacramental water on his forehead: the Church has declared this sonship to be an invalidating impediment to marriage.[9] She does not want it to be confused with the sonship of the flesh. Whence her repugnance to allow a child to be baptized by his own parents (Canon 742³). St. Paul calls the Christians whom He has brought forth to the life of grace his "children." He considers himself their father: "You have not many fathers. For in Christ Jesus, through the Gospel, did I beget you" (I Cor. 4:15).

For all these ministers of the Father in the effusion of divine life in our souls we must, making all due allowances, have veneration, docility, trust, loyalty, and filial sentiments as for our heavenly Father and because of Him.

Note on the Basis of Divine Adoption (see p. 75 above):
In his book *De l'habitation du Saint-Esprit dans les âmes des justes,* Father Froget sees as consequences of this indwelling:

---

[9] There is an invalidating impediment between the baptized person and 1) the person who has baptized him; and 2) the godfather or godmother. Cf. Canons 1079 and 768.

"forgiveness of sins, justification, and the deification of the soul" (Chapter 7). Cf. also Chapter 8 on divine adoption and the right to the inheritance; and Chapter 9 on the infused virtues, the gifts, the fruits and the beatitudes.

Father Terrien, in *La Grâce et la Gloire,* considers our adoption as the heart of the supernatural and sees two principles of this adoption: 1) a created principle, namely grace, the virtues, and the gifts (Book II); and 2) an uncreated principle, the unique indwelling of God in the souls of His children (Book IV, Chapter 3).

In the 19th century, Dr. Scheeben saw in the divine indwelling not the essential but the integrating cause of our divine adoption. This led to heated discussions with Father Granderath of Innsbruck.

Note on the Filial Spirit discussed on p. 83 above:

"It is an incomparable glory to be called the children of God." This incomprehensible union raises our condition and transforms our lowliness into an august, ineffable dignity. We become princes of royal blood, but of the blood of Jesus Christ. We are associated in an empire, but it is the empire of a God. A guardian angel is placed at our side, as an honor guard before the palace of kings. But to enter into God's family, to be associated with the Blessed Trinity, to be able to say to the First Person who is God: You are my Father; and to the Second Person who is God: You are my elder Brother; and to the Third Person, the Holy Spirit, who is God like the Father and the Son: You are the soul of my soul, and the source of a new life in me—what dignity, what splendor!

"Let us therefore call God our Father. Let us dare to do this, because He Himself commands us to dare; but let us live in such a way that He cannot address the following reproach to us: If I am your Father, where is the honor that you owe Me?" (Pichenot, *Le Pater,* 2nd Conference).

"Let us delight in calling Him by the sweet name of Father over and over. If there are names that leave a sweet savor on our lips, names that we never tire of repeating, one of them is certainly the name of Father, of a real Father, that reminds us, when it is applied to God, of infinite tenderness, absolute perfection, and a community of life of which we are proud" (Beaudenom, Meditation 33).

4 Consequences of Divine Adoption

THE consequences of our divine adoption through grace are numerous and of great interest. We shall study three of these consequences in this chapter (the following chapters will deal with others).

When we become children of God, we also become: 1) Brothers of Jesus Christ; 2) brothers of all the just; 3) objects of our Father's tenderness.

1. Brothers of Christ

Since Jesus Christ is also the Son of God, there are several differences between His Sonship and ours, which stem from the superiority of His over ours. But there are also magnificent similarities between the two sonships. Let us examine both the differences and the similarities.

(1) *Differences.* There is a difference in the *Father.* The Father of the Word is the First Person of the Blessed Trinity. Our Father is the one God: the Three Persons of the Blessed Trinity, Father, Son, and Holy Spirit, possessing the divine Nature in common. We know that all the operations of God whose effects are distinct from the divine substance and outside of it are common to the Three Persons, because the prin-

86

ciple of these operations is the nature common to all Three, as Christ Himself has told us: "For whatever [the Father] does, this the Son also does in like manner" (Jn. 5:19). And the Holy Spirit does these things as well.

Thus when Jesus speaks of the Father, He is not speaking of the same Father, depending on whether He is speaking of His or of ours. His Father is the First Person; our Father consists of all Three Persons. A distinction is called for, and our Lord Himself has made it. He never said "our Father," but intentionally said: "My Father and yours" (cf. Jn. 20:17). Obviously, His Father is our Father, but inasmuch as Jesus is the Word, He is also our Father, as is also the Third Person. And when the Church speaks to our Father in her prayers, she is usually addressing the Three Persons of the Blessed Trinity.

The difference between Christ's Father and ours stems from a difference in the mode of our generation. Only the Word is the Son of God by nature.[1] Being the Son is what constitutes His Personality. He alone exhausts the Father's natural capacity for generation. He alone receives from the First Person the same nature in its entirety, and possesses it in common with Him, as His Son. The Third Person also possesses this nature and receives it from the two others, not through the relation of Sonship but by "procession." That is why the Word is truly the Only-Begotten by this natural generation. By nature, God has only one Son; through love, He has a multitude of sons.

For this mode of generation is not the only one possible

---

[1] Did not grace produce the effect of adopted sonship in Christ, who possessed grace in the maximum degree?

A few theologians, like Scotus and Durandus, have thought that Christ as man could be called the adopted Son of God, without prejudice to His divine Sonship as the Word. However the Church forbids us to call Christ an adopted Son of God, and with good reason. For sonship relates to the person: sonship must be attributed to a person. Now, adopted sonship is unfitting to the Person of the Word: the Word is the Son of God by nature, and cannot cease being what He is.

On the other hand, to be simultaneously son by nature and adopted son, that is, to belong to the family by birth and to belong to it by adoption is a contradiction. Only a subject outside the family can be adopted. Being the Son by nature and by birth, the Word cannot be a son by adoption.

to God. There is another mode by which He can acquire children, who are less perfectly His children than His Word, but more numerous, as numerous as He wills, quantity in this instance making up in some way for what may be lacking in quality. This mode of generation seems to be the most perfect possible of realization *ad extra*. For outside of God, there can only be created and accidental reproductions of His nature, never any total or even partial communication except through the hypostatic union.

With regard to the second mode of divine generation, it is not true to say the Word is the only Son of God. He has brothers, and many of them: "among many brethren" (Rom. 8:29). He is not the Only-begotten, but the Firstborn, the first.

He is the first, because He has always been the Son and He always will be. His generation is eternal. It is of the very essence of the Father to beget Him. As for us, the Father has adopted us freely. There was nothing to oblige Him to do so. There was a time (at least before our baptism) when, since we did not yet have grace, we were not yet His children, and even now we could cease being His children through sin.

Christ is also first by reason of the perfection of His Sonship which infinitely surpasses ours, for all its excellence. He is the Son of God far more perfectly than we are. That is why He says: "My Father and your Father." For God was His Father before being ours, and God is His Father more than He is ours. Since it is by the communication of nature that one is the son of another, the bonds of sonship are the closer and the more numerous in the measure that the community of substance is more complete. Now, this community of substance could not be more complete than between the Father and the Son, since they possess the same, identical nature (*numero eadem*), and since everything between them is in common and identical, with the exception of the relation of Fatherhood for the one and of Sonship for the other, which is the only distinctive and constitutive element of their respective Personalities.

Clearly, we are far from such perfection. The grace that "deifies" us does make us divine, without however transforming us into God in the strict sense of the word. It is not a sharing with each of us of the divine substance which is possessed by the Three Persons in common. It remains a created "accident" within us, distinct from the nature of God of which it is a reproduction.

(2) *Similarities*. But these differences in Christ's Father and ours, in the basis for our sonship, in its duration and perfection, do not prevent the existence of magnificent similarities between our divine sonship and that of Christ, nor the forging of very close bonds between Him and us.

Our adoption makes us participate in the divine nature that He possesses in common with the Father and the Holy Spirit, and share in the Father's tenderness for Him, until the day when we shall be invited to share in His own felicity, His own heritage: "But if we are sons, we are . . . joint heirs with Christ" (Rom. 8:17). Our adoption is a reproduction and as it were a continuation in us of His Sonship. The Father has only one Son by nature, and He cannot communicate His divine essence in itself to others. But He can confer created imitations of it upon creatures endowed with reason, and thus give His only-begotten Son a multitude of brothers. Just as copies of masterpieces are multiplied to make these works known and give them new admirers, just as light is projected on crystals to show forth their beauty; so God has willed that the Sonship of His Word should be reflected in many souls, so that this Sonship might receive more glory. He loves this Son so much, "the object of all His pleasure," that He wants to contemplate His likeness in many creatures, discover in them His Son's beloved features, love them in Him and embrace them together with Him.

Through grace, the image of the Son as Son is impressed upon the soul, and a profound likeness with Him is realized.[2]

St. Thomas declares: "Adoptive sonship [through grace] is a certain likeness of the eternal Sonship. . . . Therefore

---

[2] This likeness is not the same as that impressed on the soul by baptismal character, the effigy of the Christ of the Passion and Resurrection. These are two very distinct likenesses of Christ, which call for and complement each other. The likeness of grace normally is added to the likeness impressed by the "character." So true is this that it is possible to receive grace only if one wants at least *"in voto"* to receive the baptismal character.

adoption, though common to the whole Trinity, is appropriated to the Father as its author; to the Son, as its exemplar;
to the Holy Spirit, as imprinting on us the likeness of this
exemplar" (IIIa, q. 23, a. 2, ad 3).

Moreover, grace demands a practical imitation of Christ.
The just man who has become a son of God must, as we
have said, strive to treat God as a Father and to live as His
son, that is, to live the way the Son par excellence lived, He
who came precisely to show how true children must behave,
think, love, and act. Grace impels us to reproduce His life,
to take on His Spirit, to practice His morality, to receive His
teachings. Anyone who did not live as a son, the way the Son
did, would cease being a son. And conversely our sonship is
all the more intense and perfect in the measure that we conform more adequately with the examples given by the Son.

Not only is Christ's sonship the final and exemplary cause
of our sonship. It is also its efficient cause.

The reason He was able to merit the grace of adoption for
us is that He Himself was the Son by nature and that the
hypostatic union of His humanity to the Person of the Word
gave His acts an infinite value. He is the instrument of our
adoption.

It was the Son, the Word, who intervened even in favor of
the sonship of our first parents. It was the Son who become
incarnate so as to merit the restoration of this sonship in
fallen humanity. "But when the fullness of time came, God
sent His Son, born of a woman, . . . that we might receive
the adoption of sons" (Gal. 4:4-5).

Grace comes to us from Christ, for "of His fullness we have
all received" (Jn. 1:16). This is not to say that His grace
passes into us, for grace cannot change its subject like a garment or a coin that can be passed from one to another. It
means that grace belongs to Him before it belongs to us. It
is He who merited it for us, who paid for it, so to speak, by
His sacrifice. Grace is the price of Christ's blood, the equivalent of His immolated corporeal life, just as bread given to
a beggar is the equivalent of the labor that earned it. In this
sense grace is a part of Christ.

And is it not Christ who also distributes grace to us? Is

grace ever given to us unless He has positively willed it? Grace comes to us the way sap flows from the vine stock into the branches, as He Himself has taught (Jn. 15:1-8).

It is He who has won for us "the power to become children of God." And with what fraternal tenderness He has done it! Our elder Brother did not regret the return of His prodigal and fallen brothers to the Father's house. On the contrary, He came Himself to seek us in our abjection, to bring us back to the Father. And with what sacrifices! He paid the ransom for our redemption and rehabilitation with His own life.

No, Christ does not cast jealous glances upon us, like those selfish and unnatural brothers who grieve or sulk because they fear their parents' love will be divided and their inheritance diminished. On the contrary, He works wholeheartedly to give His Father more children, to multiply His co-heirs and to heap good things upon His new brothers.

He was the only Son. He rejoices that He is now only the first born of a very large family. And He Himself merited that His sonship should be extended to so many through His sufferings and death.

Moreover, He has willed to educate His brothers supernaturally by living under their eyes and teaching them how real children of God must conduct themselves. He has willed to transmit to them the Father's secrets, the condition and complement of their adoption, and to reveal these secrets to them: "Nor does anyone know the Father except the Son, and him to whom the Son chooses to reveal Him" (Mt. 11:27). Christ has communicated all His possessions as a Son with the greatest generosity and the tenderest affection.

After giving us His Father, He also willed to give us His Mother, so that our brotherhood with Him might be more complete. We were His brothers as adopted sons of God. He became our brother through His sacred humanity by taking on our flesh which, through Mary, comes from the same first father. He became our brother, too, by living our laborious life, by suffering upon our earth, and by bequeathing His Mother to us before He died, the supreme gift of His fraternal affection.

Finally, through the Eucharist, He found the means of remaining with us in order to help us during our earthly sojourn.

All these things are indubitable proofs that Christ looks upon His brotherhood with us not as an empty word or a pious fancy, but as a reality whose full consequences He draws, that He takes seriously, and whose obligations He fulfills to the limit. He treats His brothers through grace as brothers, having the most ardent affection for them, covering them with His powerful protection and His vigilant solicitude, taking constant care of them, providing for their interests, especially their spiritual interests, and working for their salvation. He continues to do for them in a different and still more efficacious form what He did for them during His life. He does not stop being their brother devoted unto death, their Redeemer, and their Savior. He continues to prepare a place in heaven for us, and He always makes intercession with the Father for us (cf. Heb. 7:25).

We can depend upon Him with absolute confidence. However, on one condition: that we also take our title as brothers literally, that we have and express for Him truly fraternal sentiments. We must have for Him a fraternal affection, a fraternal devotion, fraternal trust, gratitude, and delicacy. In short, we must respect all the demands of this close and profound brotherhood.

Inasmuch as we resemble Him by our divine sonship, we must also resemble Him by our acts, draw inspiration from His example, imitate His manner of acting, pattern our behavior upon His, and become conformable to Him in all things: *conformes fieri imaginis Filii*, and strive to lead the same filial life with respect to the Father as He does. To this end, we can look to His all-powerful help. If He was willing to shed His blood for us before we were His brothers, so that we might become the children of God—"He gave the power of becoming sons of God"—what will He not do now that we are His brothers and sons of God, to help us to remain what we are and to become even better sons!

Thus grace unites us to Him in a very intimate way. It establishes powerful bonds between Him and ourselves—

bonds of love and devotion; bonds of resemblance in our divine sonship. He Himself compares these bonds to those that unite the branches to the trunk of a tree, and the vine to the vine stock (cf. Jn. 15:1-2).

Through grace, we form in union with Him one great Mystical Body, whose Head and Heart He is.

In itself, grace implies an incorporation, a union, and an identification with Christ.

2. Brothers of Other Just Men

By the very fact that the just are children of God through grace, they become brothers. The supernatural bonds that unite them are much more real, profound, and intimate than the bonds of the flesh. They all share in the same divine nature, they have the same marks of resemblance with their heavenly Father, are the objects of the same adoption and paternal solicitude, commune in the same life, and are destined to receive the same eternal heritage. Together they constitute a vast family, the family of God: the Church. The truth of this supernatural brotherhood is so evident and so clearly taught by our Lord and the Apostles—who point to it as the reason for the command of charity to our neighbor— that we need insist no further upon it. Let us rather indicate a few conclusions to which it leads us.

(1) Our supernatural brotherhood is an honor. Through grace, all the just are our brothers more authentically than we can say: all the just upon earth, all those beautiful souls whose consciences are pure, the elite of the human race; all the just in heaven and all those in heaven, all those noble Christians who have honored the world with their virtues through the centuries. It is an innumerable multitude of every tribe, race, and tongue—the apostles, martyrs, confessors, and virgins who have striven to imitate the holiness of the Master—their Brother—in their own lives, and who now form His blessed retinue in heaven. It includes all the just of the Church Militant, the Church Suffering, and the Church Triumphant. What an honor for us, and also what an advantage and consolation! For through grace, a com-

munication of services and possessions has been established among them.

(2) Our supernatural brotherhood is an advantage. Just as the blood carries to all the members of the body the life-giving and nourishing elements that are found in a few vital organs, and just as it communicates the heat and life of some members to the others; so grace, divine blood, enables all of God's children to benefit from the common treasure of all. Through grace, a wonderful and continual transfusion of satisfactions and merits (cf. Chapters 11 and 12 below), a circulation of life from some to others, occurs throughout the vast Mystical Body that is God's family. The faithful of earth can glorify the saints in heaven and relieve the souls in purgatory, and pay off their debts of temporal punishment. In return, they can receive the graces that the elect obtain for them, for it is certain that the blessed in heaven are in-terested in their "wayfaring" brothers, that they love them, want their welfare and their salvation, and help them to at-tain it through their intercession. And it is certain, more-over, that they are very powerful over the Father's heart.

It is very probable that the same can be said of the souls in purgatory. The number of the faithful who have recourse to their intercession and have experienced their powerful efficacy is constantly increasing.

There is an incessant exchange of prayers, expiations, and merits (of fittingness) among the just. And this exchange is the more intense in the measure that they are more closely united to God their Father and to Christ their Brother. There is a reciprocal interchange of light and life among them. The progress of some of them has its divine extension in the others. The upward flight of some souls is communi-cated in a certain respect to all the rest. The treasures of virtue and grace that they accumulate benefit everyone. Every just man is, as it were, a source of good for his brothers.

The Father has willed that the community of sonship among men should find expression in a community of goods.

All the just have a share in the fruits of all the Masses that are celebrated each day all over the world. These Masses are offered, in the name of all for all, by the priest, whose sublime mission it is to be the official representative of them all, the spokesman of the whole Church. For it is the priest's role to pray, to offer up sacrifice in the name of all, and thus to be the source of a universal community of worship and of spiritual goods. Everything is in common, everything belongs to everyone in a family where union and affection reign. Prayer is said in common, for each one speaks in the name of all and makes petitions for all: "Our Father, ... Give us our daily bread. Forgive us our trespasses . . . Lead us not into temptation. Deliver us from evil. . . ."

Being itself a supernatural good, grace is also a canal through which the supernatural goods of the children of God can be communicated from some to others. Grace is the foundation of the Communion of Saints.

(3) Our supernatural brotherhood is a consolation. Thus, no matter how lonely and forsaken a just man may be in this life, he must never think he is isolated, abandoned, lost in the universe, reduced to his own personal helplessness. Through grace he possesses a multitude of brothers who, from a distance and even without knowing him, protect him, sustain him, and surround him with affection and devotion. From the best of these brothers, he receives powerful help (in this family where mutual assistance is practiced with intensity). His indigence is filled from their spiritual riches. His weakness relies upon their strength. Like members of a caravan in a dangerous ascent, the members of the Father's family are "roped together" through grace and charity, and lend each other mutual support.

(4) Our supernatural brotherhood is one of basic equality. The just are brothers, regardless of their differences in race, language, culture, condition, fortune, and nationality. The illiterate man is the brother of the scholar, the poor man is the rich man's brother, the subject is his prince's brother, the slave is his master's brother. Before God, the lowly are the equals of the great, and perhaps even nobler, if they surpass them in grace.[3] St. Paul wrote to the Galatians: "For you are all the children of God through faith in Christ Jesus

---

[3] Our Lord's words, "and the last shall be first" (Mt. 20:16) can also be understood in this sense.

[the condition of grace]. . . . There is neither Jew nor Greek; there is neither slave nor freeman; there is neither male nor female. For you are all one in Christ Jesus" (Gal. 3:26-28).

If all natural diversities are as nothing and disappear before the equality established by divine adoption, must we not count them for nothing in our judgments of Christians? In our dealings among ourselves, we should banish all opposition between "classes," all haughtiness of the "great" toward the "lowly," all hatred among races and nations, all exploitation of the weak by the strong, all jealousy, rancor, and egoism. Charity, self-sacrifice, mutual support and help, meekness, union, and peace should reign.

While respecting the order of preference willed by God, our fraternal love should rise above particular societies, above frontiers, above the horizons of this world, and extend to the entire family of God. We cannot sincerely love God without loving all those whom He loves, all those who are dear to Him, all His children. We cannot love the Father without loving our brothers. These two loves are one. They stem from one and the same theological virtue, charity, whose one object is God. Christ has told us so Himself. After declaring that the first commandment was to love the Father, He said: "And the second is like it, 'Thou shalt love thy neighbor as thyself.' " (Mt. 22:39).

(5) The dogma of our supernatural brotherhood is very fruitful socially. This dogma, based on the common adoption of the just by God, was among those that made the deepest impression on the first Christians. In the simplicity of their logic they immediately drew its principal consequences and made it their duty to conform their lives to it. With a magnificent and stirring upsurge of love, they tried to share everything, even their material goods, in common. The charity that united them was so striking that the amazed pagans cried out in admiration: "See how they love one another!" And to express this charity the inspired narrator used the bold words: "The multitude of believers were of one heart and one soul" (Acts 4:32).

Many of the early Christians understood how unfitting, how offensive to the heavenly Father (as well as odious for themselves) was the slavery that degraded His adopted children to the level of beasts of burden and made them the undisputed "property" of masters to whom they were equal through grace. Little by little, in the light of this divine revelation, the chains of slavery were broken. Christians sought to imitate Philemon, to whom St. Paul had written from Rome, asking him to welcome Onesimus (his fugitive slave whom Paul had converted and baptized in prison and in whom he had seen qualities that fitted him for the service of the Church) not as a slave but "as though he were my very heart" (Philemon 1:12). Christian masters progressively liberated their slaves [4] for the Lord's sake, thereby bringing about the most far-reaching social reform the human race had ever seen. Respect and charity for the human person, until then unknown in social customs, were introduced into human relations. Thus Christ's words "And you shall know the truth, and the truth shall make you free" (Jn. 8:32) were verified to the letter and in an admirable manner.

Oblivion or ignorance of this human brotherhood, which stems from our adoption through grace, is one of the chief causes of the terrible wars that have drenched our modern times in blood and goaded peoples and individual men to destroy one another.

Hence those who have in one way or another prevented the Church from preaching the dogma of brotherhood to the world and from impressing it upon men's minds share in the responsibility for wars. Among them are all persecutors of the Church, schismatics, and heretics, the rationalistic philosophers, the fomenters of the French Revolution, secularists, etc., whose irreligion has borne fruits of blood and tears and is now contributing to the revival of slavery.

Nothing we can say or do will prevent the return of such cataclysms unless we help the Church to spread her doctrine, which alone can pacify men.[5]

---

[4] It goes without saying that slavery did not disappear everywhere in a few years. It took centuries for such a reform to become more or less universal.

[5] "I hear talk of universal brotherhood all about me. God knows what lies in the hearts of so many apostles who are preaching it, and how they practice the doctrine that they teach so vociferously! For my part, I know

3. The Father's Affection

The soul in the state of grace is the object of a special love, of a most fatherly affection, on God's part. We shall try to show: a. the reality of this love; b. its marks; and c. its consequences. (a) *The Reality*. This affection is the consequence of the effects of grace we have just studied.

To love, to give, to will and do good—all these are one and the same. It is love's imperious need to express itself by giving gifts, by proving its loyalty, by pouring itself out in benefactions. So true is this, that love is recognized and measured by its acts. The surge of love impels it out of itself toward its object. On the contrary, selfishness betrays the absence of love. Without giving, there is no love. The two are inseparable. When we give, it is because we love. We do not know how to love as long as we do not know how to give.

Now, how could God give Himself more completely than He does through grace, since grace is a communication of His nature, His life, His possessions, His beauty, His activity, His happiness, and the gift of Himself by His supernatural presence in the soul of the just man, and in heaven by the beatific vision? Is it not because of grace that He gave us His only-begotten Son and that this Son has given us His blood? If we had a better knowledge of the price of grace, we would better understand the intensity of God's love for us: "If thou didst know the gift of God!" (Jn. 4:10). This love is incomparable, far superior to the love expressed by creation.

Grace is more than a magnificent gift. It is also a powerful bond that unites us to our Father, draws Him to us like an irresistible magnet, and makes us participate in His own life

no Christian can have any doubt that true brotherhood, the brotherhood that honors us, the brotherhood that knows neither envy nor change, the brotherhood in a word that can make all hearts beat as one heart, and make all souls c e, is brotherhood in Christ. To form a race of brothers, what more is needed than a single Father, a single Mother, a single Brother, the firstborn of this Father and Mother, who surround us with one and the same love and who will assemble us, as heirs of one and the same glory, at the same eternal banquet?" (P. Terrien, *La Grâce et la Gloire*, Vol. I, Part X, Ch. 3).

even here on earth, until such time when, through the intuitive vision, grace will unite God to our understanding the way an idea is united to the intellect in the act of knowing.

This is proof enough of an unusual love, for we become united only to those we love and in the measure that we love them. We instinctively flee from those we do not love. We drive them off, we keep them at a distance when we can, just as God does with the damned. The need for union reveals love (that is the reason for marriage: a man and a woman are united because they love each other). Inasmuch as grace consists in union with God and the presence of God, it is love, and the proof of a very great love.

And yet the chief reason why grace must be considered a sure manifestation of God's special love for a soul is that it is a partaking of His nature and an incorporation into His Son. God loves creatures the more they resemble Him. He cannot help loving whatever He finds of Himself in them, whatever reflects His perfections, whatever reveals His own divine Being to Him (just as a father cannot help loving his features, his blood, and his temperament as revealed in his child). The more closely creatures resemble God, the dearer hey become to Him. Anything that increases their conformity with Him intensifies His love for them.[6]

God loves everything that exists. He has greater love for living beings, and still greater love for beings that think (the intellect being a reflection of His Mind). But He loves with

---

[6] Almost all catechisms and manuals of theology repeat that sanctifying grace "makes us pleasing in the eyes of God." That is one of the divisions of grace. It is said that grace is either *gratum faciens* or *grata data*. All grace is gratuitous, but all grace does not make the recipient pleasing. St. Thomas says: "The grace that unites man to God is the grace that makes him pleasing to God" (Ia IIae, q. 111, a. 1). And in his answer to the first objection, he explains that nevertheless "grace is said to make pleasing, not efficiently, but formally, i.e., because thereby a man is justified and is made worthy to be called pleasing to God."

This is one of the meanings of the word grace, in fact the principal one: to render pleasing and lovable, an object of love—*gratiorem reddere, gratum facere*. According to the most common interpretation, grace is used in this sense in St. Paul's Epistle to the Ephesians: "*In qua [gratia] gratificavit nos in dilecto filio suo*" (Eph. 1:6). In other words, God, by His grace, has made us pleasing, lovable, in His eyes.

an infinitely greater love those who are adorned with grace, which is a share in His own nature. True, He loves the splendid stars He created, the wondrous beauty of each individual flower, every animal from the almost invisible insect to giant mammals, man for whom He has prepared a magnificent abode and in whose soul he has placed a reflec-tion of His own Spirit, and the luminous and powerful angels. In all these creatures, even the most infinitesimal, we glimpse peremptory traces of His love which has lingered over them as it were, to adorn them, adapt them to their end, and make life easier for them. Yes, the universe is full of His love.

But it is also true that all this love gathered into one does not equal the love God has for a single soul in the state of grace, since, by a single degree of grace, He places more of Himself within us than there is in all the rest of the universe, a greater likeness to Himself, and more of His own nature: "We shall be like to Him" (I Jn. 3:2). In the words of St. Thomas: "Through grace, man receives a likeness to God which is a source of delight to Him."

In the soul that has been transformed into His like-ness by grace, marked with His effigy, molded so to speak in His own mold, God can perceive many reflections of His Godhead, notice some of His personal traits, admire a few of His own properties. In the intellect illumined by faith, He sees convictions like His own; in the will, a charity like to His, and above all, an aptitude to see Him intuitively as He sees Himself—an aptitude rooted in grace. Looking into this soul as in a mirror, He recognizes Himself.

How then could He help being pleased with this soul and cherishing it? By making us share in His nature, God necessarily makes us participate in the love He has for Him-self.

Through grace, God becomes our Father in very truth, and much more perfectly than are our earthly fathers. For the latter do not produce our souls, the principal element of our beings. And they merely helped in transforming already existent matter when our bodies were formed. God, on the other hand, is the sole author of the supernatural life within us. Now, an ordinary father finds it not only a duty but a need to love his child, to the point that even unreasoning creatures do so instinctively and any man who does not is considered a monster. What then must be the ardent affection of our heavenly Father for His children! How intense this love must be! [7]

God did not have to give us this gift, He did not have to unite Himself to us and reproduce Himself in this way within us. He did not have to beget us supernaturally: *Voluntaris nos genuit.* He did not have to incorporate us into His Son. These blessings are absolutely supernatural, that is to say, gratuitous and free on His part. But granted He has given them freely, that He has freely adopted us as His children and called us into His family, He cannot *not* love us in proportion to our dignity. If He did not love us, it would be a contradiction; for He communicated His nature to us, begot us to His life, and adopted us only because He loved us. Grace is not the cause of His love for us, but its effect.

This is what distinguishes divine love from human love. St. Thomas teaches: "The will of man is moved by the good preexisting in things; and hence man's love does not wholly cause the good [the perfection] of the thing, but presupposes it either in part or wholly." On the other hand, "since the creature's good springs from the divine will, some good in the creature flows from God's love, whereby He wishes the good of the creature" (Ia IIae, q. 110, a. 1, c). And in his answer to the first objection, he repeats: "[there is this difference between human and divine love] that what is pleasing to a man in another is presupposed to his love, but whatever is pleasing to God in a man is caused by the divine love."

It is not the perfection in us that inspires God's love; it is His love that produces the perfection. Our perfection is subsequent to His love, as its effect and consequently its proof and measure. Our love presupposes God's love and comes from it. Consequently, our perfection manifests God's love: it is the sign and measure of it.

Loves of different orders correspond to perfections of differ-

---

[7] Cf. at the end of this chapter, a passage by Bishop Pichenot on this point, p. 107 below.

ent orders. There is a natural love, common to all creatures, that corresponds to natural goods (or perfections). There is a special, supernatural, and much higher love of the same order as that with which God loves Himself, that corresponds to supernatural goods. Our Doctor explains: "According to [the] difference of good the love of God to the creature is looked at differently. For one is common, whereby He loves all things that are (Wis. 11:25), and thereby gives things their natural being. But the second is a special love, whereby He draws the rational creature above the condition of its nature to a participation of the divine good; and according to this love He is said to love anyone simply, since it is by this love that God simply wishes the eternal good, which is Himself for the creature" (Ia IIae, q. 110, a. 1, c.).

(b) *The marks of this love.* Here we have one of the marks of God's love for the just. It is *disinterested,* spontaneous, and freely given. Its cause lies in God Himself, in His absolutely free choice: *Elegit nos.*[8] There was nothing to oblige Him to choose us. It comes entirely from His personal initiative. If we have become His children, the objects of His Father's love, it is solely because He predestined us to it according to His good pleasure (cf. Eph. 1:4-5).

This is one of the ideas on which St. Paul insists, in order to bring out more forcefully the complete gratuitousness of God's love for us. This gratuitousness greatly increases the value of His love and makes it more touching. "God is love," says St. John. "In this is the love, not that we have loved God, but that He has first loved us" (I Jn. 4:9-10). His love was the inspiration for ours. Not only is it a love of dilection, it is also a love of predilection. And consequently He loved us when we were still in sin, when we were His enemies, "by nature children of wrath" (Eph. 2:3).

Clearly, this love of God is essentially efficacious, productive, creative, in contrast to our love which is too often helpless, sterile, consisting merely of sentiments or words. God actualizes whatever good He wishes for a person. His benevolence always becomes beneficence. The instant He loves,

---

[8] That is why Scripture and theology speak of the just in heaven as *"the elect."*

He gives. He communicates His treasures to those He cherishes; He protects and helps them, and fills them to overflowing. He never adopts anyone ineffectually. He never calls anyone His child without making him in fact His child: *Ut filii nominemur et simus.* Nor does He fail to surround this child with His fatherly solicitude, or fail to take care of him as a father does his child, especially in spiritual matters, until the day when He introduces him into his heavenly inheritance.[9]

His action toward His children(toward all men, but above all toward His adopted sons) is inspired only by His love. It has no other purpose than to procure their well-being, to reform, purify, and sanctify them, to allow them a more abundant share in His divine riches, His divine life, and His divine felicity. If He seems to strike them down or let them suffer, if He places the cross on their shoulders, it is only a salutary pruning, the source of still greater spiritual fruitfulness. Our Lord has made this known to us: "Every branch that bears fruit He will cleanse, that it may bear more fruit" (Jn. 15:2).

It is an all-powerful love, from which no spiritual or material power can wrest us, as long as we ourselves do not turn away from it through sin: "For . . . neither death, nor life, . . . nor height, nor depth, nor any other creature will be able to separate us from the love of God" (Rom. 8:38-39).

This love appears all the more touching when we consider its duration.

As long as I remain in the state of grace, the Father does not stop loving me. He loves me day and night, while I sleep and while I work, and even when, engrossed by creatures, I do not think of Him.

---

[9] Holy Scripture very often affirms this special protection of the just by God, for example in the passage from Psalm 36: "But the salvation of the just is from the Lord, and He is their protector in the time of trouble. And the Lord will help them and deliver them: and He will rescue them from the wicked; and save them, because they have hoped in Him" (Ps. 36:39-40).

Our series of books on the effects of the sacraments (*Les Effets du Baptême, Notre Pentecôte, Pain Vivant, Notre Messe,* etc.) shows some of the manifestations of God's paternal solicitude for His children, and points out how He helps them to live filially according to the spirit of their adoption through these divine rites.

And how long has this been going on? Since my baptism?
Yes, but in a sense much longer still! Before the creation of
the world, before the beginning of time, before the angels,
before anything existed outside of Him; as long as He has
existed; from all eternity. He has eternally loved me, dis-
cerned me, called, chosen, and predestined me to be His child
(Rom. 8:29). And I can truthfully apply to myself the words
of the Book of Wisdom that the liturgy has spoken with regard to the Blessed Virgin Mary: "I was created before all
things" (Ecclus. 1:4).

And how long will God continue to love me so? If I do
not prevent Him from loving me by reason of my sins, He
will love me eternally. He will never stop loving me: "The
truth of His love remains forever: *Et veritas Domini manet
in aeternum.*" His love is immutable, like Himself.

What fidelity as compared with our poor, fragile human
loves, that are so vulnerable, so changing, that so quickly
grow cold and die out! What assurance for our hearts to
know that He will never be the first to stop loving us. What
delight to think that He loves us, that He has loved us, and
that He will continue to love us always! What a vast treasure
of love this eternity represents. And how greatly it increases
its value!

And what are we to say of the intensity of this love? To
get an idea of it, we must remember that God loves us even
now with the same love He will have for us in heaven when
He will give Himself to us in an ineffable and eternal
embrace. The only differences are in the manifestations of
this love. Here on earth He cannot reveal Himself to our
understanding the way He will in glory, nor show Himself to
us intuitively in all the splendor of His beauty and perfection. The reason for this is that it is necessary that we have the
possibility—the liberty—to spurn Him and to choose our end
ourselves. This is the essential condition of our time of trial.
To safeguard the freedom of our love, God does not give
His own love free play. He "does violence" so to speak to
His own heart, so as not to do violence to ours. But He
already loves us as He will love us in heaven.

Moreover, the wonderful effects that this love produces

here on earth suffice to reveal its power. If the value of the gift, the intimacy of the union, the perfection of our identification with God and of the sonship of which it is the principle clearly indicate its intensity, it must rise to an incomparable height since, through grace, it gives us such precious benefits, establishes so close a union, and honors us with such lofty dignity. Truly an inestimable gift, an immeasurable love!

The love of men, passionate as it may be, cannot be compared to this love. Even paternal love—which is the deepest, the most touching, and the strongest of human loves—is nothing but "hate" compared to it. For, according to our Lord, by comparison with our heavenly Father, even the most affectionate fathers are "evil" (cf. Mt. 7:11).

Grace is such an evident sign of the Father's special and very intense love for us that St. Paul (and the Church, too) takes the effect for the cause and identifies grace with this love. To state that the grace of God has been poured into our souls, St. Paul says "the charity of God is poured forth in our hearts" (Rom. 5:5). Grace is like a boiling lava that pours forth from God's heart, to penetrate, kindle, and deify our souls.

Elsewhere (cf. II Cor. 13:13), St. Paul cites grace and charity together as being absolutely inseparable: "The grace of our Lord Jesus Christ, and the charity of God, and the fellowship of the Holy Spirit be with you all. Amen."

In the face of so much love, the heart of St. John, the Evangelist of love, explodes in enthusiastic admiration and gratitude: "Behold what manner of love the Father has bestowed upon us, that we should be called children of God; and such we are" (I Jn. 3:1) in very truth!

(c) *The Consequences.* My first obligation in the face of so great a love is first of all to *believe* in it firmly, repeating with the Apostle of charity: "And we . . . have believed the love that God has in our behalf" (I Jn. 4:16). It is also my duty to savor all its meaning, to consider its full significance, to drink in all its consoling light, to draw all the practical consequences from it and to become deeply imbued with it through meditation.

It may well be that we speak too exclusively of the love that we owe God and not enough of the love that God has for us. "We forget in practice that God loves us wondrously. We are more concerned with loving Him than with knowing that He loves us. Would not an understanding of the degree to which God loves us help us, decide us, to love Him in a special way? We quite frequently meet souls that love God, and love Him passionately. Do we meet many who think, know, and feel that God loves them passionately? It is a second stage to be passed, that many do not even suspect or admit. . . . This spectacle of God's great tenderness acting as a more-than-royal retinue to the soul—that is the great feast!" [10]

What delight in life! To know that we are loved, and so deeply loved by our heavenly Father! What can the love or hatred of miserable creatures matter, by comparison? Whether a match burns or dies out makes little difference when we can warm and light ourselves at the divine fire. Do we worry about a drop of water when we possess the ocean? Why do not men, who suffer from not being loved, quench their hearts' thirst at the infinite wellspring of God's love? If God could suffer, His great sorrow would be to see His love so little known and esteemed. Did not Christ lament this fact to the seer of Paray? Thus, the first duty of God's children is to believe in the love of the Father.

Our second duty is to answer His love with a truly filial love. This love, characteristic of Christians, has its own distinctive marks. It implies delicacies that ordinary love does not know.

A man cannot have such tenderness naturally. For the sentiment that nature, left to its own lights, inspires is a sentiment of fear of God. But the Father gives this tenderness to His children, together with grace, at the very moment He begets them to His own life and adopts them, so that a filial love in them may correspond to His own paternal love. Such is the charity—the supernatural love—that the Holy Spirit comes to kindle in their souls and that makes them say to

---

[10] De Tourville, *Lumière et vie*, p. 173.

God: "Father, Father!" (Rom. 8:15; Gal. 4:6), and it is a love they must translate into action. It is not enough for them to be children of God. They must also conduct themselves as such, "live" all the sanctifying consequences of their dignity, answer all the moral demands of their title, progressively acquire the true spirit of sons, develop within themselves the spirit of adoption, as the Church prays that they may.[11]

Note on the Intensity of the Father's Love (see p. 101 above):

Bishop Pichenot says: "Paternal affection is not a virtue, but a need, a necessity, as well as a joy. God always expects it in the heart of a father: He simply wants to govern it and prescribe laws for it, *ordinavit in me caritatem*. Now, should I not expect it eminently in God and do Him the same honor, since no one is as much a Father as He? All fatherhood comes from Him . . ." (*Le Pater*, 6th Instruction).

---

[11] Many Christians could join in making the following avowal: "Our Father! . . . Is it true that You love me like a father and look upon me as Your child? If only I really believed it! . . . O my soul, your songs are sad. . . . Do you not too often forget love? And yet it is so easy to admit its existence. The crib, the Cross, the Host, grace, heaven . . . are eloquent proofs of it." (H. Charasson, *Mon Seigneur et mon Dieu*).

5 Justification

THE effects of grace hithero discussed (especially our participation in the nature of God and our divine adoption) seem to have been of particular interest to St. John and the Greek Fathers. The effect of grace we are about to discuss, namely, *justification,* was given greater emphasis by St. Paul and St. Augustine. The temperament and antecedents of these latter saints explain their concern with justification. "For a convert, it is natural that grace should be first and above all a forgiveness. For all men, grace is mercy, but the more one has been under the domination of actual sin, the more conscious we are that grace is mercy. Paul felt more keenly than others a truth that applies to all men"[1] (P. Rousselot, *Recherches de science religieuse,* 1928, p. 98).

After the Lutherans and Jansenists had distorted the teachings of Paul and Augustine, the Church had to pursue them into the stronghold of their errors to re-establish the truth. This helps to explain the preponderant place theologians, in their fight against these heresies, have given to justification in the last few centuries, somewhat at the expense of the other effects of grace.

At any rate, it is undeniable that justification is very

[1] Cf. the continuation of this passage in the *Note* at the end of this chapter, p. 130 below.

important, especially if we take it in its fullest sense to
include: destruction of sin, reviviscence of past merits, rectification of the will, and sanctification of the soul.

1. Grace Justifies the Soul

Habitual grace can be given to those who do not have it. It
is then known as "first" grace. It can also be given to those
who already possess it, in order to increase it: it is then called
"second" grace.

In itself, it is one and the same grace. The difference
between "first" and "second" grace lies in their effects which
come from a difference in subject.

"First" grace produces a special effect that "second" grace
does not: it wipes out sin.

In the present state of the human race, anyone who is not
in the state of grace is in the state of sin, at least of original
sin. It has to be one or the other. There is no intermediary
state in which a man would be without grace, even though
without sin. Thus first grace is received only by sinners. It
always has the specific efficacy of destroying sin: an efficacy
which we can call "negative," as do certain theologians.

The Church has given the name of "justification" to the
infusion of first grace into the soul of the sinner (whence
has come the name of "just"). She has borrowed it from St.
Paul, who has frequently used the term "justify" and also
the substantive "justification" (cf. Rom. 4:25; 5:16, 18; 8:10).

The meaning of the word. A defendant justifies himself
before a tribunal if he establishes his rights, if he proves his
innocence, if he clears himself of the charges made against
him. The judge justifies him if, after an examination of the
case, he declares that the accused is not guilty or that his
guilt has not been proved. Thus, to justify a person means
to restore him at least legally to the innocence he enjoyed
before his indictment.

Men can be mistaken or deceived. Every justification is
not authentic. God, on the other hand, is infallible. His
knowledge is infinite, and He sees men's hearts. If He declares
a man to be just, that man really is just. If a man is not just,

then God makes him become so by wiping out his sin and restoring him to His friendship. Now He brings these things to pass through grace. By infusing grace, He repairs the ravages of sin, forgives sin, confers a capacity for the beatific vision, restores man to the supernatural state. In a word, He *justifies* him.

Hence *justification* is a combination of two effects: the infusion of grace and the remission of sins.[2]

There is a fundamental opposition on this point between the doctrine of the Church and that of the Protestants. The latter, realizing and reading in St. Paul the permanence of concupiscence in us, even after baptism and justification, and confusing sin with concupiscence, have concluded to the coexistence of sin and grace in the soul of the justified man.

But since, according to Scripture, justification presupposes the remission of sin, there was only one means of reconciling these two visibly contradictory things: the permanence of sin on the one hand, and on the other the remission of guilt and the infusion of grace. The only solution was to consider this remission and grace as purely extrinsic, "forensic"—as merely a juridical fiction. Thus the remission of sin, as they see it, means that the sin is no longer imputed to its author, and that it is hidden from the eyes of God in the shadow of the perfection and the infinite merits of Christ.

According to them, original sin has corrupted the very depths of our nature, and has inflicted irremediable wounds upon it. Nothing can purify man's nature from the radical corruption produced in it by original sin. Our free will has been destroyed forever. Any restoration is merely an external matter, and this suffices to make us worthy of heaven. What happens within us does not matter, provided it is hidden from God's most pure eyes through the merits of His Son.

---

[2] These two inseparable effects are symbolized and produced by the baptismal rite that is articulated in two distinct acts: 1) the *immersion*, or the disappearance of the subject in the water, which represents his death to sin (the destruction of sin), in union with the dead and buried Christ; 2) the *emersion*, or emergence from the water, which signifies the rebirth to the life of grace, in union with the divine Risen One. We have explained these matters in our work, *Les effets du Baptême*, Chapter 1.

And just as past sins are not opposed to grace, neither are present or future sins. Man can commit all the sins he pleases without ceasing to be just and to possess grace, providing he continues through an invincible faith to cover himself with the merits of Christ.

These conclusions are logical but false, because they start from an erroneous proposition.

The Church for her part teaches that through sanctifying grace we are not merely reputed to be pure and without blemish, but that we really *become* so; that we not only appear but *are* without sin; that after justification the most searching eye would seek in vain within the soul of the just even the shadow of his former sins, which have been forever wiped out, detroyed, like a filthy spot that has been so totally removed that even the sharpest eye could not detect where it had once been.

1. *De Facto*

It is an incontestable truth of faith that the infusion of grace wipes out sin at least *de facto* and through the positive will of God. The Council of Trent affirms it expressly with regard to the grace of baptism: "If anyone denies that by the grace of our Lord Jesus Christ which is conferred in baptism, the guilt of original sin is remitted, or says that the whole of that which belongs to the essence of sin is not taken away, . . . let him be anathema" (Session V, Decree Concerning Original Sin Denz. 792). True, this declaration refers explicitly only to the grace of baptism and to original sin. But all first grace must have the same effect with regard to all sin.

Moreover, the following texts from the Sixth Session of he Council of Trent have general import. Chapter IV teaches that "the justification of the sinner [is] a translation from that state in which man is born a child of the first Adam, to the state of grace and of the adoption of the sons of God" (Denz. 799).

Now, anyone who passes from A to B, does not remain in A. That would be contradictory. And so, if through justification we pass from the state of sin to the state of grace, we do not remain in the state of sin.

In Chapter VII of the Sixth Session we read: "Justification . . . is not only a remission of sins but also the sanctification and renewal of the inward man." But justification is a remission of sins. Would there really be santification if sins remained in the soul, even if covered and hidden?

The Fathers of the Council of Trent were reproducing the terms St. Paul used in writing to the Corinthians when he contrasted what they had become with what they had been, their new holiness with their former corruption: "But you have been washed, you have been sanctified, you have been justified in the name of our Lord Jesus Christ" (I Cor. 6:11). According to the Apostle, justification involves purification and sanctification, that is, the complete disappearance of the stain of sin. For if sin remained, even if carefully camouflaged, there would be neither purification nor sanctification.

St. Paul is even more explicit in addressing the Romans, and uses expressions that remove all danger of ambiguity. He opposes the just man to the sinner, justice (grace) to sin, the effect of the former being the contradiction of the effect of the latter. Our Savior's obedience has made us just in the same way that Adam's disobedience had made us sinners —intrinsically, really: "For just as by the disobedience of the one man the many were constituted sinners, so also by the obedience of the one the many will be constituted just" (Rom. 5:19).

Besides, the Apostle affirms that Christ the Redeemer did more to give us life than Adam had done to kill us, that Christ's work was more efficacious and more powerful for our welfare than what our first father did for our perdition, that He has more than repaired the ravages Adam caused. Now all these things would not be true, if the principal element, the stain of sin, remained imbedded in justified souls.

In the first centuries of Christianity, catechumens were completely immersed in water when they were baptized. This was the sign of their total death to sin, just as the white garment placed on them as they came forth from the water signified the immaculate purity of their souls, which were now completely purified of sin.

Grace drives out sin; the two are incompatible *de facto*. This is a truth of faith.

2. *De jure*

Must we go futher and affirm an incompatibility *de jure* between grace and sin, deriving from their respective natures?

According to the Scotists, this incompatibility is moral: sin would exclude grace only *demeritorie*. That is to say it would "merit" God's withdrawal of grace. Between the expulsion of sin and the infusion of grace there would be only an extrinsic, non-essential bond.

For Suarez, the incompatibility between grace and sin is natural, but through a miracle contrary to the demands of the natures of these two realities, God could make an exception to it.

The Thomist opinion, which is by far the most widely held, maintains that this incompatibility is necessary to the point that even God in His omnipotence could not make them coexist in the same subject. That would be a contradiction, and hence a work exceeding His power.

If sin and grace did cohabit in a single soul, this soul would at one and the same time merit heaven (through grace) and hell (through sin). It would be simultaneously the friend of God (through grace) and His enemy (through sin).

Through His absolute power, God could grant forgiveness without grace, but it docs not seem that He could grant grace without forgiveness. Grace is inseparable from pardon and necessarily includes it. The first meaning of grace is *mercy, forgiveness*.

There is no need to state this fact explicitly. The father of the prodigal son did not expressly declare that he forgave his son the sorrow that his arrogant demands, his departure, and his dissolute life had caused him. The Gospel does not say a word about it, and it is not necessary. Did not his paternal conduct, his affectionate welcome, his kisses and tears of joy, the feast, and his command to clothe him in his own brother's garments proclaim his forgiveness loudly enough?

Could those who saw the old man run out to meet his son as soon as he caught sight of him in the distance, "fall upon his neck" according to St. Luke's expression (Lk. 15:20), and hold him tightly against his heart, have any doubt that he fully forgave him? And was it not even clearer when he quickly pulled off his son's tattered garments and commanded that he should be clothed in the best garment, be given shoes for his feet and a ring for his finger as a symbol of their mutual affection, and ordered that a fattened calf be killed for a feast of rejoicing? Obviously, the father no longer remembered his son's shameful mistakes, and did not even want to hear of them. And when the elder brother called them to mind to justify his jealousy, he answered only by giving reasons for joy: "We were bound to make merry and rejoice, for this thy brother was dead, and has come to life; he was lost and is found" (Lk. 15:32). There was no longer any question of sins, wrongs, or grievances. His father's heart had wiped out, forgotten, and forgiven everything, and forever. Just as the fire destroyed the filthy rags his son had worn, so his tenderness consumed all of his guilty past. For all time to come, he would cast aside this painful memory, as if it had never been.

How much greater and more touching proofs of love does God give the converted sinner in conferring grace upon him! He clothes him in the precious garment which is a participation in His own nature, and He restores to him all the rights and privileges of a son: the right to the divine inheritance, the right to share in His own happiness, the right to act supernaturally, divinely, past rights and future rights. God does more than embrace him warmly. He takes up His residence within his soul, surrounds him with His paternal tenderness, and imbues his whole being with His divinity. And what delight for His heart, because "there will be joy in heaven over one sinner who repents, more than over ninety-nine just who have no need of repentance" (Lk. 15:7). Henceforth, God welcomes him into the loving intimacy of His own life.

Could He give more eloquent proofs of His complete and final forgiveness? How could He manifest more clearly that He no longer remembers the sins of this pampered child, that He no longer thinks or even wants to think of them, that He will never bring them up again, that He wipes them out as if they had never been?

Yes, God forgives since He gives so generously what is most precious and personal to Himself: His own life, His own happiness. Yes, He forgives, since He gives Himself with such eagerness and love. Yes, He justifies, since He purifies and sanctifies. Yes, He has mercy, since He infuses His grace. Grace is the sure sign of His forgiveness, its indubitable manifestation. Grace contains His forgiveness just as heat contains the disappearance of cold, and as being contains the disappearance of non-being. Grace is the principle, the formal cause of forgiveness.[3] "*Quia ipse [Spiritus Sanctus] est remissio omnium peccatorum*—for it is the Holy Spirit [grace] given to the soul who is Himself the remission of sins."

Grace bears within itself the divine power to extirpate sin. Deep as the roots of sin may be, grace pursues them into the hidden recesses of conscience. It has the power to wipe out all stains, just as a powerful washing soda dissolves the dirt in clothes. Nothing can resist its purifying action, which is like a fire that burns its way into the soul's very depths to destroy all evil that may be in it.

Do we give fitting esteem to this effect of grace, this total liberation, this profound purification of our conscience, this disappearance of the monstrous disorder that oppressed our soul, this destruction of the horrible stain that disfigured it? "For by grace you have been saved" (Eph. 2:8). Do we suf-

---

[3] In one of his Lenten sermons for 1910, Father Janvier said: "Even if you fall back into your former state, you will not be called to account. Your sins have become foreign to your personality, as if they had never existed. You have escaped forever the responsibility that overwhelmed you. Even if you should be condemned on judgment day (for future sins), your past sins (now forgiven) will not be the reason for your condemnation, nor will they be the reason for your sufferings in hell. Mercy does not revoke the pardons it has granted."

ficiently realize the terrible disaster from which grace saves us, the tragic misfortune from which it wrests us?

In our present state—and probably in every possible state—grace involves the remission of sins. Grace is the principle, the reason for, and the cause of the remission of sins. Grace justifies.

* * *

Is the reverse true? Just as grace always involves forgiveness of the sinner, can we say that there is no forgiveness that does not proceed from grace? Is there no remission of (mortal) sins without the infusion of grace?

De facto, there is not. This is a doctrine defined by the Council of Trent: "If anyone says that men are justified . . . by the sole remission of sins, to the exclusion of grace and charity . . . let him be anathema" (Sixth Session, Canon 11, Denz. 821).

This is a question of *fact,* a law of the existing order that does not seem to be demanded by the nature of things as was the case mentioned earlier. Absolutely speaking, God could have arranged things differently: He could have granted His forgiveness, renounced His right to punish, without infusing grace, as would have happened in the state of pure nature. The sinner could thus have avoided hell without winning heaven. He would have been adapted only to his natural end, and would have received a happiness of the same order in the life beyond. Or again, God could have been content to remit the offense and to restore grace only after death. But He decided that these two benefits (the remission of sin and the infusion of grace) were to be inseparably united, the first to be realized only through the second.

What were God's reasons for this decision? We can surmise some of them. Could the Savior, the new Adam, do less for reparation than the first man and Satan had done for destruction? Was He not called upon to affirm the superiority of His power and love? He willed to repair all the evil of sin, and to destroy the work of the devil completely. His heart could not be content with an incomplete pardon, with a partial reconciliation (as it would have been if He had not restored everything that sin had caused man to lose),[4] if He had not returned the converted sinner to his state prior to the offense, if He had not resumed His former paternal relationship toward him,—in a word, if He had not clothed him in the divine garment of grace.

If the father of the prodigal son had treated him not as a son of the family but as a servant, as the latter asked in his repentance, could it have been said that he had sincerely forgotten his wrongs and granted perfect pardon? Would not this disgrace have been testimony of a certain rancor and of an incomplete reconciliation? This was well understood by the father who, overlooking his wretched son's humble request, received him as his child, restored all his privileges as a son, and greeted his return with festivities.

Thus in the present order, there is only one end for man, at least for the adult: a supernatural end. There is no intermediary state between the state of sin and the state of grace, no state in which one would be without grace and without sin, adapted solely to the natural end in the strict sense.

The adult in the theological sense, the man who has enough understanding of God and of the moral law to incur responsibility and to commit formal sins, cannot obtain remission for such sins without an infusion of grace. Either he will do penance and be restored to justice, or else he will be damned: for him there is either justification or damnation, either heaven or hell.

Should we go further and maintain that every adult (in the theological sense) is necessarily in the state of grace or in the state of personal sin, without any possible middle ground, because at the moment when he arrived at this knowledge of God that made him an adult and was sufficiently instructed in one way or another on his destiny to a supernatural end, he had to speak out either for or against it, sinning gravely if he refused or receiving grace if he consented? That is the opinion commonly held by those authors who say that the commandment of charity toward God obligates us from the start of our spiritual life. As soon as man

---

[4] At least with regard to the essentials, for He had good reasons, born of wisdom and love, not to restore the preternatural gifts during this life.

knows that God is his supernatural end, he must choose. By cleaving to God, he makes an act of charity that justifies him even before baptism. By rejecting God in order to give himself to creatures, he grievously offends Him and commits a personal sin.

It may be asked whether God makes known man's supernatural end, and if so by what means, to the one who has concluded to His existence and to the existence of moral obligations through the light of reason and natural criteria. That is a question that does not come within our purview in the present study.

As for non-adults (*infantes*), they too are either in the state of grace or in the state of original sin. There is no middle ground for them, either. If they die before baptism, their only means of justification will not be hell as in the case of the guilty adult, nor will it be heaven. It is generally admitted that they will not suffer, and that they will even enjoy a certain natural happiness, but one that will be a "privation" in the strict philosophical sense of the word, just as it is a privation for them not to have grace here on earth. But for Adam's sin, they would have grace, and according to God's original plan they should have it. Since this privation results from sin (either personal or original), it constitutes one of the essentials of the state of sin. And that is why anyone who does not have grace is in the state of sin (in the strict or analogical sense).

Thus the infusion of grace in someone deprived of it always has this particular effect that it would not have had among the angels, in our first parents before their sin, or in our Lord or in the Blessed Virgin Mary: namely, grace wipes out sin, it *justifies*.[5] Grace has this power even in the child, for his justification also involves a remission of sin—original sin.

But it is in the adult guilty of personal sin that the infusion of grace produces this effect in the full sense of the

---

[5] That is one of the differences between their grace and ours: a difference in efficacy and not in nature. Grace would have wiped out sin if it had encountered it in them as it does in us. But *de facto* grace was not required to produce in them this effect which it had the power to produce.

word. Grace brings him back from a greater distance, and
raises him up from greater depths. Grace wrests him from the
hell that he deserves, and presses him against God's heart.
The distance to cover is greater, the effect to be produced
more extensive and more arduous; just as it is harder to heat
an object to a temperature of 100° if it is 100° below zero to
start with than if its temperature is zero. Grace must make
the sinner pass not only from natural love, but from supernatural enmity, to supernatural friendship.

Actually, the infusion of grace and the remission of sins
cannot be accomplished separately. They are produced together.

That is why the Church often speaks of them interchangeably, and is often content to speak of the remission of sins
when she means to speak of justification. In the Post Communion of Lent, she asks that the Eucharist may be "the
remission of sins" for the "living" faithful. In the formula
of absolution that justifies, she refers only to the remission
of sins: "I absolve thee of thy sins." Likewise, in the sacrament of Extreme Unction she says: "May God forgive thee
all the sins that thou hast committed through this sense."
But whenever there is a remission of sin, there is an infusion
of grace.[6]

Should we attribute to the production of grace a priority
over the remission of sins and over all the conditions required for justification? And is this a priority of nature or
of causality? We answer both questions affirmatively, for St.
Thomas says that the cause is naturally anterior to the effect.
Now the infusion of grace is the cause of all that is required
for justification. . . . It is therefore anterior to justification
by its very nature (cf. Ia IIae, q. 113, a. 1).

However, this is not a chronological priority: "The infusion of grace and the remission of sin, . . . with respect to
the substance of the act, . . . are the same; for by the same
act God bestows grace and remits sin. . . . [But] considered
on the part of the objects, . . . they differ by the difference
between guilt, which is taken away, and grace, which is in-

---

[6] Cf. the author's work, *Dans les bras du Père,* pp. 61 and 62.

fused; just as in natural things generation and corruption differ, although the generation of one thing is the corruption of another" (Ia IIae, q. 113, a. 6, ad 2). The infusion of grace appears at the same instant that sin disappears.[7]

In natural mutations (such as chemical compounds, for example) the production of one element, and consequently the destruction of the other, occur successively and require a certain length of time. The infusion of grace and the remission of sin are produced instantaneously and simultaneously: there can be no question of a priority in time.[8]

2. Grace Vivifies

We know that mortal sin deprives the sinner of the merits he has acquired. And yet it cannot destroy these merits completely. Sin prevents merits from having effect by destroying grace in the soul; as long as sin endures it makes impossible the possession and reward of these merits, as would a circumstance that prevents the payment of a debt. How can a man continue to merit heaven when he deserves hell? How can he remain the child of God when he has become His enemy?

What a disaster for the sinner who thus loses the fruit of all his past efforts, rendered eternally useless if death should strike him in this state! He is spiritually ruined, brought back to zero, as if he had never done any good at all.

However by contrast with financial "crashes," the debacle of sin can be repaired by penance. When grace returns to

---

[7] The Angelic Doctor also says: "Since the infusion of grace and the remission of sin regard God who justifies, hence in the order of nature the infusion of grace is prior to the freeing from sin. But if we look at what is on the part of the man justified, it is the other way about, since in the order of nature the being freed from sin is prior to the obtaining of justifying grace" (Ia IIae, q. 113, a. 8, ad 1). God forgives by giving grace, the way darkness is banished from a room by the turning of a light switch.
Certain catechisms put the matter this way: "Baptism frees us from original sin and gives us grace." It would be more accurate to say: "Baptism frees us from original sin by giving us grace."

[8] This is not the place to study the conditions required on the part of the subject for his justification, namely: the exercise of his free will (q. 113, a. 3); a movement of faith (q. 113, a. 4); contrition for personal sins (q. 113, a. 5). Nor is there need to discuss the process by which this justification takes place.

the soul, it removes the obstacle to reward. Former rights, with all their exigencies, are restored. It is commonly said that they *"revive."* [9]

Now these merits revive totally, at least to the degree of glory due them before sin. For, according to the Council of Trent, the only condition necessary for a just man to obtain all the glory merited by his good works is that he die in the state of grace (cf. Canon 82, Denz. 842). The only condition for recovering all the rights already acquired is the restoration of the state of grace. All theologians agree on this point.[10]

St. Francis de Sales has written luminous and exquisite pages on this subject, concluding as follows: "When Naburzardan destroyed Jerusalem and Israel was driven into captivity, the sacred fire of the altar was hidden in a well where it was transformed into mud. But when, after the return from captivity, this mud was taken out of the well and replaced in the sun, the dead fire rekindled and this mud was transformed into flames. When the just man is made a slave of sin, all the good works that he has performed are forgotten and reduced to mud. But when he emerges from captivity, when, through penance, he returns to the grace of divine love, his preceding good works are drawn out of the well of oblivion and, touched by the rays of heavenly mercy, they revive and are converted into flames as bright as they ever were, to be replaced upon the sacred altar of divine approbation and restored to their original dignity, worth, and value" (*Oeuvres*, Vol. V, 282).

Indeed, if to lose one's merits is a disaster, to recover them is an immense gain. The entire result of a lifetime, and perhaps a long lifetime, of effort revives. The fruit of years, perhaps many years, of struggles, trials, and sacrifices is regained. Past riches can once more be added to present riches and be increased with future riches as well. The whole of a man's life, except the time spent in sin (cf. Council of Trent,

---

[9] Grace makes past merits revive, and makes possible the acquisition of new merits, as we shall explain in Chapter XI below.

[10] In a *Note* at the end of this chapter, we shall state another point on which they do not agree, cf. pp. 131-132 below.

Session VI, Chapter 7, Denz. 817) contributes to the building up of his eternal happiness.

And all this is due to grace.

The instant grace enters a soul, all the acquisitions of the past, reduced to nothing by sin, spring to life again. It is as if, by a miraculous command, trees and plants mortified by winter's ice were suddenly clothed in their beautiful vegetation, or as if a body reduced to lethargy suddenly regained movement and life. Grace bears within it a divine power of resurrection. Grace is life; it vivifies.

Grace does still more. By repairing the past, it prepares the future. By wiping out sins committed, it helps, through the dispositions of soul that it presupposes or produces, to prevent the commission of future sins. This is what we mean when we say that *grace rectifies*.

3. Grace Rectifies

1. *The Meaning of This Proposition*

Protestants have maintained that all the works of the sinner are evil and that, without the grace of justification, no one can perform even a single morally good act. This doctrine has been condemned as heretical by the Council of Trent (Session VI, Chapter 7, Denz. 817). It is clearly contrary to the affirmations of Scripture, in which God is shown to us as inviting, exhorting, and obligating the sinner to perform certain acts, and praising and rewarding him for certain works—something He would not do if all the sinner's works were evil.

But while the sinner can perform a few good actions, it is not morally possible for him to avoid new falls as long as he remains in his sinful state. If he is not to fall back into sin, he must emerge from the state of sin, that is, be restored to grace. The same is true of him as of the sick man so debilitated and exhausted by dieting, fever, and suffering, that he cannot escape serious danger of contagion unless he takes the indispensable precaution of regaining his health and of becoming capable of resisting epidemics. To fail to do this when he could do so would be to deliberately court certain death. Likewise, if the sinner neglects to regain the health of soul that consists in the state of grace, he is voluntarily condemning himself to all sorts of moral contagion and to new defeats.

2. The Proofs

Such is the common teaching of the theologians. It is a certain doctrine that cannot be called into question without temerity.[11]

Aristotle laid down the principle which St. Thomas took up after him, namely, that "in unforeseen matters we act in conformity with the end that we have set for ourselves and in accordance with our habits." By taking thought and making a vigorous effort of the will, we can of course act differently and follow the path of duty. But we are rarely capable of this reflection, this rectification, this effort, and it is hard for us to persevere long without yielding to the soul's inclination.

As long as we remain in the psychological state of sin, we retain the disposition to prefer a forbidden good to God, because we are practically convinced that as far as we are concerned this good is worth more than God. Should a new temptation arise that opposes this good to God and places the will thus disposed in the necessity to choose, is it not very likely that, granted our notion of God and our undue love of creatures, we shall choose in favor of the latter? A change in our present behavior would presuppose a retraction of the past: contrition.

Moreover, the motives for avoiding a second fall are less compelling than are those for avoiding the first. Before falling the first time, we might have said to ourselves: "If I fall, I shall lose grace, God's friendship, the right to heaven, the capacity to merit, virginity. . . . I am exposing myself to damnation in hell." Once sin has been committed, these reasons no longer hold good. God's friendship, grace, heaven, merit, virginity? They are already lost. Hell? What does a little more or less matter! In very truth, it is only the first

---

11 Cf. the *Note* on St. Thomas' doctrine on this point on pp. 132-133 below.

step that is hard. We fall the second and third times with increasing ease; and then we allow ourselves to slide down the steep slope that sometimes leads to the depths. "Depth cries out to depth." Sin cries out to sin, and here too the law of the acceleration of speed holds true.

To this must be added the fact that sin diminishes not only the force of motives for good but also the divine helps which are certainly less abundant for those without sanctifying grace because prayer is less efficacious, because merit is dead, and because the sacraments of the living can no longer be a source of merit. There is a reduction in the strength that comes from outside (from God) and from within (motives and practical judgments). There is a reduction in the will's energy and in its authority over the evil instincts of nature, and a more powerful attraction to evil. Under such circumstances it is hard to remain unscathed by the claws of temptation and to avoid new sins. The crushing weight of the sins already burdening the conscience drags the soul down and prevents its flight upward toward the summits of virtue. Through these past sins the evil spirit has a stranglehold on the soul and keeps it under his dominion. The word "Redemption," which presupposes an enslaved sinner, is not merely a metaphor.

And yet since his redemption by Christ, the sinner has voluntarily remained a slave to sin. For he has infallibly vowed himself to relapses and he is entirely responsible for them, inasmuch as he could have received the necessary help to overcome his sins and to return to the state of grace. If he has not returned to grace and instead has remained helpless in the face of temptation, he has done so of his own free will, as St. Thomas points out: "Since it is by his own shortcoming that he [man] does not prepare himself to have grace, the fact that he cannot avoid sin without grace does not excuse him from sin" (Ia IIae, q. 109, a. 8, ad 1).

Thus the weight of his sins inclines the sinner to become a greater sinner. "The tree falls as it leans." The will slides in the direction it has chosen.

Likewise, the just man tends to remain, to become rooted, perfected in his justice, and to be progressively borne upward toward God. He tends to follow the habitual disposition of his will, the ordinary inclination of his heart, the unretracted judgment of his intellect. Grace presupposes contrition, *conversio ad Deum, aversio a creaturis,* in the soul that it enters. It presupposes the rectification of the will led astray by sin, a total orientation toward God that it completes and impels to its term by bringing with it hope and charity.

The just man realizes that God alone can *"terminate"* his being and bring him the happiness to which he aspires by uniting him to Himself in the beatific vision. In short, he realizes that God is his end, preferable to every other good. And he loves God, yearns for Him more than anything else, and cleaves to Him more than to anything else. He has orientated his whole being toward Him, directly toward Him. *"Justum deduxit per vias rectas*—He led the just man by straight paths."* When temptation raises its head, it finds him on guard, ready for combat, disposed to resist it. To yield to it, he would have to go against the inclination of his will, reform the judgment of his intellect, and go against the current that is carrying him toward God. He would have to fight against himself and do himself violence in some way. What is true of the sinner in the case of sin, is equally true in reverse of the just man, with regard to virtue.

3. *The Consequences*

Two consequences flow from this doctrine, that are of capital importance from the moral and practical point of view.

The first consequence is that the majority of the actual helps granted to sinners and pagans are only mediately concerned with triumph over temptations. Their purpose is above all to bring or restore these souls to the state of grace. It is by helping these souls to give up the state of sin that God wants to help them not to fall again. Father Billot says: "The purpose of actual graces given the sinner is not to make up for the rectitude that justification produces, but only (or especially) to arouse in him dispositions that will restore this health of soul" (*De gratia,* Thes. IV).

This does not mean that God absolutely refuses to give the sinner His help to avoid falling into sin again, if he asks for it. Nor does it mean that God cannot, absolutely speaking, confer upon him a series of graces that will preserve him from sin. But the help that God gives the sinner ordinarily and above all is meant to bring him to contrition, to the sacraments, and through them, to justification.[12] Instead of supporting a sick man as soon as he wants to make a step, is it not better, if possible, to help him to regain his health and, together with it, the strength to walk by himself?[13] Instead of giving a beggar the bread he needs each day and leaving him in a state of idleness, is it not wiser, when possible, to furnish him the means of earning his own bread and of providing for his subsistence by his own labor?

Moreover, this continual intervention that resistance to temptations requires on God's part is not normal in a subject who stubbornly remains His enemy, scorns His will, and prefers creatures to Him. Such a close collaboration, such intimate contacts are suitable only for a son, a friend, who is united to Him by bonds of affection.

Second consequence: there is nothing more dangerous than to persist in the state of sin, and to reject calls to penance which God makes to the conscience through His inward grace or through external graces such as preaching. God makes the conscience understand that to deliberately remain in sin is to willfully invite inevitable relapses into sin because one thereby voluntarily deprives oneself of the sufficient means of escaping sin; and that this amounts to refusing to take on the necessary dispositions for triumphing over temptations.

The longer the sinner waits to return to God's friendship,

---

[12] This also shows us to what extent the state of grace is the normal state for the Christian.

[13] Habitual grace does not take the place of actual *"sanans"* (medicinal) grace, which may continue to be necessary. But it is habitual grace that does most to *heal* the soul, according to St. Thomas (Ia IIae, q. 109, a. 9 and 10): "A habitual gift whereby corrupted human nature is healed, and after being healed is lifted up so as to work deeds meritorious of everlasting life" (a. 9, c). It is habitual grace that "restores to the fitting order," to "the state of health" by reason of which the soul can resist the contagion of sin.

the weaker he becomes, and the more he exposes himself to danger. By deferring his conversion and his justification, he defers receiving the help he needs, he defers the healing of his soul, he defers the hour of deliverance when he will triumph over the powers of evil. On the contrary, he proceeds toward the blinding of his mind and the hardening of his heart, toward final impenitence, toward hell. He multiplies the probabilities of his damnation, not only because of the danger that death may surprise him in this state, but above all because of the progressive stranglehold he allows sin to acquire upon his soul by reason of his growing impotence to resist the assaults of the devil.

The necessary means for him to avoid relapses is to stir himself to contrition as soon as possible and to seek the grace of the sacraments. Through confession he will not only abjure his sins, but also persevere in grace.

Therefore the priest must not hesitate to invite the sinner to confess his sins and to absolve him without delay, provided he fulfills the necessary conditions. The practice, formerly prevalent in certain areas and in great part inspired by Jansenism, of deferring absolution for a long time was a most dangerous one.

In addition to the three effects of grace we have already discussed, we must mention a fourth which flows from the others: *sanctification.*

4. Grace Sanctifies

The Council of Trent teaches that justification is not only "the remission of sins, but also the sanctification and renewal of the inward man, through the free reception of grace and the gifts."

We have already seen that "justification" implies "purification" and "sanctification," according to St. Paul.

Christian terminology speaks interchangeably of "habitual" grace or "sanctifying" grace, but more frequently it uses the term "sanctifying grace." In the first centuries of the Church, all baptized persons were called *"saints."* The words "Christian" and "saint" were synonymous.

The word "saint" has two meanings: a primitive meaning that essentially implies the absence of mortal sin and the presence of the state of grace. It also has a meaning, that we might call modern, that presupposes a heroic degree of virtue. In both instances, grace is sanctifying.

In the ancient sense of the word, God is holy: *Sanctus, sanctus, sanctus, Dominus Deus.* He is holiness in person, the source of all holiness. His creatures are holy in the measure that they share in His divinity. The more of the divine there is in them, the more holiness there is as well. Everything that units them to God, everything that brings them closer to Him, everything that makes them resemble Him and commune in His holiness. To deify is to sanctify. That is the function, the role, and the effect of sanctifying grace.

Sanctifying grace rectifies the will of the just man, as we have already said. It converts his will, detaches it from creatures, at least from those that are directly opposed to God and that the will cannot want without grievously offending and turning away from Him. Grace brings the will back to God and makes it cleave to Him, and it identifies God's will with man's. But is not this essential conformity to the will of God, the supreme measure of all good, also the mark of holiness? The role of grace is to imbue the soul with the divine.

According to St. Thomas, holiness includes two elements: an absence of stain (according to the name that the Greeks gave this word: "not mixed with earth"); and a consecration. To sanctify means to purify and to consecrate to God. Our Lord said: "Sanctify them in the truth" (Jn. 17:17). And Fillion explains: "To sanctify them is to set them apart, to preserve them in view of their very lofty ministry."

Habitual grace embraces these two meanings. Not only does it wipe out the stain of sin and put an end to the moral disorder that sin presupposes, but it also unites to God by a kind of consecration. When a prince marks an object with his seal, his image, he thereby expresses that he reserves it for himself and makes it his own. Grace is the seal of God, the image of God upon the soul, the sign that He makes it His own, that He reserves it for Himself and consecrates it to Himself. Like the Bride of the Canticle, it becomes "a garden enclosed, a fountain sealed up: *hortus conclusus, fons signatus*" (Cant. 4:12). Having become a divine thing, it shares in God's majesty and in the respect due to Him, as do all blessed or consecrated objects: vestments, sacred vessels, sacred places, sacramentals, etc. If our churches are holy because Christ dwells in them, how much holier are our souls in which, through grace, the Holy Spirit has chosen to reside!

Whether canonized or not by the Church that celebrates their collective feast on All Saints Day, all the elect in heaven are saints, supernaturally united to God by the beatific vision and beatific love, participants in His action, His nature, and His divinity. Their beings are totally filled, imbued with Him.

The same is proportionally true of the just here on earth, since they have the right and the capacity for this vision, and thereby already share in the divine nature. If grace is the seed of glory, the just are the seeds of the saints. Their holiness is not yet apparent and does not possess its full splendor and bloom here on earth. But it is really in them, hidden until the time of the manifestation of the children of God. All of them are saints and wear an invisible halo. Grace confers upon them at least the minimum of holiness, which is the condition of eternal life.

And yet grace tends to do more than that.

In the modern sense of the word, we say that grace raises the soul higher, always higher, toward perfection, through the infused theological and moral virtues that it produces within it.

The Spirit who comes with grace makes use of His loving action to sustain it, to spur it on, and to help it to strip itself of the old man and his lusts, and to put on the new man who is holy, as St. Paul writes to the Ephesians: "You are to put off the old man, which is being corrupted through its deceptive lusts. But be renewed in the spirit of your mind, and put on the new man, which has been created according to God in justice and holiness of truth" (Eph. 4:22-24).

Grace is a seed of holiness thrown into the furrows of the soul and which must, under the action of the Spirit, grow, spread, and shoot up divine branches of virtue in every direction, like the mustard seed of the parable (Mt. 13:31-32). Or again grace is like a leaven of perfection which has been placed by God into the helplessness of our nature, to raise the whole dough, to warm and quicken the whole inert mass, and elevate all its energies toward goodness.

Through grace, every just man bears within himself the principle of holiness. Through it, he possesses the initial holiness that he need only develop in order to attain to holiness in the modern sense of high moral perfection and of the heroic virtues. Grace has started him on his way, guides him toward these summits, and provides him with the means of reaching them. The saints are just men and women in whom grace has reached its full stature, and who have not resisted its impulsion but have docilely yielded to it, allowing it to progressively flow into and imbue their being and inform all their actions. They are just men and women who have made this precious talent bear fruit within them, instead of letting it lie useless and forgotten through laziness and fear of sacrifice.

All the just would achieve this same magnificent result, that is, they would all become saints, if they devoted the same care, ardor, and generosity to offering themselves to the influence of grace. For grace is not something inert. Being a participation in the life of God who is pure act, incessant and infinite activity, it impels to action. Through a powerful dynamism, grace tends to blossom out in acts of virtue and to produce fruits of perfection.

In the literal sense of the word, grace is *sanctifying*.

Grace *justifies*, it *vivifies*, it *rectifies*, and it *sanctifies*.

Note on St. Paul's emphasis on justification as an effect of grace (see p. 108 above):

"We need not expect to find in him [St. Paul] the calm contemplation of the supernatural order that characterized St. John: *Gratia et veritas per Jesus Christum facta est.* . . . St. John's emotion is certainly no less profound; but St. Paul's is more vibrant. After a catastrophe that had threatened to annihilate everything, even though safety was now assured, a shudder of horror and fear went through the flesh of the survivor.

"An experience of this sort was perhaps necessary to enter fully into the thought of St. Paul and to exploit its riches in the same spirit in which they had been acquired. Could this have been expected of the devout Origen?

"Could this have been expected of the Cappadocians, those fine young people who had never known anything but the paths to school and church? Chrysostom read Paul assiduously. He saw in him not so much the interior tragedy that first catches our attention as the moral tragedy. . . . Then came Augustine of Africa, whose story was altogether different. He had been converted slowly. Even after his reason had been convinced, his heart remained rebellious. He had experienced captivity to passions, *retinebant nugae nugarum.* He had long continued to yield to the enticing whispers of the old habits of his flesh which, as he said, pulled at the hem of his garment and said: 'How will you live without us?' And so God chose him to lead the Church to a deeper understanding of the mystery of grace and of the human heart, a mystery that He had already revealed to St. Paul" (P. Rousselot, *Recherches de science religieuse,* 1928, p. 98).

Note on the Reviviscence of Grace (see p. 121 above):

Theologians are not agreed as to whether the reviviscence applies to the degree of grace possessed at the moment of sin or whether the grace that is produced by the sacrament of penance or by justifying charity is added to all the graces possessed at the moment of sin, thereby resulting in a greater degree of grace after justification than before the commission of the sin.

a. Many modern theologians hold to the latter view, following Suarez. Lugo says: "Through penance man receives more grace than he had before: in fact, he recovers all this grace and receives in addition the grace that comes to him through perfect contrition or through the sacrament" (*De Poenitentia,* Disp. II, S. 3, 454).

According to the Council of Trent, man regains all the degrees of glory merited before sin, since the only condition posed for the acquisition of these degrees of glory is to be in the state of grace at the moment of death.

But if the rights to glory revive, the rights to the corresponding grace must also revive: whoever merits the end, merits the means, and no one has the right to set more conditions for this "reviviscence" than the Council of Trent has already done.

b. Despite this and other arguments, the disciples of St. Thomas continue to follow their master's opinion, maintaining that grace is restored and merits revive only in proportion to the dispositions of the subject at the moment of justification. It is a general principle that variable forms (and grace is one of them) vary in degree, in intensity, according to the subject's capacity, that is, according to the dispositions of the subject at the time he receives them (cf. Chapter X, below).

The reasons set forth in both of these opinions are not convincing. Hence, both opinions remain more or less probable, and the controversy which began long before the Council of Trent, and continued since then, has not yet been resolved.

In practice, it is safer to follow the Thomists, even though we do not have the right to teach that justification does not restore all past merits. Sinners should be exhorted to receive the sacrament of reconciliation with the most fervent dispositions, so as to make more certain the complete recovery of all their merits. But we are not permitted to say, given the present state of the question, that these fervent dispositions are the indispensable condition for their recovery. That would be a breach of the truth, as would the categorical affirmation of the contrary opinion.

Father Billot gives the following advice, not without a tinge of irony, to the partisans of the first view: "We must beware of attributing too much to consoling arguments and of embracing the contrary opinion because it would be more consoling. True consolation does not rest upon the desires of the imagination but upon the truth" (*De Poenit.* Th. X).

Notwithstanding this controversial point, it is incontestable that grace vivifies past merits, totally with regard to glory, and at least partially with regard to grace. And if merits are not totally restored, it is only because of the inadequacy of the subject's dispositions.

Note on the Doctrine of St. Thomas on the Power of Grace to Rectify Man's Inclinations (see p. 123 above):

St. Thomas has set forth this doctrine with penetrating psychological insight in Ia IIae, q. 109, a. 8. He begins by pointing out that: "In the state of perfect nature, man, without habitual grace, could avoid sinning either mortally or venially; since to sin is nothing else than to stray from what is according to our nature,—and in the state of perfect nature man could avoid this.

Nevertheless he could not have done it without God's help to uphold him in good, since if this had been withdrawn, even his nature would have fallen back into nothingness."

St. Thomas then notes that even with this grace, we cannot, in the present state of our corrupted nature, avoid all venial sin. This is a truth of faith.

Then our doctor explains the necessity of the state of grace to avoid new sins: "But in the state of corrupt nature man needs grace to heal his nature in order that he may entirely abstain from sin. And in the present life this healing is wrought in the mind,—the carnal appetite being not yet restored. . . .

"So, too, before man's reason, wherein is mortal sin, is restored by justifying grace, he can avoid each mortal sin, and for a time, since it is not necessary that he should be always actually sinning. But it cannot be that he remains for a long time without mortal sin. Hence Gregory says . . . that *a sin not at once taken away by repentance, by its weight drags us down to other sins:* and this because, as the lower appetite ought to be subject to the reason, so should the reason be subject to God, and should place in Him the end of its will. Now it is by the end that all human acts ought to be regulated, even as it is by the judgment of the reason that the movements of the lower appetite should be regulated. And thus, even as inordinate movements of the sensitive appetite cannot help occurring since the lower appetite is not subject to reason, so likewise, since man's reason is not entirely subject to God, the consequence is that many disorders occur in the reason.

"For when man's heart is not so fixed on God as to be unwilling to be parted from Him for the sake of finding any good or avoiding any evil, many things happen for the achieving or avoiding of which a man strays from God and breaks His commandments, and thus sins mortally: especially since, when surprised, a man acts according to his preconceived end and his pre-existing habits, as the Philosopher says (*Ethic* III); although with premeditation of his reason a man may do something outside the order of his preconceived end and the inclination of his habit. But because a man cannot always have this premeditation it cannot help occurring that he acts in accordance with his will turned aside from God, unless, by grace, he is quickly brought back to the due order" (*Summa*, Ia IIae, q. 109, a. 8, c.).

PART TWO

THE EFFECTS

OF GRACE

DISTINCT

FROM IT

THE EFFECTS STUDIED in the earlier chapters are not distinct from grace, and are called its "formal" effects.

The effects we are now about to discuss stem from grace necessarily and prolong it, but are not identical with it. Grace calls for these effects, demands them. One of them is the uncreated gift of God Himself to the soul. The others—the infused virtues, actual graces, the gifts of the Holy Ghost—are created gifts that spring from grace like branches from the vine-stock. All of these effects are required by grace, but only the virtues and the gifts flow from it the way the faculties—the intellect and free will—flow from the essence of the soul. The uncreated gift of God is not an "accident" of the soul, since it is God Himself dwelling in the soul. It is by far the greatest of these effects, both in dignity and value. That is why we shall give it first place here.

6 God's Special Presence in the Soul

THIS chapter will deal with the *fact* of this special presence, its *explanation*, and its principal *consequences*.

1. The Fact

This is one of the most touching dogmas of the Christian religion, one that is most conducive to piety and that contains the most fertile seeds of holiness. Who can count the fruits of perfection that it has produced in souls through the ages? How many hearts wounded by inevitable separations or the faithlessness of men have been consoled by this thought of the continuous presence of their Father! How many voids of loneliness it has filled! The realization that God is the perpetual witness of our efforts has stirred up courage and inspired good deeds. Faith in this special indwelling has drawn and kept many Christians in a sweet and life-giving intimacy with God, and at times led them to the heights of joyous contemplation. It has inspired many affectionate conversations, and made many a prayer easy and sincere. It has certainly been one of the most efficacious causes of the holiness of those in whom the Church glories and whom she offers to us as examples to be imitated.

137

And what we say of the past must also be said of the present. For the fruitfulness of this dogma has not diminished in the Church of the present day.

The power of this dogma could be felt still more widely if it were better known. Many of the faithful are delightfully surprised when they first hear of it. They have only one regret: the regret that they have too long been ignorant or only vaguely aware of it, without suspecting the vast resources it held for their souls. Fortunately, theologians are insisting upon it more and more, and fine works of popularization are striving to bring it within the reach of all.

The doctrine of God's special presence was very familiar to the first Christians. The Apostles rested their exhortations upon it as a truth present to the minds of all (and this presupposed that they had stressed it in their preaching).

St. Paul appealed to this doctrine to warn the Corinthians against those who were trying to destroy his work: "Do you not know that you are the temple of God and that the Spirit of God dwells in you? If anyone destroys the temple of God, him will God destroy; for holy is the temple of God, and this temple you are" (I Cor. 3:16-17).

In preaching against impurity he said: "Or do you not know that your members are the temple of the Holy Spirit, who is in you? ... Glorify God and bear Him in your body" (I Cor. 6:1-20). Every word of this text is a proof. He was clearly speaking of individuals, and of a presence that applied to Christians in a special way after they had been "washed, ... sanctified, ... justified in the name of our Lord Jesus Christ, and in the Spirit of our God" (I Cor. 6:11). It is a presence that consecrates the bodies of Christians to God-like temples (and in the language of Scripture a temple always implies a special presence of God). And so that no one should doubt that this was the meaning he intended to give the word, the Apostle added: "You are the temple of the Holy Spirit, who is in you, whom you have from God, and ... you are not your own" (I Cor. 6:19).[1] Thus the Christian is con-

---

[1] We should note the use of the pronoun *you* placed at the beginning of the sentence to better demonstrate that it is the privilege of Christians, as contrasted with unbelievers, to be the temples of God.

secrated to his divine Guest, and, like a temple consecrated to God, no longer belongs to men nor can he be put to profane uses.

Likewise, to deter Christians from associating with unbelievers, Paul said: "And what agreement has the temple of God with idols? For you are the temple of the living God" (II Cor. 6:16).

St. John proceeded in like manner in his Epistles, and presupposed the same knowledge of this truth among the faithful to whom he addressed himself: "If we love one another, God abides in us .... Whoever confesses that Jesus is the Son of God, God abides in him and he in God. ... God is love, and he who abides in love abides in God, and God in him" (I Jn. 4:12,15-16). Thus God's indwelling is the privilege of those who have faith in Christ and who have charity.

St. John understood and remembered the Master's explicit teaching on this subject in His discourse after the Last Supper. To dispel the sadness that the announcement of His imminent departure caused His Apostles, Jesus had promised them the Advocate: "But I speak the truth to you; it is expedient for you that I depart. For if I do not go, the Advocate will not come to you; but if I go, I will send him to you" (Jn. 16:7). And not only would the Holy Spirit come, but also Jesus Himself and His Father would come and make their abode in them. "If anyone love me, he will keep My word, and My Father will love him, and We will come to him and make our abode with him" (Jn. 14:23). It is a presence that is limited to those who love Him; and it is a permanent presence: "We will make our abode with him."

The Fathers of the Church have faithfully transmitted and enthusiastically explained this magnificent and fruitful doctrine. Perhaps the most beautiful pages they have written were on this subject. Like the Apostles, they appealed to this doctrine to throw light on their pious exhortations and to refute errors.

In his letters, St. Ignatius of Antioch (†107), a contemporary of St. John, called Christians "*Theophors,*" "Christophors." We know his proud answer to Trajan, who treated

him as if he were an evil demon: "Let no one call Theophor
(he who bears God) an evil demon!" And when Trajan asked:
"Well then, do you bear the Crucified within you?" he an-
answered: "Yes, without any doubt." And so Trajan commanded that Ignatius, who boasted he carried Christ within
him, be led to Rome to become the food of wild beasts and
an object of ridicule for the masses.

St. Cyril of Alexandria (†444) used this same truth to
prove the divinity of the Holy Spirit against the disciples
of Macedonius: "No one of sound mind can doubt that the
Spirit is God, and one with the Father and the Son in nature.
If anyone denies it, let them tell us how man can participate
in the nature of God by very reason of the fact that he has
received the Spirit, or how we become temples of God by
receiving a Spirit who is not God!" (P.G., 74; *In Joannis
Evang.*, I, IX, 14, 17).

We find similar arguments used by St. Athanasius against
the Arians a century earlier (between 356 and 362): "If the
Spirit is absent we are not of God; but when we are participants of the Spirit, we are united to the Godhead." "He who
falls (through sin) is no longer in God, because the Holy
Spirit and Paraclete who is in God has gone out of him"
(P.G., 26; Or. 3 contra Arianos, 24).

Father Froget declares: "This beautiful doctrine, which
the Fathers loved so dearly and so often discussed, either in
their exhortations to the faithful under the form of homilies
or in their controversies against heretics who denied the
divinity of the Word or of the Holy Spirit, was piously accepted by medieval theologians, and notably by the greatest
among them, the prince of scholasticism, the Angelic Doctor.
In fact St. Thomas Aquinas may be said to have appropriated
it and as it were marked it with his seal by formulating it
with all the precision of theological language."

St. Thomas did not speak of the indwelling of the Holy
Spirit in connection with grace, but in his study of the
invisible mission of the Holy Spirit (Ia, q. 43, a. 3), and of the
ordinary presence of God in all things (Ia, q. 8, a. 3). Most
other scholastics followed the same procedure.

Father Froget goes on to say: "We find this doctrine again

later on, set forth with love and an emotion that can be felt beneath the frigidity of the letter, by the principal representatives of sacred science, such as Gonet, John of Saint-Thomas, Suarez, and the theologians of Salamanca. In their works, this doctrine is like an oasis of coolness that is an agreeable change from the aridity and dryness of theological discussions. Peteau and Thomassin adorned it with the treasures of their erudition in their commentaries on some of the most beautiful passages by the Fathers relating to it."

Several contemporary authors have brought this doctrine down to the level of the general public in very interesting books, and the souls that nourish their devotion upon it are constantly increasing in number.

While the Greek Fathers may be said to have laid particular emphasis on this divine presence in our souls, the Latin Fathers did not neglect it either. St. Augustine devoted a special work to it which he addressed to Dardanus.

The liturgy makes many allusions to it in the divine worship for Pentecost, especially with reference to the Holy Spirit whom she calls "our soul's sweet Guest." In the Collect for the Wednesday after this feast, she asks: "Grant, we beseech Thee, almighty and merciful God, that the Holy Spirit, coming to us, may make us the temple of His glory."

We have ample proofs that the Church believes God is present in a special way in the soul of the just as truly as He is present in the tabernacle. For example there are the striking similarities between the ancient ceremonies of baptism and of the dedication of churches, and the parallelism between their twofold rites, which include first a purification and then a dedication to God through anointings. Moreover, she clearly expresses this belief in the first exorcism of baptism: "Unclean spirit ... depart from this servant of God, . . . and give honor to . . . the Holy Spirit." The exorcism that precedes the consignation of the senses is expressed in these words: "I exorcise thee, unclean spirit, ... that thou depart from this creature of God, N. . . . , whom our Lord has vouchsafed to call to His holy temple, that he may become the temple of the living God, and that the Holy Spirit may dwell in him."

The reality of this indwelling of God in the soul of the just [2] is a truth of our faith that we must rank among those that have been most clearly revealed. From the very beginning of the Church until now, every succeeding generation of Christians has accepted it without question and nourished its devotion upon it. The Church has given it a place of honor in her teaching. It should cause no surprise, therefore, if we stress it here with a view to explaining it and pointing out a few of its practical consequences.

2. The Explanation

This explanation will offer proofs of theological reason or fittingness, confirming the fact already established upon the authority of Revelation.

(1) There is a presence of God common to all creatures. All creatures receive their existence from Him, being unable to cause their existence or to preserve themselves in being of themselves. It is God who unceasingly communicates being to them, and if He should stop for a second they would be reduced to nothingness.

Besides, even creatures that appear inert, like minerals, act and react upon one another (as certain atomic discoveries have proven) by all the forces of affinity, repulsion, or attraction that the sciences investigate. And this also presupposes the intervention of the First Cause, for without its "concurrence" they cannot pass "from potency to act." God must act within them, that is, He must be present in them, either to maintain them in existence or to bring them out of their inertia (for God's presence is inseparable from His action). We can exercise our action at a distance; we can entrust it to intermediaries, for example moving a ball by means of another that we throw at it. But no creature can transport the action of God, the First Cause. He must exercise His action Himself. He must be where He acts. In Him, operation, power, and substance are one. He is therefore substantially in every place where His power operates. He is in every

_____
[2] Cf. the *Note* on pp. 166-167 at the end of this chapter, comparing this presence with the Eucharistic Presence.

creature; He is in heaven, upon earth, in hell; He is in the depths of the sea, in the solitude of the deserts, in the silent night of space, in the innumerable solar systems, in the bowels of the earth, in the atoms of ether that separate the stars, in the smallest bit of pollen in the fields. He is in all these places in His entirety, as wholly in a drop of water as He is in the ocean, somewhat the way the soul, the principle of life, is wholly in every part of the body that it quickens.

"Whither shall I go," asks the Psalmist, "from Thy spirit? or whither shall I flee from Thy face? If I ascend into heaven, Thou art there: if I descend into hell, Thou art present. If I take my wings early in the morning and dwell in the uttermost parts of the sea: Even there also shall Thy hand lead me: and Thy right hand shall hold me" (Ps. 138:7-10).

This is what St. Paul preached to the astonished Athenians: "He is not far from any one of us. For in Him we live and move and have our being" (Acts 17:27 28).

Thus God is everywhere, He is present in all created things as their efficient cause.

Is His special presence in the just due to the same reason? Can we explain His indwelling in their souls by the supernatural action He exercises within them? Certain authors (Peteau, Lessius, Cornelius de Lapide, Vasquez, and Father Ramière) have thought so. Grace, the infused virtues, and the gifts of the Holy Spirit are supernatural realities that cannot be preserved in existence or become principles of operations without the intervention of the First Cause.

Moreover, these supernatural realities imply a more intense action on God's part. For He has greater interest in the just than He does in sinners and in other creatures.

His providence is more active over the just, surrounds them with more vigilant care, and gives them many more actual graces. In a word, His paternal love makes Him act in them with a much greater intensity, and this implies a much more perfect presence on His part. For God is more perfectly present in the measure that He is more intensely active.

We must admit all this, but even that is not enough. For God also intervenes within the sinner to preserve him and to cause the infused virtues of faith and hope to pass from potency to act within him, providing sin has not destroyed them, and to help him through actual graces to be restored to grace. Now this intervention calls for a special presence of God in the sinner that is not very different from the presence the just enjoy, inasmuch as it has the same foundation. Between the two there would only be differences in degree, certainly insufficient to account for the categorical affirmations in Revelation that describe the divine presence in the just as far superior to God's common presence, as transcending it in value and perfection, and as an ineffable reward for their fidelity in keeping the commandments and for their love of God; something so precious that it is meant to console them for the sensible absence of Christ; and so perfect that they truly become the temples of the Holy Spirit and that their very bodies no longer belong to them but to God. Revealed docrine implies a difference not only in degree, but also in species and mode.

(2) Certain theologians (such as Suarez and Froget) see the foundation of this indwelling as the love of God for the just. "Through charity, a very perfect friendship is contracted between God and man. Now friendship demands, of its very nature, a union between the friends that is not only a conformity of sentiment, but an inseparable presence and fellowship. Such a perfect friendship, inasmuch as it is spiritual, thus wins the intimate presence of God in the sanctified soul by virtue of a divine right and as a due." [3]

But even if the union realized by love is always at least affective, it is not always effective, physical, and real. Our love for absent ones does not make them present to us, despite our ardent desires.

That is true, but the reason lies in our impotence. If we had the power, we would certainly satisfy this desire of our heart and of the hearts of those we love. We would certainly put an end to the distance that separates us, so as to be present to them and to have them present to us, so as to be with them, near them, in them, and so that they might be with

---

[3] Suarez, De Trinitate, Vol. I, XII, *De missione divinarum personarum.*

us, near us, in us. We would certainly, if we could, yield to this law of love that draws the lover toward the object of his love.

Now, God possesses this power. Why then, would He not realize it, after He has kindled in us, together with charity, the desire for His presence? Above all, why would He resist the attraction, the inclination that impels Him toward us and within us? Why would He do violence to the ardent, intense, paternal love that makes Him desire to live with us, in the closest union and the most affectionate intimacy?

These remarks are correct, but they prove the *fact* of God's special presence in the soul in the state of grace. They do not indicate the mode of this presence, nor do they explain it.[4]

(3) Is the explanation to be found in the fact that grace is the beginning of glory—*inchoatio gloria*—and that God's special presence in the just on earth is the beginning of that union with Him which is perfected in glory?

Certain authors have thought so. Grace confers the capacity for the immediate union of the intellect with God through the beatific vision, and that is why we have said it contains the seed of glory. But this capacity is not exercised, i.e., it does not pass into act here on earth. Hence the union, the actuation of the mind by God, the possession of the Blessed Trinity that it implies, cannot be realized in this life. We do not yet enjoy the beatific vision, but possess only the means necessary to enjoy it later on.

It is none the less true that grace already brings with it a beginning of union with God through glory.

Grace unites man's *intellect* to God's, since through the faith and hope that grace presupposes, the believer accepts God's affirmations and decisions, makes his own a few of His ideas, and shares in His own knowledge, that is, in Himself inasmuch as He Himself is the principal object of His thought and knowledge. The just man thinks like God and with God.

Moreover, the reason the intellect cleaves to God through

---

[4] Cf. the *Note* at the end of this chapter, containing a passage by Father Froget on this subject, p. 167 below.

grace is the authority of His testimony, the infallibility of His knowledge and veracity. This union of man's intellect to God's is actually "something" of God. And nothing is more personal or more closely united to the intellect than the motive for its assent, the thing that applies it to the truth. The believer thinks through God (without speaking of His actual intervention). His faith unites him to God. That is why St. Thomas calls faith the beginning of eternal life (IIa IIae, q. 4, a. 1).

However this is an imperfect union that does not make God present to the soul, because we can believe in the testimony of an absent person and on his authority. Besides, sinners deprived of grace by a sin that is not contrary to faith preserve this virtue and the union that it establishes with Him, even though they do not enjoy His special presence.

But the just man possesses charity, in addition to faith and hope. And even though he cannot see God here and now face to face as He really is, the virtue of charity enables him to love Him directly, in Himself, and to unite himself to Him without any intermediary, just as he will be united to Him later on in heaven. St. Paul tells us that charity is the same here on earth as it will be in heaven. Faith and hope will cease, because they are incompatible with vision. But charity will remain: "Charity never fails" (I Cor. 13:8).

It is true that we can love persons who are absent, we can love at a distance, but with a natural love. Supernatural love or charity possesses the privilege and virtue of fulfilling the deep yearning of all love, by making God, its first and principal object, present. It has the power, like a divine magnet, of drawing God into the soul, of contacting Him in His essence directly. That is why St. Thomas teaches: "In the wayfaring state, love is more perfect than knowledge. We can love God in His very essence, but we cannot know Him in this way. That is why, in heaven love will be of the same nature as it is now, and be different only in degree. Knowledge of God, however, will be of a different species" (III *Sent.*, dist. XX, 11, q. 3, a. 1, ad 3).

Charity is like one of the arms with which we can grasp and embrace our heavenly Father even here on earth, and thus possess and enjoy Him in a certain respect. As St. Paul told the Romans: "Charity . . . is poured forth into our hearts by the Holy Spirit who has been given to us [through it]" (Rom. 5:5), and who allows Himself to be embraced by us. Through charity, a supernatural and direct union of our will with Him is accomplished. The supernaturalized faculty of our will takes possession of God, and God actuates this power in very much the same way He will actuate the intellect in the beatific vision.

Inasmuch as, according to Revelation, charity is identical here on earth with what it will be in heaven, it follows by the strictest logic that its nature is the same, its role is essentially the same, and its action is the same, and that in heaven charity will be a principle of union with God, of possession of God. It is through charity that grace is really the beginning of glory. And that is one of the reasons for the splendor of this virtue, so enthusiastically praised by the Apostle.

(4) A few theologians (cf. de la Taille, *Recherches religieuses,* 1928, p. 253) go further and teach that through grace God *"actuates"* the essence of the soul, without informing it. In other words, they say that God unites Himself to the soul, gives Himself to it (actuation being "a union, a gift of self"), the way He will unite Himself and give Himself to our intellect in the beatific vision.

In the words of de la Taille: "There is even now in the just an actuation of the soul, understood as a previously existing substance living its own rational life under the influence of an added divine life stemming from a vital, uncreated principle. And this principle communicates itself to the soul (also without informing it), gives it the fundamental capacity to fulfill the functions of this new life whose plenitude is the beatific vision." [5]

By whatever name we call it, it is certain that grace is the principle of a very intimate supernatural union between God and the soul. It is a very close bond that links them, a

---

[5] Cf. *Note* on p. 168, at the end of this chapter, containing a citation on this question by the same author.

powerful magnet that draws them together. A multitude of wonderful unions are possible to God that we do not even surmise but that are known to His infinite omniscience. The union realized by grace is one of these. It is not a hypostatic union such as exists between the divine and human natures of Christ through the person of the Son. The union through grace is similar to the one that unites the Eucharistic species to the Body and to the whole Being of our Lord. Just as transubstantiation eliminates the distance that separates the consecrated Host from Him, so grace eliminates the distance between God and the soul and makes Him present in the soul.

The union wrought by grace is much closer and more perfect than all possible natural unions between distinct persons or substances. God compenetrates every portion of the soul, to the very depths of its being. He is one with the soul.

When we speak of presence, we are speaking of union: a supernatural presence implies a supernatural union.

And through God grace unites us to all those who are united to Him, and the more closely in the measure of their union with Him. It unites us to the Blessed who are united to Him by the beatific vision, according to the degree of their union. Hence it unites us first of all to Christ; to the Blessed Virgin; to the souls in purgatory, also united to Him by grace (and it is a consolation for our bereaved hearts to know that we are united to those we mourn); to the just on this earth in proportion to the intensity of their grace, especially to the holiest and most beautiful of these souls. Grace is one of the foundations of this community and communication of spiritual goods known as the *Communion of Saints*.

Thus through grace a supernatural union is accomplished between God and the soul. But union means a gift of self. God gives Himself to the soul in the state of grace; He gives Himself to it in a much more perfect way than to others. He gives Himself personally. He is not only *in* the soul, but He *belongs to* the soul; and He is in the soul because He belongs to it. The soul possesses Him as its property, its possession.

He is within its reach, at its service: *"datus est nobis—*He has been given to us." [6]

Presence signifies possession as well as union.

The soul possessing grace can already in a certain respect enjoy and possess God. Is it not one of the effects of ownership to confer the right to enjoy the thing possessed? The Angelic Doctor declares: "By the gift of sanctifying grace, the rational creature becomes capable of enjoying not only the created gift but even the divine Person [of the Holy Spirit]."

The soul does not yet see God as it will in glory. But it knows with certitude through faith that He is in the depths of its being; that they are reciprocally present to one another. A father and son, sitting close to each other in the darkness, do not see each other but each knows the other is near, and this thought delights their love. If they should suddenly see each other in bright light, their joy would be perfect. To their happiness in knowing they are close together would be added the joy of seeing one another, of gazing at each other's beloved features, of revealing their souls in their eager eyes.

That is how we possess God here on earth—in the darkness, without seeing Him. And for our hearts this possession is already an imperfect beginning of eternal beatitude: "a kind of perfect inchoation of future happiness . . . even in this life" (*Summa,* Ia IIae, q. 69, a. 2).

When the sun of glory some day allows us to perceive Him in all the splendor of His infinite beauty, our love will be kindled to still greater intensity by this vision. But the difference is one of degree and not of nature. Hence, while grace will give God to us in plentitude later on, it already gives

---

[6] St. Bonaventure teaches: "The Holy Spirit gives Himself to us both in His own Person and in the created gift of grace: *Spiritus Sanctus datur tum in propria Persona, tum in dono creato quod est gratia.*" (I *Sent.,* dist. XIV, art. 2, q. 1).

St. Thomas also explains the expressions "The Holy Ghost is sent," "He is given:" "The mission of a Divine Person is a fitting thing, as meaning in one way the procession of origin from the sender, and as meaning a new way of existing in another: *neutreum autem horum est nisi secundum gratiam facientem*" (Ia, q. 43, a. 1). (The Latin quoted above is not found translated in the English version.) [Translator's note].

Him now in the obscurity of faith and in the expectation of hope. And while it will bring us closer to God later on, it already brings us close to Him now. And therefore to the extent that grace is meant to make God present to the soul, it begins to do so even in this life.

This is all the more true because God is not illogical with Himself as we too often are. He always wants to perfect what He has begun. When He makes Himself present and unites Himself with another, it is no vain gesture on His part. If He gives Himself, if He makes Himself present, if He unites Himself to a soul, He tends to reveal His presence to it in some way, to make it feel His love and His paternal embrace, to make it delight in Him and to join with Him in a common life of affectionate and intense intimacy, as a foretaste of heaven's close union. He tends to manifest Himself to the soul, according to our Lord's promise recorded by St. John: "He who loves Me will be loved by My Father, and I will love him and manifest Myself to him" (Jn. 14:21).

The soul in the state of grace, that is, in the state of charity and filial affection, possesses as it were a supernatural sense, a special flair, a hidden affinity, spiritual "antennae," to apprehend within itself the presence and action of its heavenly Father. It acquires a quasi-experimental knowledge of this presence, according to St. Thomas.[7]

Father Garrigou-Lagrange teaches: "Through the special inspiration of His gift of wisdom, God makes Himself felt in a certain respect as the radical principle of our whole life, more personal to us than we ourselves are. To produce this quasi-experimental and not discursive knowledge within us, the Holy Spirit, through His illumination and inspira-

---

[7] "Non qualiscumque cognito sufficit ad rationem missionis . . . sed solum . . . cognitio ista (quae) est quasi experimentalis" (Ia, dist. 14, q. 2, a.   , ad 3).

Now those who do not enjoy the use of reason (children, adults while asleep, etc.) do not possess this knowledge, but they possess the principle of it. When the conditions for this knowledge are realized, they will be capable of it. Besides, they possess the virtue of charity by which their soul apprehends God. God is intimately united to their souls (as He is to all others in the state of grace), and is taking care of them and preparing them for future intimacy with Himself.

tion, makes admirable use of our connaturality or affinity with divine things, founded on charity.

". . . This knowledge (through lively faith and the gifts of the Holy Spirit related to charity) makes contact with God not as a distant or merely pictured reality, but as a present reality possessed and enjoyed here and now" (*Revue Thomiste*, 1928, Vol. XI, p. 468, 457).

The Angelic Doctor explains: "God is said to dwell spiritually as in His intimate habitation in the saints whose souls are capable of possessing Him by knowledge and of delighting in Him through love, even when they are not actively knowing and loving, providing that through grace they have the *habitus* of faith and charity, as is evidently the case in infants that have been baptized" (*In I Cor.* 3:16).

St. Teresa of Avila declares: "The Lord wants to give the soul a glimpse of the land it is to inhabit some day, so that the perspective of rest that awaits it may make the fatigue of such a difficult journey more endurable" (*Interior Castle*, 6th Dwelling).

"In His munificence, He wants to make this soul understand that He is very close, so close that it no longer needs to send Him any messages. It can speak to Him without raising its voice. What I am saying here may seem strange since, as we know very well, God is always with us. On this point, no doubt is possible. But our divine Monarch, our Master, wants us to realize that He hears us, that we are experiencing the effects of His presence" (*The Path to Perfection*, Chapter 28).

The veil that hides the Father's face from the soul has not yet fallen, but it is less opaque. We cannot yet see the full sunlight of vision, but there is already a ray of dawn, *inchoatio gloriae*.

True, all souls in the state of grace do not reach these heights. All of them do not experience this sentiment that God dwells within them and that they intimately possess Him. In fact, many do not even suspect it, and have no experimental knowledge of His presence. The reason for this is more often than not the dissipation of their heart, their lack of purification. For, in order to sense the nearness of

God we must impose silence on our passions, recollect our
thoughts in Him, calm our souls, and place ourselves in a
state of receptivity to the delicate inspirations of the Spirit.
We must push aside everything that engrosses the attention
and turns it away from Him. We must free ourselves of everything that obstructs, disturbs, hardens, preoccupies, everything
that comes from below in the way of self-love, sensuality,
and more or less conscious egoism. We must pacify,
purify, illumine, and mellow our souls like rich soil in which
the heavenly seed can germinate and grow. We must remain
in a state of docility to God's action, like taut bowstrings,
ready to vibrate under the divine bow. We must allow ourselves to be penetrated and made supple by the gifts of the
Holy Spirit. "The clean of heart . . . shall see God" (Mt.
5:8).

Is this not precisely what many of the just lack? Overwhelmed by earthly concerns, they live in the incessant tu-
mult of the passions and human anxieties. Their attention
is dispersed in every direction, and the eye of their heart is
never fixed on their divine Guest. Under these conditions,
no perception of the divine presence is possible.

But they could be aware of God's presence within them
if they decided once and for all to have done with this life
of dispersion, and imposed upon themselves indispensable
purifications of heart. Grace implants in them the principle
of this mystical experience, and gives them the aptitude for
it. The sense of God's presence, so it seems, is the normal
fulfillment of grace in the soul, and if this sense does not
develop it is because they have not fulfilled the necessary
conditions. They are like rosebuds that have been prevented
from blossoming by a killing frost. Alas! Many are those in
whom grace is never more than a "bud"! And how many
souls would have attained to the highest mystical graces if
they had cooperated with grace with a little more generosity
and vigilance! [8]

Thus we can distinguish three degrees of perfection in the
presence of God in our souls through grace.

---

[8] Cf. the *Note* at the end of this chapter, giving the teaching of several
theologians on this question, pp. 168 and 169 below.

The first degree is the lowest, involving the minimum of awareness. God is habitually present in the soul, without being consciously enjoyed. Neither the mind nor the heart are aware of His presence. This is the case of baptized persons deprived of the use of reason or dissipated persons who live in a state of continual distraction with respect to the divine Guest of their soul. Alas, there are many of them.

The third degree is the one of maximum awareness, and will not be achieved until the life to come. It is the degree of beatific vision, love, and possession. God is unceasingly and supernaturally present to the soul, immediately grasped by the mind and heart through an intuitive vision and burning charity. It is an ineffable intimacy, an incessant conversation, a delightful possession.

Between these extremes there is a second degree, that varies according to the state of souls. It is not vision, but a more or less intense foretaste of it. God gives a keen sense of His presence, a delightful, almost direct knowledge, like that of the senses in relation to sensible objects, a *"quasi-experimental"* knowledge, midway between obscure knowledge through faith and the clear vision of the blessed in heaven.

3. Its Consequences

We have now to draw a few dogmatic and practical conclusions that follow from this divine presence in the soul, whose reality we have tried to prove and explain.

1 Dogmatic Consequences

(a) Grace implies a twofold gift. Grace itself is a gift of God, produced by God in the soul: it is God who gives grace.

But grace is also the gift of God Himself: God gives Himself to us through grace. Hence, grace is a twofold gift: a created, finite gift, a supernatural "accident" by way of participation (grace in itself); it is also an uncreated, infinite, supernatural, substantial gift (God Himself). Grace is a twofold divine reality that enters the soul. Thus, through grace, God gives Himself to us in two ways. He makes us participate in His own nature, by communicating His own life to us.

When He confers grace upon us, He transmits something of Himself to us; and He gives Himself personally to us, by uniting Himself to us, by surrendering Himself to us, by dwelling within us.

When conceived in its plenitude, grace is not only something, it is also and above all *Someone*. It is not only a precious, supernatural "accident"; it is also a still more precious living Being. Grace is something divine, and it is God. It is God surrounded by divine things, ensconced in divine things; it is something divine accompanied by God.[9] Grace fixes God within us. It brings with it the One who is its author and its object, like a gift that would include its giver.

To quote Bishop Gay, grace is "like a river whose wellsprings follow its course and swell its flowing tide; like a ray of light which contains the source of light in its entirety. When God creates, He works, thinks, wills, or says a word: that is enough, and everything is accomplished. The same is true when He governs. In the case of grace, that is not enough. His operations produce men and angels; but He can make gods only by communicating His divine substance. It is to make us share in this substance that Jesus comes to dwell in us. . . .

"This is the great mystery of life that every justified Christian bears within himself and that is the cornerstone of the Christian state. This is the real and immediate union with God which, not as an effect of our natural instinct but as a consequence of our predestination to grace and of the revelation of it that we have received, has been the universal, constant, persistent dream of the human race, to the point of becoming its obsession wherever it has remained only a dream" (*De la vie chrétienne*, First Conference).

Grace is really the gift of God (that our Lord wished the Samaritan woman to know); and according to the Seraphic Doctor, it is the excellent and perfect gift: *"datum optimum*

---

[9] To define grace, as some do, as "God within us," is not enough. Grace is God within us, and something else: a reproduction within us of the divine nature.

et datum perfectum—the best and perfect gift" of which St. James speaks (Jas. 1:17).

(b) God's presence is inseparable from grace. Grace remains distinct from God but it is inseparable from Him. It cannot enter the soul without Him, and He in turn comes into the soul only if He sees in it the resplendent reflections of His essence. Whenever God gives grace, He gives Himself.

Thus, theologians like Peteau, who thought that this effect was not produced in the just of the Old Law, were mistaken. Inasmuch as the presence of God in the just soul had not been expressly revealed, this and other wonders of the supernatural life were not too clearly understood before Christianity. But the fact that this presence was known only imperfectly did not prevent it from being real, any more than imperfect knowledge of it prevents it from existing in the souls of ignorant Christians. As is true today, fervent, recollected, and purified souls under the Old Law experienced the presence of God within them. Grace, all sanctifying grace, implies this indwelling, which will one day be perfected by the beatific vision. And grace is the foundation, the reason for, and the *principle* of the beatific vision.

(c) This presence is common to the Three Persons. What we have said so far gives us the necessary light to judge the opinions of a few authors who hold that this indwelling applies only to the Third Person of the Blessed Trinity.

According to Peter Lombard, the Holy Spirit takes the place of charity in the souls of the just (and his disciples added that He takes the place of grace as well).

For Peteau, grace and charity are distinct from the Holy Spirit, but through them the soul is directly united only to the Third Person of the Blessed Trinity, and united by concomitance to the other Two. As he sees it, the union of the soul with the Father and the Son is somewhat like the union in the Eucharist between the substance of Christ's body and the accidents of bread by virtue of the first transubstantiation, the rest of His divine being (its accidents, His soul, His divinity, the Trinity) being united to the bread only by concomitance. And Peteau compares this union between the Holy Spirit and the soul to the union of the Word with the humanity of Christ, not in the sense that union by grace is hypostatic but in the sense that it relates directly to one Person only.[10]

Some authors, and above all St. Cyril among the Fathers, admit that the union between the soul and God through grace relates to the Three Persons, but to the Holy Spirit in a special way. And this special way is none other than the mode of origin of this union, the basis for the appropriation to the Holy Spirit of this special indwelling, as transmitted to us by Revelation.

This opinion leads us back to that of St. Thomas, which is by far the one most commonly held by theologians. The Angelic Doctor declares: "The union accomplished by the grace of adoption is common to the Three Persons, both in its principle and in its term." Not only are all Three the efficient cause of grace (for grace is a work *ad extra,* stemming from the divine nature common to the Three Persons). The Three Persons are also the term to which grace tends, inasmuch as all Three are the object of this knowledge (*ut cognitum in cognoscente*) and of this love (*ut amatum in amante*), which are the foundations of the indwelling of God in the soul.

Grace makes us love the Three Persons by means of the charity that it implants in us; it gives us a clear and intuitive vision of the Three in the next life, and a quasi-experimental vision of Them in this. St. John Chrysostom says: "The [Holy] Spirit cannot be present unless Christ is present also. Wherever one of the Persons of the Trinity is present, there is the Trinity. There can be no separation in the Trinity, it is perfectly united" (P.G., 60, *In Ep. ad Rom.,* homil. 13:8).

---

10 It is not the humanity of Jesus that is in us through grace. This presence is realized only by Communion, as long as the sacred species remain intact within us.

Through grace we possess Jesus in His divinity only, Jesus the Word (as well as the other Persons). To speak of the presence of Jesus within us through grace can sometimes lead to ambiguity. However, it is permissible to speak of this presence, as does Bishop Gay in the passages cited above, on condition that we understand it to refer only to His divinity, distinct from His Eucharistic presence in us through Communion.

Moreover, we cannot see how this presence could be limited to one of the Persons of the Blessed Trinity.

Every union is accomplished by something that passes from one of the terms to the other, by a connecting link. Now the foundation of union through grace is a supernatural participation not in the Person of the Holy Spirit but in the divine nature common to the Three Persons. A special union to one Person could be accomplished directly only by the communication of whatever constitutes that Person (the only thing the divine Persons possess individually is what constitutes them as Persons). As Father Prat points out, "Indeed we do not see what a divine Person can give in His own name to a finite nature, except His personality, since that is the only thing He possesses as a Person" (*The Theology of St. Paul*). But what difference is there between the communication of a Person and a hypostatic union? Inasmuch as union through grace is not a hypostatic union, it cannot relate exclusively to one Person.

It may be objected that in a number of passages Scripture seems to reserve the union through grace to the Holy Spirit, such as for example the following passage of St. Paul: "Do you not know that your members are the temple of the Holy Spirit?" (I Cor. 6:19). We answer that in other passages Scripture attributes this union only to the Father and the Son, for example: "If anyone love Me, . . . My Father will love him, and We will come to him and make our abode with him" (Jn. 14:23). And in still others it attributes the union to Christ alone: "to have Christ dwelling through faith in your hearts" (Eph. 3:17); "Do you not know that your bodies are members of Christ" (I Cor. 6:15). Does this mean we are to exclude the Holy Spirit?

Any reasonable exegesis demands that we complement and explain these texts in terms of each other. It must be admitted that the texts that reserve the presence of God through grace to the Holy Spirit by far outnumber the others. But this attribution is adequately explained by the procedure frequently used in the language of Scripture and Theology, known as *appropriation,* and which consists in attributing to one Person of the Blessed Trinity operations or properties which really belong to all Three, because they call to mind the mode of origin proper to that Person. It is like a procedure of divine rhetoric, in accordance with the laws of psychology, since it stimulates the mind, obliging it to correct, to supplement or to imply, as in the case of rhetorical figures. Indeed, it is a procedure perfectly adapted to Oriental habits of language. It is a very useful means of calling to mind the existence of the Three Persons in God and the mode of origin that constitutes each of them.

When we "appropriate" to the Holy Spirit this indwelling of God in the just soul (as well as the "gifts" which we shall discuss later), we evoke the mode of "procession" that is characteristic of this Person. Both the Holy Spirit and the indwelling of God in the soul, as well as grace and the gifts, have a common origin: love—God's love for the soul, on the one hand; the mutual love of the Father and of the Son, on the other. Inasmuch as the Holy Spirit comes through love, everything that comes through love is attributed to Him: this is *appropriation* through similarity of origin. We can now understand in what sense we must take the affirmation that grace establishes special relationships between the soul and each of the Persons of the Blessed Trinity by making us children of the Father, brothers of the Son, and temples of the Holy Spirit.

Through grace, we become not only children of the Father and temples of the Holy Spirit, but children and temples of the Three Persons of the Blessed Trinity, and brothers of Christ in the sense we have explained above (p. 86). It is an axiom in theology that everything that is "ad extra" in God, everything that does not specifically constitute a Person, is common to the Three Persons, as is the divine nature from which it stems.

2. *Practical Consequences*

There is no dogma more fruitful in practice than that of the indwelling of the Holy Spirit in our souls. Innumerable consequences derive from it in terms of piety.

It can be said that this divine presence through grace imposes all the duties demanded by the Eucharistic Presence.

We shall discuss two of these duties here: *respect and close friendship*. It is by fulfilling both of these duties that we can glorify God in His temple, as the Apostle asks us to do (I Cor. 6:19). And St. Paul shows the implications of this first consequence by demanding chastity and the renunciation of idols.

(a) *Respect*. Since God dwells in our hearts we must free them from idols, and these idols are not all made of wood or iron. There are living idols that are called a woman, a child, a man. There are idols of pleasure, idols of ambition, idols of money. Everything that we prefer to God, that we love more than God, that we want to keep or obtain even if it means offending God, everything that we place in opposition to God, that we esteem in practice above God, everything that we treasure in our hearts as a rival to God, is an idol. And when an idol enters a soul, God leaves it. We drive Him out scandalously, and we profane His temple.

Yes, we are His temples, for after justification our members no longer belong to us but to the Holy Spirit. They belong to Christ through grace; they have been consecrated and dedicated to Him with the holy oil of baptism.

Since he has become a member of Christ and the temple of the Holy Spirit, the just man must avoid all mortal sin, and above all the sin of *unchastity,* for whether in desire or in fact the unchaste person unites his body, which has become Christ's, to an unworthy creature [11] and violates the temple of the Holy Spirit.

Is it not a sacrilege to use a consecrated temple for purposes that are not only profane but actually evil and forbidden by divine law? And yet that is what the person who yields his body to illicit pleasures is doing. "Do you not know that your members are the temple of the Holy Spirit, . . . and that you are not your own?" (I Cor. 6:19).

---

[11] "Do you not know that your bodies are members of Christ? Shall I then take the members of Christ and make them members of a harlot?" (I Cor. 6:15).

"Or do you not know that he who cleaves to a harlot, becomes one body with her? 'For the two,' it says, 'shall be one flesh.' " (I Cor. 6:16).

"Flee immorality . . . the immoral man sins against his own body." (I Cor. 6:18).

Therefore "glorify God and bear Him in your body" (I Cor. 6:20).

Surely this is a supernatural and powerful motive for practicing chastity, which every Christian should understand and turn to for inspiration.

The just man will extend the respect he owes to his divine Guest to his own body and to the bodies of others, as if they were churches. Because God dwells in him, he will keep his body clean, and give it reasonable care and respect.[12] He will not rig it out in garments that deform it or leave it half naked, as do those men and women who are the slaves of ridiculous or inhuman fashions and torture their bodies out of foolish vanity. He will not degrade his body by grotesque manners, by yielding to debasing purposes or actions, by buffoonery, or intemperance in food and drink. He will never allow his body to be used for purposes unworthy of its nobility.

The Church has drawn all these very logical conclusions. How great is her veneration for the bodies of Christians!

In baptism, she blesses the body, anoints it with sacred oil, clothes it in white. At death, she blesses it again, incenses it, surrounds it with lighted candles and ceremonies, accompanies it reverently to its final resting place, wants it to be buried in consecrated ground, and, as if to preserve it longer, prohibits its incineration after the manner of unbelievers (Canons 1203, 1240[5], 2339).

Since our bodies are the temples of God, our souls are His sanctuaries or tabernacles. Let us strive by our good works to adorn our souls with merits, with the beautiful flowers of all the virtues, and above all to keep constantly lighted within them the lamp of love, the candles of sacrifice and renunciation, sending forth often the incense of prayer, and immolating on the altar of charity our passions, our preferences, our aversion to duty and effort, our sensuality, our pride, and our selfishness.

It is a great honor for subjects to be received in their prince's palace, and a still greater honor for them to receive

---

[12] We have already pointed out another motive, at the end of Chapter 1, p. 43 above.

him in their homes. How much greater is the honor, not only of receiving the passing visit of our Creator, our infinitely perfect God, but of having Him as our permanent guest not only in our home, but in our hearts, within the depths of our beings!

May we give Him a reception worthy of Him, and may our gratitude be proportionate to so great a favor! To quote St. Gregory, "Consider what an honor it is to give hospitality to God in our hearts. Certainly, if a rich and powerful man were to enter our home, we would hasten to clean it from top to bottom so that nothing might offend the eyes of this friend. Therefore let him who wants his soul to be the dwelling of God purify it from all stain of evil works." [13]

But it is not enough to avoid all that could displease the most pure eyes of the divine Guest. That is a negative aspect. There is also something positive to do. In addition to our effort of purification, we must make an effort toward close friendship which will be most profitable.

(b) *This close friendship* is the fruit of two presences: the presence of God (which grace always accomplishes); and the presence of the soul (which we must assure by recollection). There are so many reasons that command us to make our souls present to God by recollection!

There are reasons of fittingness. If some great personage deigned to pay us a friendly visit in our home, would we dare leave him alone, absent ourselves for long hours, and pay no attention at all to him? But think of it! The Almighty does us the very great honor of becoming our guest because He loves us and wants to be with us, and we would think of committing the unfitting sacrilege of not staying with Him, of continually absenting ourselves, of traveling the paths of dissipation in our ingratitude and thoughtlessness, of devoting to trifling matters the attention that should belong to Him alone? We have time for everything, for things that are useless or even dangerous, for frivolities, for the dust of events that each day's wind carries away, and yet no

---

[13] Ninth Lesson for the Office of Pentecost.

time, or almost none, for the One who should hold first place in our lives!

If God lives with us, must we not also live with Him? If He abides within us, must we not abide in Him, too? *Manet in eo et Deus in eo?* Must we not answer the movements of His heart toward us by the movements of ours toward Him, so that the affectionate union may be established for which He comes within us and which both His charity and ours commands? [14]

Even if friendship were lacking, the most elementary politeness should hold us close to Him, full of attention and courtesy, for politeness also has rights with regard to the One who "alone is great."

If we love the Father with a filial love, our hearts, our sons' hearts, should be able to keep us in His presence. Can we claim to love someone if we experience no need of union with him?

But our recollected awareness of God's presence is not merely fitting. It is also useful and easy.

It greatly benefits the soul to live this life of affectionate union with "the God of its heart." What joy, what inspiration this friendship brings!

There is joy, for a family is happy when the father is home. The friend delights in possessing the one he loves. The soul in the state of grace should be filled with rapture at the thought of possessing its God in such a perfect way! Do what we may, the creatures that are dear to us do not remain at our beck and call. The necessities of life force us or them to go away. Distance separates us. And even when they are present, their presence is only exterior. How much more perfect is God's presence in us through grace! Nothing can take God away from us, no power on earth or in hell, not even death. As St. Paul cries out: "Who shall separate us from the love of Christ?" (Rom. 8:35). He remains with us and in us constantly, compenetrating the depths of our being. This is the union our hearts dream about.

Oh! To know that He is there within us, and we in Him,

---

[14] Cf. *Note* containing a remark of Bishop de Ségur and a letter from Father de Foucauld, on p. 169 below, at the end of this chapter.

to know that we are continually under His loving eye, at His feet, in His arms, and yet not be lulled into lethargy by this thought! When isolation weighs upon us, and when by the force of circumstance or the wickedness of men a painful void seems to surround us and we have the agonizing impression that we are alone in a land of exile, what consolation to say to ourselves: "No, the exile is not alone; since he is in the state of grace he carries about within himself everywhere and always the One who makes up for everything else but whom nothing could replace." When our hearts are wounded or when, tired of struggling against ourselves, trials, or injustices, we are at the end of our tether and close to despair, what a solace to remind ourselves that He whom the Church calls "the best of comforters," "the soul's delightful Guest," is right there within us.

Why, O poor humans, do you seek from creatures the answer to your hearts' thirst when you bear within yourselves the One who alone can satisfy it? Why do you search so far in vain when He is so near?

"Many are the souls that have expressed . . . the inexpressible joy of this discovery of God (within themselves), after finally emerging from their abysmal unawareness of God's presence! . . . What rapture to realize that God is within the soul through grace and that we possess Him substantially within us! That surpasses all the rest" (De Tourville, *Vie et lumière*, p. 171).

This exercise does not merely bear fruits of joy. It is also a principle of sanctification, a source of consolation and a stimulant to devotion for all.

It inspires us to prayer, and is itself a prayer. How can we think that God is there out of love, like a benevolent father, to live and act with us, and not be filled with affectionate gratitude, and not feel the desire to speak to Him, to pour our hearts into His, to adore Him, thank Him, ask His forgiveness, beg His graces and His all-powerful help. At the very least, how can we fail to fix our gaze upon Him with filial and trusting tenderness?

When I remember that He is witness to my efforts, how can I fail to feel inspired to do good? He sees me, not only

from His distant heaven or through walls, but at very close
range from the depths of my soul, being as present to me as
I am to myself. He knows all my thoughts, affections, intentions, and all the movements of my heart. There is nothing,
not even my most secret desire or activity, that escapes His
eye, for His gaze is constantly fixed on me and penetrates
my innermost soul. Should not this conviction turn me away
from evil and inspire me to good? What a safeguard!

And besides, how heartening it is to say to myself: "He is
there to love me, to help me, to enlighten me, to defend me
in time of danger and to stimulate and sustain my efforts!"
Is this not a powerful means of spiritual progress? *"Quaerite
faciem ejus semper,* and *confirmamini*—Seek ye the Lord, and
be strengthened: seek His face evermore!" (Ps. 104:1).

When November comes in our mountains, and the wind
whistles grimly in the pines, shepherds light a little fire in
the shelter of some rock, and take turns warming their
numbed limbs by it before they return to their watch. Our
souls also quickly grow cold and numb in the face of the
temptations, difficulties, and trials of the world. They, too,
have a strong need to come back often through the day to
regain heat, vigor, and courage at the divine fire that burns
within them through the action of grace.

St. Francis de Sales tells us that there is no practice more
necessary or fruitful for the spiritual life, and he constantly
recommends it:

"My dear Philothea, in this matter I urge you very strongly
to follow my advice, for in this consists one of the surest
means for your spiritual progress. As often as you can during
the day, draw your mind back to the presence of God . . .
consider what God does and what you are doing: you will
see His eyes turned toward you and perpetually fixed upon
you through incomparable love. O my God, you will say,
why do I not always look upon You as You look upon me?
Why do You think of me so often, my Lord, and why do I
think so little of You? Where are we, O my soul? Our true
place is God, and where are we in fact?" [15]

---

[15] *Oeuvres,* Vol. III, p. 91. And St. Francis de Sales goes on: "Remember,
Philothea, to make several retreats into the solitude of your heart while you

Besides, this fruitful exercise is *easy* and within the reach of all, even those who have the most to do. We can do it when we are walking, working, going about our duties. It would not seem to be incompatible with any occupation. "And thus," our holy Doctor teaches, "conversations are not usually so serious that we cannot from time to time withdraw our hearts from them to plunge them in this divine solitude.

"This exercise is not difficult, for it can be interwoven into all our affairs and occupations without hampering them in any way; providing that, whether in spiritual retreat or in these interior upsurges of the soul, we turn away only for short periods that do not hinder but on the contrary are very helpful to us in our pursuits. Even though the pilgrim who sips a little wine to rejoice his heart and refresh his lips pauses for a short while, he does not terminate his journey but regains strength to complete it more quickly and easily, stopping only to go forward more surely" (*Oeuvres*, Vol. III, p. 95).

This practice demands no intellectual training. The simplest minds are just as capable of it as the learned (if not more so). They know how to love, and that is enough. In fact, many more simple souls than we imagine practice it without being aware of it, under the inspiration of the Holy Spirit.[16]

It does not fatigue us: a quick glance with the eyes of the heart, a rapid thought, suffices to restore the contact. Even when we are unable to do other exercises, we can always do that one.

---

are corporeally amid conversations and occupations; and this mental solitude can in no way be prevented by the multitude of those who are around you, for they are not around your heart but around your body so that your heart remains alone in the presence of God alone. That is the exercise King David carried on amid his many preoccupations, as witness many passages of his Psalms, such as: 'To Thee, O Lord, have I lifted up my soul. . . . My eyes are ever toward the Lord' (Ps. 24:1,15)." (*Oeuvres*, ibid., p. 92).

[16] The author takes the liberty of recording the following personal experience: "In 1926 I visited my aged mother who had been living alone since the death of two of my brothers and of my father in the war. When I asked her if she were not lonely, she answered: 'Oh! not at all. I live with God and I speak to Him all day long.' And yet she had never studied the dogma that we are explaining here."

Let us cultivate the holy desire of gathering up all the benefits of this divine presence within us, and of trying to exploit as effectively as possible the treasures this gift of God brings to our souls, by placing ourselves in a position to enjoy His presence and receive His divine communications.

Pascal has written: "Faith is God felt by the heart." No, faith is not sentiment, it is not the experimental awareness of God's presence. But this sentiment, this awareness, is certainly one of the effects of the spirit of faith, one of the rewards of the just man who has learned to "live" one of the most radiant dogmas of his faith, the dogma of the indwelling of the Holy Spirit in his soul.

The Christian must be a man who lives in his Father's intimate friendship.

Note Comparing the Special Presence of God in the Soul Through Grace and the Eucharistic Presence (see p. 142 above):

This presence is as *real* as the Eucharistic presence. When we reserve the term "real presence" for the Eucharist, we do not mean to oppose it to God's presence in the soul through grace but to the Protestant error according to which the consecrated bread and wine are merely the figure, the symbol, of the body and blood of our Lord.

The differences between these two presences relate not to their *reality,* but to other points.

The *reason* for the divine presence in the consecrated species, as in the womb of the Blessed Virgin Mary when she was carrying Jesus, is the hypostatic union of the Word with the humanity of Christ. The reason for the divine presence in the soul of the just man is grace, which is also a very perfect union. The principle of the first presence is the sacrament of the Eucharist, whereas the principle of the second is the sacrament of baptism or of penance.

God's presence through grace is incompatible with the sin that destroys it. The Eucharist may enter a sinful heart, but without spiritual fruit. Of its nature, God's presence through grace is *permanent,* and comes to an end only through sin on the part of the subject. The Eucharistic presence, on the contrary, is *transitory,* and is terminated with the corruption of the sacred species.

Normally, the grace of God's presence in the soul is necessary in order to receive the grace of the Eucharistic presence: the state of grace is *required* for Communion. But the purpose and effect of Communion are to intensify God's presence in the soul by increasing grace. In heaven, Christ will be visibly present but there will be no Communion, whereas grace will subsist. "Better still, heaven will *be* this presence seen in its full light. Rather than a place, heaven is a *state,* the state of those who are no longer reduced to possessing the Blessed Trinity within themselves without enjoying it, but who henceforth possess it with beatifying intensity" (Raoûl Plus, *Messager du Coeur de Jesus,* 1926, p. 29).

Presence through Communion is necessary only through moral necessity, whereas the presence of God through grace is as absolutely necessary as grace itself. It is possible to go to heaven without ever having received Holy Communion (provided one has not violated any moral law); but without grace no one can enter heaven, even if he has not committed any personal sins: witness the case of children who die without being baptized.

These two presences do not detract from or replace one another. On the contrary, each one complements and calls for the other. Both of them are precious gifts of the Father for which Christians should thank Him.

Note Explaining the Mode of God's Special Presence in the Soul (see p. 145 above):

Father Froget says: "Charity fulfills all the conditions of a true and perfect friendship between God and man. It is a love of benevolence, a mutual love, a love founded on a community of nature until such time as it attains to the community of happiness of which it is the pledge. Being a true friendship, it must have the prerogatives and fulfill the demands of friendship. Now, what does friendship require? What mode of union does it demand between those whom it unites? Is it satisfied with mere conformity in thoughts and desires, with a community of external goods and a bond of affection? Is that the final goal of all its aims and aspirations? No. What friendship wants and demands, what it strives toward with all its strength, what it effectuates insofar as possible is a real and intimate union, it is life in common, the reciprocal possession of the two lovers" (Froget, *op. cit.,* Chapter IV, 6).

Note on the Actuation of the Soul by Grace (see p. 147 above):

Father de la Taille says: "Sanctifying grace is the created communication of the Spirit of life to the essence of the soul, just as the light of glory is the created communication of the divine Intelligible to the intellective faculty. It is the infused receptiveness of the soul to uncreated Grace (God), just as glory is the infused receptiveness of the intellective faculty to uncreated Truth. . . . Both make God dwell in us; the former (grace) in the essence of the just man, the latter (the light of glory) in the intellect of the blessed. Finally, in both cases, the actuation is habitual, that is, both accidental and permanent, and neither transitory on the one hand nor substantial on the other."

Must we go further and say that God actuates the essence of the soul in order to become the co-principle with it of its supernatural and meritorious acts? If He produces these acts insofar as they are supernatural, they are not ours, since in themselves they do not come from us. No, if our acts are to belong to us in their supernaturality, this supernaturality must come from a principle placed in us by God but that is really our own and stems from our own personality.

"It is the function of the just in this world to journey toward the homeland where they will see God. Now, the movement toward the Object of the beatific vision is accomplished by charity." But this charity is friendship, and all friendship presupposes between the lovers a certain community of life that permits each one to look upon the other as another self—*Pares invenit aut facit amicitia*—whence the necessity of a fundamental union that underlies the love itself between the soul of the just man and the God of the life to come . . . Now, underlying the faculties, the intellect and the will, there is only the essence of the soul. And therefore it is this essence, already existing in its own right and living its own life, that is henceforth united, espoused, to the divine Essence, associated with the divine Life, the beneficiary of the divine Nature (*divinae consortes naturae*). This union of essences is called sanctifying grace. And it implies, in addition to the created gift that constitutes it, an uncreated gift without which it disappears" (de la Taille, *ibid.*).

Note on the Development of Grace to Mystical Heights (see p. 152 above):

Father Gardeil says: "The mystical experience is the final development of the life of the Christian in the state of grace. . . .

[It is] the mystical knowledge, the supreme but normal development of the state of grace" (*The Structure of the Soul and Mystical Experience*).

It is essentially in this experience that mystical graces consist.

"The indwelling of the Blessed Trinity in the soul is not a privilege reserved for a few souls that have attained the highest degrees of union. It is granted to every just soul, it is bound up with the state of grace. But the mark of lofty mystical graces is to make the soul aware of it" (*Etudes*, 1928, Vol. 117, p. 649).

It has even been suggested that the mystical life be defined as: "The life of grace become conscious" (Bainvel), that is, experimentally known.

"The essential of the mystical state consists in a knowledge of God received in the soul passively, a quasi-experimental knowledge that differs not only in degree but in genus from the knowledge that can be acquired by the natural exercise of the intellect, and accompanied by a loving union that is also very different from ordinary prayer" (de Grandmaison and Rousselot, in *Christus*).

Note on the Necessity of our Abiding in God (see p. 162 above):

Bishop de Ségur once said: "Life with the heart's divine Guest is the normal state in which all baptized souls should remain" (*Le chrétien vivant en Jésus*). This can be pointed to as one of the guiding ideas of Christian devotion.

That is the advice Father de Foucauld gave his sister: "And besides, God is in us, in the depths of our souls . . . always, always there, listening to us and asking us to talk with Him a little. . . . Accustom your children to converse with the divine Guest of their souls. . . . remind them often that for us Christians there is no solitude. . . . God, our sweet Jesus, is within us. . . . Oh! Magdalen was not alone at Sainte-Baume, she was no more alone than she had been in Bethany: instead of having God visible before her in mortal form, she had Him invisibly within her heart, but He was no less present. She was seated at His feet here as well as there. . . . That is as much as my weakness, my indigence, and my own life is capable of. . . . : try to make this life more and more your own. That will not distract you or turn you away from your other occupations. It will take you only a minute. The only difference will be that instead of being alone, there will be two of you to accomplish your duties.

"From time to time lower your eyes to your breast, recollect yourself for a quarter of a minute, and say: "You are there, my God, I love You." It won't take you any longer than that, and everything you do will be done much better when you have a helper, and what a helper! Little by little it will become a habit, and in the end you will always sense within you this sweet companion, this God of our hearts. And then we shall be more closely united than ever, for we shall live identically the same life . . . Our time will be spent in the same way, with the same very sweet companion" (*Ecrits spirituels*, Bazin, Nos. 191-192).

And he sought the grace of this continual intimacy with God for himself: "My God, deign to give me this continual sentiment of Your presence in me and around me . . . and, at the same time, the fearful love that we experience in the presence of one we love passionately, and that makes us stand before the beloved person without being able to take our eyes from him, with the great desire and a wholehearted will to do everything that pleases him, and a great fear of saying or thinking anything that may displease him" (*ibid.*, No. 51).

7 The Infused Virtues

GRACE supernaturalizes the very essence of the soul, and this sums up the effects which we have studied so far.

But action follows the laws of being: *Operari sequitur esse.* Faculties or principles of action must be of the same species as the essence from which they emanate, if the operations are also to be of the same nature. Operations, faculty, and essence go together, to the point that the scientific procedure for knowing the essence of a subject is to examine the nature of its operations, and to infer from them the nature of the faculties and of the essence itself. Being is necessarily the principle of an activity of the same order as itself. Whoever participates in the nature of God also participates in His life and in His divine activity.

The following chapters will deal with this deification of the activities of the just man, with his transcendent energies.

In the present chapter, we shall seek to establish the following facts concerning these new faculties whose principle is grace and that are called the infused virtues: 1. their *reality;* 2. their *supernatural character;* and 3. their *value.*

1. The Infused Virtues are Real

It is an axiom in theology that the supernatural is grafted upon nature, perfects it, and raises it to a superior level; and

171

that consequently the supernatural adapts itself to and ensconses itself within nature. If the graft is to "take," all of its elements must correspond to those in the "subject," bark to bark and stem to stem, and be their prolongation. In like manner the elements of the supernatural life, the divine graft, must correspond to those of the natural life.

Now, in the natural life, the soul acts not by itself but through its faculties—the intellect and the will, and through its external and internal senses. The soul is not the proximate, immediate principle of operations, but their mediate or remote principle: it operates through those of its powers that are directly ordered to action.

So too with the supernatural life. It contains these same two elements. The principle of being, corresponding to the essence of the soul that it supernaturalizes, is grace itself. And the element through which grace acts, the proximate principle of operations which corresponds to the faculties of the soul, consists of the *infused virtues*.

It is not enough that the trunk and the roots of the spiritual tree of our soul be divinized. The branches (faculties) and the vegetation they bear (actions) must be divinized as well. "Grace is the root or the trunk of the (spiritual) tree, the supernatural virtues are its branches. Now, as everyone knows, it is the branches that ordinarily bear flowers and fruit" (P. Froget, *op. cit.*, Chapter 11).

The purpose of the infused virtues is to supernaturalize the faculties of the just man, and thereby supernaturalize his acts. For acts can belong to a subject perfectly and be totally imputed to him only if they come totally from him even in their supernaturalness. The subject must possess in himself and in his own right the principle of these acts if this supernaturalness is to become in some manner *connatural* to him.

Inasmuch as the essence of the soul is distinct from its faculties, the principle that supernaturalizes its faculties must be distinct from the one that supernaturalizes the soul itself: the virtues must be distinct from grace.

But why several virtues? Would not one and the same vir-

tue suffice to supernaturalize all the faculties and good acts
of the just man?

Categories of acts that are mutually irreducible, and specifically distinct by virtue of their objects, must have specifically distinct principles; for objects specify acts, and acts
specify faculties. Now the good acts that the just man accomplishes differ too widely and are grouped in categories
that are too dissimilar to be confused or identified.

By comparing the good acts of the just man, it has been
found that they could be divided into seven categories, in
turn divided into two groups: the three *infused theological*
virtues and the four *infused moral* virtues.

(1) *The theological virtues.* The first group includes all
the acts (and hence all the virtues) that relate directly to God
as their supernatural end, that is, that have God as their
formal and even their material (at least principal) object.

These acts are of three kinds:

The acts by which we steadfastly accept, on God's infallible authority alone, all the truths affirmed by Him.
The virtue that supernaturalizes these acts is *faith*.

The acts by which the believer desires the happiness of
heaven and confidently expects to possess them some day and
to receive from God, who is faithful to His promises, the
necessary helps to attain this end. The virtue that supernaturalizes these acts is *hope*.

The acts by which the believer loves God as a Father for
His own sake, and his fellows as brothers for God's sake. The
virtue that supernaturalizes these acts is *charity*.

It is certain that these three supernatural virtues exist in
the soul of the just man. In its Sixth Session, Chapter 7, the
Council of Trent affirmed (but did not define) the infusion
of these virtues simultaneously with the infusion of grace:
"Whence man through Jesus Christ, in whom he is ingrafted,
receives in . . . justification, together with the remission of
sins, all these infused at the same time, namely, faith, hope,
and charity. For faith, unless hope and charity be added to
it, neither unites man perfectly with Christ nor makes him
a living member of His body" (Denz. 900).

Scripture is no less explicit. St. Paul says: "So there abide faith, hope and charity, these three; but the greatest of these is charity" (I Cor. 13:13).[1]

No adult, being a free person, goes toward his end, i.e., his supernatural end, unless he freely consents to it and wills it. But to want it, he must love it—and that is *charity;* he must desire it, strive to attain it, and consider it possible— and that is *hope;* he must know it, realize that he is destined for it, that it is worthy of love and desire, that it can be obtained (these are all truths that only Revelation can teach and which he must accept)—and this is *faith.*

These acts of faith, hope, and charity can lead to the supernatural end and serve to obtain and merit it only if they are of the same order as this end, that is, only if they are supernatural. They must be supernaturalized by those principles (supernatural and distinct, like the acts that they specify) that are the theological virtues of faith, hope, and charity (*Summa,* Ia IIae, q. 62, a. 3). It is by practicing these three virtues that we reach the heights of the spiritual life here on earth.

(2) *The cardinal virtues.* However, the practice of faith, hope, and charity is possible and easy only if the soul knows how to govern itself in its use of creatures in accordance with faith, so as not to make them obstacles to the attainment of its supernatural end. This is the effect of the *moral virtues.*

Moreover, the theological virtues do not extend to all the good acts of the just man, they do not embrace the entire field of his moral activities. Man has duties not only toward God, but also toward his neighbor and himself. Many of his good acts relate directly not to the Creator but to creatures. Is it admissible that these acts should be outside the supernatural sphere, and consequently without merit, when the Father has promised to reward all virtuous acts? Is it admissible that a vast area of the moral activity of God's children should be excluded from divine influence, without

---

[1] In heaven, faith and hope will cease. The former will be superseded by the intuitive vision, and the latter by possession. Our Lord had neither faith nor hope, since He enjoyed Vision from the beginning of His mortal life.

utility for their life's goal because disproportionate to this goal?

The Scotists offer the following objection: Does it not suffice, for these acts to be supernaturalized and meritorious, that they be "inspired" by charity and directed toward God by this virtue? Is it not charity (as St. Thomas himself declares) that gives all these acts their supernatural orientation? [2]

Charity does indeed accomplish these things. But our Doctor answers: for an act to be adequately supernatural, it is not enough that it be supernatural in its motive; it must also be supernatural in its principle (presupposing that the former can pass into the latter). Nothing can be in the effect that is not in the cause. Now the effect of the meritorious act (vision) is absolutely supernatural, that is, above the powers and rights of every created nature. The act of a natural virtue remains natural in itself and can only merit a natural reward. Charity does not change the order of an act of natural virtue merely by inspiring it. Charity may give such an act a necessary orientation, but this is not enough. A supernatural principle must also supernaturalize the act in itself.

It may further be objected: Why should a permanent principle be required, and why would not actual graces suffice since they suffice for the good acts of the sinner that prepare him for justification?

We answer: The reason they suffice is that the merit in question here is not the same as the one we are discussing. The merit of acts that dispose to justification is only a merit of fittingness (*de congruo*). The merit earned by the good acts of the just man is merit in *justice:* it demands that the whole person, his essence and his faculties be elevated above their natural level, deified, in a permanent manner.

There is a peremptory reason why all the infused virtues cannot be given to the sinner. Since the sinner's "being" is not Godlike, how can his "to act" be Godlike? How could he possess properties of a superior order to that of his essence? For the just man, the reverse is true: since his essence belongs

---

[2] Cf. the *Note* at the end of this chapter, containing an opinion on the views of St. Francis de Sales on this subject, p. 183 below.

to the supernatural order, it is fitting that he be capable of performing acts of the same order.

We know that even the lowest forms of life possess properties and principles of action that correspond to their essence, and that knowledge of essences through properties and operations of a being is accepted as an infallible scientific procedure. How, then, could this harmony between essence and operation be lacking to the children of God, whose life is the most perfect of all, the supernatural life? Grace calls for the virtues to supernaturalize the good acts of its subject.

This doctrine of St. Thomas has been the one most commonly accepted in the Church since the Middle Ages. In 1201 Pope Innocent III concluded: "The view that is affirmed by some, to wit: that neither faith nor charity nor the other virtues are infused in baptized children for lack of their consent, is not generally approved" (Denz. 410). Now, what can these "other virtues" distinct from faith and charity be, except the moral virtues?

Father Billot declares: "The Scotist opinion has gradually been discredited, to the point that the opposite view, the one that has been most common since ancient times, has in time become common and almost universal" (De virtutibus, Thesis 2).

It may perhaps be objected: We admit permanent principles are necessary to supernaturalize all the acts of the just man. But inasmuch as they are principles of operations, like the faculties, why do we need more of these principles than we have faculties? For there are seven such principles, but only two spiritual faculties: the intellect and the will.

Like the faculties, the infused virtues relate directly to the operations, and they are therefore received in the faculties. These virtues are modifications, perfections, habits of the faculties. Now there can be more habits than there are faculties, several habits for each faculty—in fact as many habits as there are groups of acts distinct by their object. The same faculty can be engrafted with different virtues, like a fruit tree that has been engrafted with several varieties of fruit.

Thus most theologians agree that in addition to the theological virtues there are four species of infused moral virtues that correspond to the four natural or acquired virtues. These virtues are called *"cardinal virtues"* because they are as it were nuclei around which all the other virtues group themselves; "hinges" (*cardines*) that support the moral life. These four virtues are:

Prudence, which supernaturalizes the acts by which we wisely choose the means for attaining the supernatural end and the intermediary ends.

Justice, which supernaturalizes the acts by which we render to everyone his due.

Fortitude, which supernaturalizes the acts by which we triumph over fear and dread.

Temperance, which supernaturalizes the acts of moderation of the sensible appetites, taste, and above all touch.

The infused virtues accomplish approximately the same function for the faculties in a permanent manner that actual grace accomplishes in a transitory way at the moment of the act itself.

2. The Infused Virtues are Supernatural

Being supernatural in their effects, the infused virtues must also be supernatural in their essence (since the effect cannot be greater than its cause) and in their principle. God alone can produce them, for supernatural effects cannot come from a natural cause. That is why we say these virtues are *infused,* as though poured into us by God without our active participation. At the utmost we can merely merit the infusion and increase of these virtues, as is true of grace; whereas we ourselves are really the efficient, physical, and immediate causes of our natural virtues. When we practice the natural virtues we acquire them by repeating acts of these virtues: they are *acquired* (although they may be infused "by accident." For instance, it may please God to create within us the facility for acts of virtue that is normally acquired only by habit resulting from exercise.)

While the infused virtues can increase through repeated acts, they do not increase in the same manner as the acquired virtues. The good acts of the just man (cf. Chapter XII below) merit an increase in sanctifying grace and, together with it, an increase in all the infused virtues and gifts. There are at least two differences between the efficacy of good acts in increasing the infused virtues and their efficacy in increasing the acquired virtues:

1. In the case of the acquired virtues, good acts are an efficient, physical, and immediate cause; in the case of the infused virtues, they are a moral and indirect cause. Good acts do not of themselves increase the infused virtues, but they *merit that God increase them*.
2. Good acts develop only the particular virtue from which they stem, whereas good acts of specific infused virtues merit an increase in *all* the infused virtues as well as an increase in grace.

Thus there is a difference in cause or origin between the supernatural and the natural virtues. There are also differences in their object, their conditions, and their effects.

Differences in their object. The object of the infused virtues is supernatural, that is, above the natural powers of the human soul. It can be known only through Revelation, and this knowledge is given only as a gratuitous gift. For all the infused virtues, this object consists in our elevation to the supernatural order and presupposes our divine adoption. The object of charity is to make us love God like a Father; the object of hope is to make us desire and hope for the Father's inheritance, and the means of acceding to it; the object of faith is a wholly filial trust in the word of the Father; the object of the moral virtues enables us to judge the righteousness of human acts, not only with respect to their conformity with our nature as rational animals but with our *super-nature* as adopted children of God. This provides the infused virtues with possibilities of perfection unknown to the acquired virtues. For example, the virtue of religion rises above the motive of justice due to God; it is imbued with filial piety, thus receiving a stimulus toward horizons that are beyond the scope of natural virtue.

There are also differences in *condition* and *existence* between these two species of virtue.

In the first place, the infused and the natural virtues do not necessarily coincide. They may or may not exist simultaneously. The soul that has received the supernatural virtues, together with grace, does not always have the natural virtues or the acquired capacity to perform with ease acts supernaturalized by the infused virtues. Thus, the day after a man has been brought back to God by a mission and has regained grace by a sincere confession, all the vicious tendencies created by his former sins may still be quivering within him. If before his recent conversion he was inclined to impurity, anger, intemperance, pride, he has not yet had time to acquire the opposite habit or virtue. This will probably take much effort and many weeks!

Through penance, he has rectified the general orientation of his will, which is now united to God and prefers Him to the satisfaction of his passions. But he still has within his being a propensity toward these passions, and his very organism impels him toward these satisfactions. We cannot with impunity cultivate familiarity with evil. We cannot taste the forbidden fruit without being penetrated with its poisons which are hard to eliminate.

On the other hand, a person in the state of sin can very well possess one or another of the natural virtues (although it would be difficult to possess them all!) without having the infused virtues, that is, without being in the state of grace. For example, there are sinners, even pagans, who have strongly developed the virtue of patriotism, justice, respect for professional duty, for their pledged word, and for secrets entrusted to them. But splendid as their intentions and actions may be, their value is still infinitely less than the value of actions, even if less brilliant supernaturally speaking, performed by the just man armed with the supernatural virtues.

We know of course that the infused virtues and grace are closely interrelated. The infused virtues are produced only in conjunction with grace; they all grow equally, in union with grace; and they disappear when grace is driven from the soul by mortal sin [3] (except faith and hope, which can exist "without form" [4] with sins that are directly opposed to them).

The infused virtues cannot diminish directly, any more than grace can. A single evil act, mortal sin, suffices to destroy them, whereas it takes continued repetition to uproot the acquired virtues by a process of progressive diminution.

Finally there is a difference in the effects of the supernatural and the natural virtues, and this is a consequence of their mode of origin. The acquired virtues facilitate the acts to which they relate. The more intense these virtues, the easier it is to exercise them; for they are habits, and the proper function of habit is to incline a power, that is indifferent in itself, to certain acts, and thus enable it to perform these acts with more uniformity, promptness, pleasure, and sureness. "Not only does habit increase the aptitude of the organs and faculties for certain determinate acts, but it brings an absolute increase in the strength, the power of these organs and faculties" (Ribot, *Psychologie*).

Now this does not seem to be precisely the effect of the supernatural virtues. These virtues give the power to perform good acts supernaturally, but not to perform them easily. They are principles of supernaturality and not of psychological facility. The reason the just man finds it easier to overcome temptations than does the sinner is because of the rectification of his will worked by justification (cf. Chapter 5, p. 122 ff., above); it also comes from the more numerous actual graces placed at his disposal (cf. Chapter 8), but not directly from the infused virtues themselves.

---

[3] These virtues (except faith and hope in the case of those who enjoy the beatific vision) always accompany grace, but they do not all have a chance to be used. Those who have never committed any sin (for example, our Lord, the Blessed Virgin, Adam before his sin, the good angels) cannot perform acts of penance (contrition), nor can those who are not subject to concupiscence (the angels) perform acts of chastity. But their dispositions are such that if they were called upon to perform acts of these virtues, they would not fail to perform them. That is what theologians mean when they say that in such individuals the virtues are "habits but not as to the act: *quantum ad habitum et non secundum actum*" (Ia, q. 95, a. 3, c.).

[4] Theologians apply the description "without form" to these virtues when they are not accompanied by charity. For charity is the "soul," the "form" of the virtues, in the Scholastic sense.

True, each of the acts of the infused virtues creates in the faculty from which it emanates a tendency to repeat the act. It implants in the faculty the seed of a habit (that is natural in its origins) to reproduce whatever is natural in the act. For let us not forget that every supernatural act presupposes the exercise of a supernaturalized natural faculty, that is, the combination of natural and supernatural activity. It is like the fruit of a grafted tree produced from the sap of the wild subject mixed with that of the graft, the effect of their twofold activity being so intermingled as to form a single principle of production. The supernatural act has a twofold result: one effect is in the faculty (the facility to reproduce whatever is natural in the act); the other effect is in the supernatural virtue from which it stems (and simultaneously in all the other virtues and in grace itself). This latter effect is the "infusion" by God of new degrees of the virtues and of grace merited by the supernatural act.

Each supernatural act strengthens the subject's inclination to repeat the act. But the supernatural virtues are not like the natural virtues in that they do not of themselves directly increase facility in practicing them. The proper and immediate function of the supernatural virtues is simply to supernaturalize the faculties and their operations.

For this reason we would be justified in calling the supernatural virtues *powers*, principles of operation. We choose to call them virtues, that is, qualities affecting the powers, in order to indicate that they are received in our faculties to enrich, perfect, and supernaturalize them. Even though limited to the effect of supernaturalizing our faculties and their operations, their function is no less sublime and precious.

3. The Infused Virtues are Precious

The infused virtues divinize the actions of the just man just as grace deifies his essence. Thus all his faculties and good actions are supernaturalized, as well as his "being." Everything in him and everything that he does is raised to the divine order, partakes of the divine nature, receives the divine impress and likeness. All of him, both his "to be" and his "to act," is lined with divinity, just as the ark of the covenant was lined with gold. All of him has God for a coefficient.

A good action performed in the state of grace, even if it is humanly insignificant, the dust of despised daily duty, is impregnated with the supernatural by an infused virtue and has far greater value than the most brilliant exploits of a sinner (even if they are of capital importance to the human race).

"Through grace man performs divine works. Hence these works have greater value than those that stem solely from nature or in which nature is merely the separated instrument of the Godhead. Discover the secrets of the universe, harness the energies of nature, found great empires, govern peoples, save them from death, foretell the future, work miracles. All these things are of less moment than handling a crude tool while offering to God work sanctified by grace. Understand this truth, you scholars and public men who are so proud of your achievements. Do what you will, you will not take them beyond the limits of time and nature, whereas the lowly work of a divinized worker is, according to the forceful words of an ancient author, pregnant with the eternal felicity it is to produce in due time" (Monsabré, Lenten Sermons of 1875, 18th Conference).

Just men, you cannot value too highly this new benefit that grace brings you, transforming your poor natural energies and elevating your faculties almost to the level of God's. Grace makes you sons of God. Through the virtues that accompany it, you can act like sons of God; your acts take on a value and dignity that are truly divine.

But if you value this benefit, do not let it lie fallow. In conferring the power to act supernaturally it also imposes the duty of using this power.

Does not the perfection of every power consist in its actualization, in its bearing fruit in an act? Of what use are power, talent, and genius, if they are never used? Or rich mineral veins if they are never exploited? To what purpose is the power to produce supernatural acts if we never make use of it? The virtues are precious faculties, but on condition that they be stimulated, exercised, and thus produce the actions for which they were intended. And for those who know how to make their virtues bear fruit by persevering effort, the Master increases their virtues, as we learn in the parable of the talents. As for those, on the contrary, who are lazy and bury their virtues, He takes away what He has given. Exercise of the virtues is the condition for their preservation, the meritorious cause of their increase, and the means of making easy the acts they supernaturalize.

We should make use of all the virtues, but above all, charity. For, as St. Paul tells us (I Cor. 13:13), charity is the greatest virtue. Its merit surpasses that of the others, and it has more powerful effects.

Given equal effort, an act of the virtue of charity increases all the other virtues more than does the act of any of the other virtues, for it brings a greater increase in grace.

Charity moreover has the singular privilege of possessing the queenly power to move and "command" the other virtues. When we make charity intervene in the action of the other virtues, we add its efficacy to theirs and multiply their value. As St. Francis de Sales tells us: "If the love in a heart is zealous, powerful, and excellent, it will also enrich and perfect the works of the virtues that proceed from it" (*Oeuvres*, V, p. 251).

*   *   *

Note on the role of charity with regard to the other virtues, according to St. Francis de Sales (see p. 175 above):

According to certain authors, it seems that in the second and definitive edition of his *Treatise on the Love of God* St. Francis de Sales did not admit the existence of any infused virtue except charity: "The second edition of the *Treatise* no longer mentions the infused moral virtues because it denies their existence: at the close of his research and reflections, Francis de Sales teaches that charity, when it encounters natural moral virtues in a soul, perfects them immediately without the intermediary of any other infused 'habitus'" (P. Mogenet, *Rev. d'Asc. et de Myst.*, April-June, 1940, pp. 117 and 121). Charity would then take the place of all the others, just as a bishop can perform all the functions that he has empowered various ordinands to perform.

8 The Source of Actual Graces

ACTUAL graces (or the supernatural helps given to us in our actions) can come to us from four sources: 1) from the merit of our good works;[1] 2) through prayer; 3) through the sacraments; 4) by reason of our divine adoption.

We shall limit ourselves in this chapter to the two last-named sources and explain how sanctifying grace is the principle of the actual graces that flow from them.

1. Through the Sacraments

It is the universal teaching of the Church that each sacrament produces, in addition to first or second sanctifying grace, a special grace called "sacramental grace," meant to help the subject fulfill the obligations that the sacrament entails.

It is the common opinion that this supernatural help is not, as Capreolus once taught and as Father Billot has held more recently,[2] a "habitus" or permanent quality, or a dis-

---

[1] We shall discuss the role of sanctifying grace in prayer and merit in Chapters 10 and 11 below.

[2] *De sacramentis,* Thes. 5:2: *"Auxilium habituale, id est dispositiones in potentiis animae receptae contra defectus particulares ad quas reparandas*

position of the powers of the soul, specifically distinct from habitual grace and from the virtues and gifts. For there is no supernatural "habitus" other than that of habitual grace, or of the virtues, and of the gifts.

Everyone agrees that sacramental grace implies at least a permanent right to receive, when the need arises, actual helps or graces to attain the moral goal of the sacrament.

Must we go along with Cajetan and many modern thinkers who see nothing more than this right to special helps related to the purpose of the sacrament? Or must we admit, with a number of Thomists, the existence of something intrinsic and permanent in addition to the right, which would be the source of these special helps? Sacramental grace would thus be "sanctifying grace, to which a modification has been intrinsically added conferring a special power with regard to the effects proper to the sacrament, and moreover constituting a demand for and a right to the particular helps that would help us attain the end of each sacrament" (*L'Ami du Clergé*, 1929, p. 326).

This question does not concern us here. One thing seems certain (regardless of the opinion we adopt concerning its nature): sacramental grace and the helps it implies are never produced apart from sanctifying grace (first or second, depending on whether the sacrament is a sacrament of the dead or of the living). Sanctifying grace and sacramental grace are inseparable; one is never conferred without the other.

Such is St. Thomas' explicit teaching concerning the sacramental grace of baptism. In his view, when there is a "fiction" by reason of an attachment to mortal sin on the part of the catechumen, this sacrament (and the same is true of all the others) produces no grace, whether sanctifying or sacramental. The production of grace will be accomplished (for this sacrament as well as for the others) only at the moment when the obstacle (*fictio*) is removed through adequate contrition.

But if sacramental grace is not given apart from sanctify-

---

singula sacramenta sunt ordinata: it is an habitual aid consisting of dispositions received in the powers of the soul to make up for the particular weaknesses that each sacrament is intended to correct."

ing grace, it seems logical to conclude that it disappears when the latter is destroyed through sin, and that it reappears when sanctifying grace returns through justification. Not only is the production of sacramental grace inseparable from the production of sanctifying grace, but these two species of grace cease and "revive" as one.

This is completely evident to those who consider sacramental grace as a "simple modality" of sanctifying grace.

And it is very understandable that the fatherly help, cooperation, and solicitude that sacramental graces imply are reserved by the Father for those who are His children through sanctifying grace. For example, it is obvious that the precious helps required by the sacrament of matrimony are the privilege of husbands and wives in the state of sanctifying grace.

For all these reasons we can hold as *very probable* the opinion concerning the interrelationship between sacramental and sanctifying grace. (We are assuming, of course, that the sinner is not deprived of the necessary helps for conversion and for overcoming this dangerous "fiction," and that God watches over those souls whose welfare is the responsibility of baptized, confirmed, ordained, or married persons who are devoid of sacramental grace.) [3] This is what Suarez teaches with regard to the sacramental grace of confirmation, and it applies to the other sacraments as well.

The Consequence

Sin, insofar as it destroys the sacramental grace of all the sacraments hitherto received, deprives the sinner of all these precious helps. For example, husbands and wives who have received the sacrament of matrimony in the state of mortal sin, or who have fallen into this state afterwards, do not receive the sacramental helps of marriage, confirmation, or baptism. Deprived of the numerous and morally indispensable actual graces to which these sacraments normally give the right, they are reduced to their own strength, that is to say, to their own natural weakness, in fulfilling their often

---

[3] Cf. the *Note* at the end of this chapter, p. 195, containing the passage of Suarez to which we allude here, and an opinion published in *L'Ami du Clergé*.

arduous obligations as married persons, parents, Christians, and confessors of the faith, which they incurred through these sacraments. In order to make up for this lack, they would have to pray a great deal in order to obtain through impetration graces to which they no longer have a right sacramentally. But how many of them do pray?

Is it surprising, therefore, that there are so many unhappy married couples as a result of unfaithfulness, dissensions, suspicions, loss of interest, and so many parents unfitted for their difficult mission as educators and who refuse to accept the responsibilities of parenthood? Is it surprising that so many Christians live as if they had never received baptism, continually violating the promises they made in that sacrament and the nobility with which it endowed them? And that so many confirmed Catholics are ashamed of their faith, and do not have the courage to confess and defend it as is their duty, but are slaves of human respect and of stupid fear? All this is inevitable when so many married couples and parents, so many baptized and confirmed Christians, wallow in mortal sin and are thus deprived, through their own fault, of the supernatural and necessary helps that God has linked to sanctifying grace. God is not with them to help them accomplish their heavy responsibilities. The organ is no longer adopted to the function, the means is no longer adequate to the goal.

Thus baptized, confirmed, and married Catholics may be scarcely better than pagans in spite of the sacraments they have received. Thus sin prevents the sacraments, which are in themselves fruitful sources of energy, principles of transformation and sanctification, from producing their full effect and from obtaining their utmost efficacy. Thus there may be a serious obligation [4] for certain persons to return to the state of grace in order not to commit new sins. And this is one of the reasons why the Church has made confession obligatory at least once a year.

But sanctifying grace is not only the condition for the actual graces that come through the sacraments. It is also,

---

[4] We have already pointed to another reason on p. 126 above.

in itself, the cause and source of divine helps: it actually obtains some of them.[5]

2. Through Sanctifying Grace Itself

By the very fact of his justice, the just man has a special right to God's help.

Our Lord has declared this truth Himself: "He who abides in Me [through grace] . . . My Father will cleanse that [he] may bear more fruit" (cf. Jn. 15:5,2). In other words, the Father will cultivate him, purify him, surround him with solicitude in order to make him progress in holiness, like a gardener who wants to stimulate one of his favorite trees to become a heavy producer. St. Paul affirms that it belongs to the children of God to be led by the Spirit of God (cf. Rom. 8:14). The Spirit impels them, helps them to look at God and to love and treat Him as a Father, and to behave like true sons in their dealings with Him: "You have received a spirit of adoption as sons, by virtue of which we cry, 'Abba! Father!' " (Rom. 8:15). In fact it is this Spirit who inspires us with the conviction that we are His children.

He works to turn us away from the things of the flesh in order to make us take delight in the things of heaven. "They who are according to the Spirit mind the things of the Spirit" (Rom. 8:5). He works to make the works of the flesh cease in us: "If you live . . . by the Spirit you put to death the deeds of the flesh" (Rom. 8:13).[6]

---

[5] It is also the principle of the actual graces that our meritorious actions win for us (cf. Chapter 12 below), and whose production sin prevents.

[6] The Psalms had already forcefully described the attentions that God showers upon the just:

"The Lord . . . saveth the upright of heart" (Ps. 7:11).

"The Lord is in the just generation" (Ps. 13:6).

"The salvation of the just is from the Lord" (Ps. 36:39).

"The Lord keepeth all them that love Him" (Ps. 144:20).

He protects the souls of His faithful, and He gives light and joy to the righteous (cf. Ps. 15:7-11).

Christian tradition does not limit the meaning of these passages to a purely material protection, but understands them to include a spiritual providence. And rightly so, for if God is thus concerned for the corporeal welfare of the just, how much greater is His interest in the welfare of their souls, which is the only thing that really matters.

The divine Guest does not abide in our souls to remain an inactive visitor who comes to find rest, or to be like the idols on pagan altars who "have eyes and see not, ears and hear not" (Ps. 113:5,6). He is essentially active, since He is "pure act." He is the living God, the Creator Spirit: *Creator Spiritus*. And He comes and abides within us to work toward our sanctification through His actual graces and His gifts.[7]

In the words of Father Gardeil, "All the testimonies of the New Testament reveal that from the first moment Christianity appeared there existed a very affirmative doctrine concerning the normal, continuous, and efficacious influence of the Holy Spirit on the souls of the just, concerning the gift of Himself, as well as the gift of His enlightenment, and His help in the struggle against evil, with a view to promoting their supernatural sanctification and assuring their salvation" (D.T.C., "Dons du Saint-Esprit," column 1752).

In making man an adopted son of God, sanctifying grace demands that God in turn surround him with a special providence and take a most fatherly care of him. Can a father help being intensely interested in the welfare of his child? Can he refuse to provide for his needs if he has the means to do so? Can he fail to bring abundant helps to his indigence and weakness, or to work zealously to perfect him?

It is an instinct and a duty for parents to provide their progeny the helps they need, and this duty is more rigorous and continues for a longer time the higher one rises in the hierarchy of living beings. How, then, could the case of our heavenly Father be different, with regard to His children whose life (being supernatural and therefore far superior to every other type of life) makes more imperious demands on His help for its preservation and growth? Being more loving, more devoted, more powerful, and wiser than other fathers, God takes a far greater interest than they in those who are born of Him, in order to bring them abundant help in their necessities.

---

[7] We shall discuss this in the following chapter, which is essentially a continuation of the present one. "The Holy Spirit abides in us to sanctify us, to guide our entire supernatural activity . . . ; He makes His abode within our hearts only to help us, to enlighten us, to strengthen us" (Dom Marmion, *Christ in His Mysteries,* Chapter 17, No. 5).

If He requires them to trust Him like sons (Mt. 5:24), and commands them to be at peace and free of anxiety, is it not because they can indeed depend upon Him for the needs of their souls, even more than for those of their bodies? And if He flings the treasures of His goodness to beings without reason or duration, will He not do at least as much for those who will remain the children of His love for all eternity? St. Paul concludes: If God has manifested His love for us (by giving us grace) when we were still sinners and His enemies, ... how much more will He save us now that we have been justified, reconciled, and have become His children! (Cf. Rom. 5:7-11).

According to the Council of Trent: "For they who are the sons of God love Christ, but they who love Him, keep His commandments, as He Himself testifies (Jn. 14:23); which, indeed, with the divine help they can do. . . . For God does not forsake those who have been once justified by His grace, unless He be first forsaken by them" (Sixth Session, Chapter 11). These are the very words of St. Augustine.

In Canon 18, it defines "that there is no commandment the just man is incapable of obeying. . . ." The reason it does not include other men in this statement is that in its opinion the evidence is more perfect, the certitude is greater, and the reasons are more compelling that God always sustains the just man by His grace (Denz. 828). Father J. de Guilbert affirms: "The state of grace, far from being in itself—as is sometimes imagined—a merely static element of the spiritual life, is also an element of continual progress, a principle of uninterrupted ascent toward a more perfect supernatural life" (*Revue d'Asc. et de Myst.*, 1933, p. 26).

In the dome of the Sistine Chapel, Michelangelo depicts the Creator communicating life to the first man simply by bringing the tip of His finger near him. Can He unite Himself with a soul by the close bonds of grace without transmitting to it something of His own powers? Can total weakness approach omnipotence without being supported? Can a frozen object approach fire without being warmed, or night approach day without being illumined? Or can arid soil be touched by a flowing spring without being watered? Or utter indigence approach infinite riches without being aided? [8]

As we have said, the infused virtues do not by themselves facilitate virtuous acts. They give the power to accomplish these acts supernaturally in a connatural manner, without lessening the moral difficulties involved, as do the acquired virtues (whose specific effect is to make good actions easier, quicker, and more pleasant).

But is it fitting that our supernatural moralization should not be as perfect as our natural moralization, and that our supernatural life should have deficiencies unknown to the natural life? This would seem unworthy of the Holy Spirit from whom our supernatural life comes. It would seem therefore that He must make up for its lacks by some normal aid, and by stimulations and impulsions that succor the impotence of our faculties.

All life must be capable of defending itself, repairing its losses, exercising itself, and developing. Even the humblest of living things, the plant, heals its wounds, defends itself against the germs of death, and develops. Therefore, must not the much more perfect and superior life which is the supernatural life, the highest form of life, also have this power in an eminent degree? Let no one say that grace is a dead thing, placed in the soul as if it were devoid of life. Grace, on the contrary, is essentially active through the principles of operation, i.e., virtues and actual graces, that it demands or that emanate from it. Grace is a powerful, dynamic leaven, buried in the cold, inert mass of our nature, penetrating, raising, stimulating, and quickening it. Like the kingdom of heaven, it resembles a seed that wants to grow and spread in every direction, and become "a tree, so that the birds of the air [may] come and dwell in its branches" (Mt. 13:32).

Grace is sanctifying. Does not the sonship that grace establishes place special obligations upon the just man? [9] Once he

---

[8] Cf. *Note* at the end of the chapter containing a passage by Bishop Gay on this subject, p. 197 below.

[9] Cf. the author's work, *L'Enfant de Dieu*, 2nd edition.

has become the son of God, must he not act, think, judge, love, and will as a son? Does he not owe fraternal charity to his fellows, and to the Father filial affection and total trust? He must trust His teachings with unshakable faith, even if they contain unfathomable mysteries; trust His wishes by perfect submission to everything that expresses them, whether they be commandments, counsels, or events; trust His promises, even if their fulfillment seems hard and remote, with a hope that never hesitates. He must work for the glory of the Father and direct all his actions toward this goal, remain in His close friendship, and strive to prolong in his own moral life the likeness to God that grace impresses upon his soul. He must strive to imitate Him and to live in His friendship.

Now this devotion, this love, and this trust are morally impossible without the help of the Holy Spirit, who alone can make a success of His child's education by infusing in him this filial spirit, destroying the old man and producing the new, conformable to the image of the only-begotten Son. While grace imposes obligations on its children, it calls forth helps that are not refused.[10] The just man can count on these helps. But he is not thereby dispensed from using the means to obtain them: i.e., the sacraments, merit, and prayer. For it is above all through these sources that he will receive grace in abundance.

Let us admit that God gives these helps more liberally to the just who belong not merely to the soul of the Church, but to her "body," that is, to those who have received the external, official, and sacramental sign of the children of God: baptismal character. In other words, He is more solicitous of those who are *Catholics,* for according to the Vatican Council holiness is a distinctive mark of our Church, a special proof of her divinity. The heroism of virtue and the abundance of grace that the Catholic Church's holiness presuppose are not found elsewhere, at least in the same degree. The reason for this no doubt lies in her greater number of sacraments and her more efficacious means of obtaining

---

10 Cf. at the end of this chapter, a citation by Father d'Herbigny, p. 197 below.

grace. At any rate, God appears to be less generous to those of His children who live outside His visible family, the Church, even if they are in good faith. And it would seem that this is in order to preserve the Church's unique privilege, her glorious mark: her holiness.

Granted this difference, it remains no less certain that God has intense solicitude for all His children, and that He surrounds them with a very special and continual providence.

Actually His children are not always aware of it, and they often fail to recognize His fatherly action under human guise and commonplace appearances. They imagine that God's help can be given only in elegant dress or extraordinary forms. They refuse to see it in the humble costume of the daily events or creatures about them. Indeed they are like the scandalized Pharisees who refused to admit God could hide under the lowly humanity of Christ the poor workman. Or else, like our modern rationalists, they cannot accept the fact that a priest, who is only a man like themselves, can be invested with divine powers! They are willing to see authentic grace and indubitable interventions of God in the sudden inspiration to heroic acts, in an influx of blinding light in the intellect, an unexpected transformation of the will, an irresistible impulse of the Spirit impelling the soul to goodness. But how, they ask, recognize His action and His supernatural stamp in the things that make up the drab routine of our days, or under the plain outer shell of creatures and events obviously unworthy of being bearers of divinity?

And yet, are the paltry Eucharistic species of bread and wine worthier of the God they contain? Were the dove and the tongues of fire worthier of the Holy Spirit who borrowed their fragile form when He descended from heaven? Are the baptismal water and the sacred oil worthier of the supernatural wonders whose fruitful instruments they are? It would seem that the power of God shines forth most clearly when He realizes great effects through lowly and feeble means.

It is unquestionable that He makes use of creatures and events to assist the spiritual progress of His children. He makes all things contribute to their welfare. [11] The whole of humanity works for them, under the guidance of His invisible hand. For them empires are born and die; for them peoples rise up; for them persecutors and even the demons themselves strive to convulse nations. It might be said that grace automatically places the just at the center of God's action upon the world. God concentrates upon them the beneficent effort of His Providence, the flow of His many varieties of graces. From within and from without, through His direct action or through secondary causes, He never ceases seeking their consent to partake ever more fully of His divinity.[12]

The fact is that God makes great plans for His children. He dreams of bringing them by a progressive ascent to the radiant summits of mystical love where He can reveal Himself to them and give them a foretaste of the beatific vision. He dreams of entering deeper and deeper into their lives, of descending ever further into their beings, of possessing their faculties so completely that He Himself acts in them and they can in truth repeat the Apostle's words: "It is now no longer I that live, but Christ lives in me" (Gal. 2:20)—in other words, "it is Christ who acts, thinks, loves, wills, and does all things in me and for me." The realization of this dream demands their attentive and generous cooperation: trusting docility to God's action; recollection so they will grasp it as it passes; a spirit of renunciation that will help them to yield to this action, or at least remove the obstacles to it.

Alas! How many good men refuse to accept these conditions and thus prevent sanctifying grace from ever attaining its full stature within them! It is their own fault, however. For grace tends of its own accord to develop fully, and it is a source of actual graces. Besides, it cannot be denied that the just receive more actual graces than do sinners. The reason for this is no doubt the fact that their prayers are more

---

[11] Has not St. Paul affirmed that "for those who love God all things work together unto good, for those who, according to His purpose, are saints through His call" (Rom. 8:28)?

[12] Cf. *L'Enfant de Dieu,* 2nd edition.

efficacious in obtaining actual graces (cf. Chapter X), that the sacramental sources of grace closed to the sinner, especially the Holy Eucharist, are open to them (cf. Chapter VIII), and that all their good actions merit new and more abundant graces (cf. Chapter XI). But the reason also lies in the fact that they are in the state of grace, and therefore children of God and temples of the Holy Spirit.

They can count on the Father's help, and this certitude opens up brilliant prospects. If they really want to, they can be "all powerful in the One who strengthens them" (cf. Phil. 4:13), they can hope for all things, dare all things, and undertake all things in the name of goodness.

Indeed, has anyone been more daring than the saints, all of whom have accomplished great things?

It is this abundance of divine helps and this confidence that are responsible for the prodigious progress of the human race under Christianity.[13]

Awareness of the powerful and life-giving action of God (and of His presence) [14] in the soul is precisely what the highest mystical graces consist in. The mystical life, outside its exterior manifestations, is the awareness of God's operations within us, and of our operations in Him, in the order of nature and in the order of grace.[15]

Once it has reached this state, the soul experiences the delicate motions that the Spirit inspires, constantly impelling it to greater heights. It is very sensitive to the touches of His powerful love. This results from the perfection the gifts of the Holy Spirit have reached within it. We shall study these gifts in the following chapter.

* * *

Note concerning the interrelationship between sacramental and sanctifying grace (see p. 186 above):

Quotation from Suarez: "Ut autem tunc (temporibus oppor-

---

[13] Cf. the *Note* at the end of this chapter, p. 198 below.

[14] Cf. what has already been said concerning the special presence of God in the souls of the just, Chapter 6 above.

[15] "Mystical lights reveal to us the operation of God in us and our operations in God, of which we are ordinarily unaware in the course of our everyday life" (Etudes, 1928, Vol. CXVII, p. 643).

tunis) detur (auxilium) necesse est, hominem non opponere obicem peccati, sicut in ipsa susceptione sacramenti necessarium hoc fuit ad gratiam ipsam, quae est veluti fundamentum hujus protectionis et auxilii divini, quia si homo ponat obicem peccati mortalis, fit indignus hoc auxilio et ineptus, vel indispositus ad finem, hujus sacramenti, quia, et fides mortua infirma valde est, et homo in eo statu existens caret habitatore Spiritu Sancto" (cf. *Notre Pentecôte*, p. 126).

L'*Ami du Clergé* (1937, p. 276) takes a different view. In answer to the question: "When common sanctifying grace disappears, is sacramental grace by this very fact totally destroyed?" it says: "The question seems quite delicate and cannot be formulated in a uniform manner for all the sacraments." According to this editor, in the case of the sacraments that confer a permanent right to grace (baptism, confirmation, holy orders, extreme unction, and matrimony) "the sinful Christian may retain certain sacramental graces." However he admits that it is evidently very important to induce parents to live in the state of grace so that they may possess the sacramental grace of marriage as completely as possible.

But we do not see:

1. Why this right (*res et sacramentum*) can bring about the production, in the state of sin, of certain graces and not others.

2. Nor why, if it brings about the production of certain graces after sin has followed the fruitful reception of a sacrament, it could not do the same in cases in which the sacrament has remained "without form." No one admits this latter possibility, for the sacrament "without form" is precisely the one that is valid and produces only the *res et sacramentum,* but not grace.

3. Moreover this opinion destroys the bond that unites sacramental grace and sanctifying grace, since the former could (at least in individual cases) be conferred without the latter.

It will be objected that it is contrary to God's goodness to abandon these sinners without help in the face of their heavy responsibilities.

We answer:

a. That God is not obliged to do more for them than for those who have not received the sacrament.

b. That His chief effort is to bring them back to the state of grace (cf. pp. 126-127).

c. That they can still have recourse of prayer to obtain His help.

Note on the just man's assurance of God's help (see p. 191 above):

"For adorable reasons which relate in part to His justice but which are inspired above all by His wisdom and love, God allows the redeemed and divinized soul to retain an inner core of indigence in this life. . . .

"But when the soul is clothed by its divine Guest in life-giving splendor as in a defensive and offensive armor, it can always and quite easily hold concupiscence in hand. By thus turning its struggles into victories, it reduces its enemy to the condition of being the cooperator with its virtues and the purveyor of its glory." And all this is the result of grace.

"The state of grace becomes a principle of action. Life is given only to be lived, strength only to be exercised, and seed only that it may bear fruit. The soul in grace is a field full of divine seeds. The heavenly Adam has made His abode in it as in an earthly paradise. He has also come to defend and cultivate His domain. The first Adam fell down in his task; but there is no danger that the second Adam will default. On the other hand, the new Adam cannot ordinarily accomplish everything in the soul by Himself. The soul, which is His garden, is also His Eve, His "help like unto Himself." While the soul cannot seduce Him, it can betray Him and thereby bring His works to naught. His work succeeds only in conjunction with the operation and co-operation of the soul. Christ and the soul must be united in all things. That is the law. Their separation infallibly means sterility and death. Thus when Jesus consecrates and deifies our being, He also deifies our works."

Note on God's help to the just (see p. 192 above):

"The Master stands at the door of the sinner's soul and knocks. Since He cannot do violence to liberty or force His friendship, it is only from the outside that He can ask the soul to receive Him, project His light into it, or appeal to its good will. As long as the heart created by Him has not given itself to Him, He waits, He hopes, and He works, but He does not force. He refuses to obtrude Himself as a master upon wills that reject Him.

"But within the just man, He lives as a welcome and beloved Guest. He manifests His good pleasure without the noise of words—by a sign, a look, or a suggestion, that is the gentler in the measure that He knows He is loved. He no longer asks admittance since He has already been accepted by the soul. He simply extends, universalizes, and intensifies His action. He would like to adorn and vivify the very last ramifications of the soul's human activities and intentions. By means of this union of love the soul lives by God, it is deified. And yet *everything* in the soul must be won over to the dominion of its divine Guest. Every movement of the soul should merit His divine pleasure. Of course the soul's activity is human, but it is also divine. It is the fruit of two lives made one by love. It should be worthy of acceptance and be accepted. . . .

"Every increase, every act of this divine life in man requires a new gift of God. Only God's *actual* help can confer divine value upon the exercise of human vitality. But in the case of the just man, this divine influence is normally the result of a permanent graft [sanctifying grace]. The Master of all help rules in his soul, as a present and active Guest, as a King known and loved. His support compenetrates, as if by natural endosmosis, the activities of the supernaturalized soul. Enemies will attack, but He is sure to conquer them if the soul does not betray Him. In the case of other men, however, the enemy is within, and divine help arrives from without. The Master besieges the soul and at first has only one end in view: to prepare the inauguration of the divine kingdom or its restoration" (d'Herbigny, *Recherches de S. R.*, 1920, p. 163).

Note on the divine helps Christianity brings the soul (see p. 195 above):
"The Christian is the man of bold initiatives and invincible resistance.

"He is the man of bold initiatives, for the more intense a life the more it tends to manifest itself brilliantly in every domain. Grace borrows its energy from God Himself, who is always acting, who acts in all things; and therefore it must prove the supernatural character of its origins by the courage of its undertakings.

"He is the man of invincible resistance who never draws back, for the stronger a being the more unflinchingly it confronts the combat in which all of life unfolds. Now, there is something infinite in our virtue. When we make use of it, we triumph over the greatest difficulties and, like St. Paul, we defy created forces to overcome our courage. We sense the support of the Spirit who breaks cedars and crumbles mountains. The true Christian, therefore, is not a feckless being, like the Gospel character who had buried his talent and allowed it to remain unproductive. He uses the gift he has received and makes it bear fruit" (Father Janvier).

9 The Gifts of the Holy Spirit

THE just must be attentive to God's incessant and fatherly action upon them. They must respond to Him with a most filial docility, yield tractably to His movements, receive His impulsions joyfully, and obey His suggestions trustingly and promptly. And yet these dispositions are supernatural. God alone can implant them in the souls of the just, and He owes it to His wisdom to do so. He provides for these dispositions by the *Gifts* that we are to study in the present chapter.

In the first part of this chapter we shall deal with the gifts *in general* (their role and existence, their subject, division, and number, their relationship with grace and with the virtues, their value). In the second part, we shall deal with each of the gifts *individually*.

1. The Gifts in General [1]

1. *Their role and existence.* Before using his wicker, a basket-maker is careful to soak it in water to make it flexible. When an intelligent gardener plans to water the soil, he loosens it so that the water may penetrate it more easily. The

---

[1] For a summary of the various opinions of theologians on the distinctions between the gifts, the virtues, and grace, cf. de Guibert, *Revue d'Ascétique et de Mystique,* January, 1933.

blacksmith heats the iron he intends to bend. An electrician prepares his electrical wires to increase their ductibility, so they will transmit the current with the least resistance and waste. Every good orator strives to make his audience like him, so it will accept his ideas more readily. These are examples of a law of common sense: it is necessary to prepare, to adapt material before working on it intensely. God, who is the perfect Artisan, could not omit this necessary precaution in the souls He plans to bend and forge to virtue, and to draw to Himself. His way of preparing souls is through His gifts, which are infused and therefore supernatural dispositions that impel the faculties of the just man to cooperate promptly with His actual graces.

Through the gifts, God communicates to the faculties of the just man an affinity, an instinct for His action, that permits his faculties to receive divine influences connaturally. Henceforth these faculties possess more delicate sensitivity to the touches of grace; they have a new sense for discovering and following God's impulsions. They are more alert to His calls, and answer them with greater docility. They become adapted, attuned to God in a permanent way.

The gifts are "habitus," or stable dispositions, but they are exercised only through the impulse of actual graces. They are like the strings of a lyre, taut and ready to resound, but that emit sound only under an artist's fingers.

These dispositions come into play as soon as God's action begins and continue as long as it does. They are active even before the will's consent, during the making of a choice, and later during its execution. They are operative in the case of prevenient or operating grace as well as of consequent or cooperating grace.

The inclination they impress upon the will does not force it to follow the impulsion of grace. It impels, but without violence. It facilitates the consent of the will, but leaves it free to abuse its freedom and refuse grace, thus making the gifts useless.

2. *The subject of the gifts.* The gifts affect the spiritual faculties on which God's supernatural action can be exercised: the intellect and the will.

They affect the intellect because the graces can be sources of light. It is through the intellect that God most often influences the will. The gifts make the intellect more transparent to the rays of the divine sun, allowing them to penetrate the mind as light permeates pure water.

Several of the gifts—understanding, knowledge, and wisdom—relate chiefly to the intellect, as do the actual graces that stem from them. The others are directly related to the will. It is the will that decides to obey or to resist the suggestions of the Holy Spirit. It is the will above all that needs to be moved to follow them promptly and docilely, and hence with greater facility and perfection.

It goes without saying that there are circumstances in which the gifts are more necessary than others, for instance when there is need of positing with ease acts that are difficult and heroic. At such times, in order to overcome the resistances of nature and the repugnance of the flesh, an intense impulsion by the Holy Spirit and extraordinary divine helps are needed. The role of the gifts in such cases is particularly opportune in helping the soul to respond.

But is the role of the gifts to be limited to these heroic acts? We do not think so, and while we agree that the gifts evidently play a more intense role with regard to these acts, we believe their role should be extended to all the motions of the Holy Spirit without exception, to all actual graces, to all acts accomplished with the help of God. For "the same need that cries out for the exterior helps of the Holy Spirit also calls for the influence of His gifts, since these gifts predispose minds and hearts to receive the divine impulsions. What are heroic acts? What are those victorious instincts that suddenly awaken in the depths of souls, take hold of them and dominate them? They are a clearer and more brilliant manifestation of the Holy Spirit, the divine Mover, and of His gifts." [2]

---

[2] Terrien, *op. cit.*, Vol. III, Chapter 4.

Do Christ and the blessed in heaven possess the gifts? They do inasmuch as the gifts consist in habitual dispositions of filial docility to the motions of the Father, for these motions can still occur in heaven in that they presuppose "the existence of no imperfection in a created being other than

3. *The division and number of the gifts.* The gifts are not divided in exactly the same way as the virtues. Thus the same gift can relate to several virtues: for example, the gift of fortitude relates both to charity and to temperance. On the other hand, several gifts can relate to a single virtue: the gifts of understanding, knowledge, and wisdom, are related above all to the virtue of faith.

It would be difficult to prove by reason alone that the sevenfold division of the gifts is absolutely irreducible. But since some division is necessary, this particular division has the great advantage of being hallowed by Catholic tradition, which has taken it from the famous text of Isaias: "And there shall come forth a rod out of the root of Jesse [the Messias], . . . And the spirit of the Lord shall rest upon Him: the spirit of wisdom, and of understanding, the spirit of counsel, and of fortitude, the spirit of knowledge, and of godliness. And He shall be filled with the spirit of the fear of the Lord" (Is. 11:1-3). Since Christ is the spiritual model that the Father wants us to imitate and the vine-stock from which we receive life-giving grace, the Fathers and theologians have rightly concluded that we, too, were meant to receive these same glorious faculties.

It is true that several exegetes, including Father Condamin (cf. *Le Livre d'Isaïe,* p. 90), claim that this passage speaks only of six gifts, and not of seven. They hold that Is. 11:3— "And He shall be filled with the spirit of the fear of the Lord"—cannot be taken to refer to a seventh gift. They argue:

1. It is not a new gift, since fear of the Lord has already been mentioned in Is. 11:2 (cf. Tobac, *D. T. C.,* art., "Isaïe," col. 66).
2. The gifts are enumerated in pairs. The phrases in verse 3 are not included in the enumeration.

---

that which belongs to him as a finite and contingent creature" (de Guibert, p. 22).

Pope Leo XIII teaches in the Encyclical *Divinum illud:* "Horum [donorum], beneficio instruitur et munitur ejus [Spiritus Sancti] vocibus atque impulsioni facilius promptiusque obsequatur; haec propterea dona tantae sunt efficacitis ut eum fastigium sanctimoniae adducant, tantae que excellentiae ut in caelesti regno eadem, quamquam perfectius perseverunt."

3. The LXX, and the Vulgate after them, have translated the same word by two others: piety, and fear of the Lord, a procedure that is not permissible.

Following Knabenbauer and Touzard (cf. *Revue biblique,* 1889, p. 232; also Gardeil in D. T. C., art. "Dons du Saint-Esprit," cols. 1750 and 1751), the partisans of the traditional interpretation point out that these arguments are not apodictic. The word "fear" in the Old Testament has a very broad meaning, and can include piety in addition to fear in the strict sense of the word. Hence, two words were needed to translate it. It often happens that the full significance of a term can be rendered only by two or more words in another language.

This translation rests on the authority of several Fathers, and upon the authors of the Vulgate and the Septuagint, who must have known the Hebrew text.

What matters here is not so much the number as the assurance of the universality of the gifts, of their adaptation to all the graces. And that is probably what tradition has sought to signify by using this sevenfold division which is very ancient in the Church and hallowed by the liturgy (*Sacrum septenarium,* Pentecost hymn).

The existence of the gifts can be regarded as a truth of *Catholic doctrine* by the ordinary magisterium at least with regard to heroic acts, and abstracting from the differences among the gifts themselves and their generic distinction from the virtues.

The number seven is the *more common* doctrine; and the opinion that affirms a real distinction between them and the virtues, and extends their role to all actual graces seems to be *more probable.*

4. *The relationship between the gifts and grace.* As we have already said, the gifts are the privilege of the children of God. Like the infused virtues, they emanate from sanctifying grace and are a development of grace. They follow all the phases by which grace is produced, disappears, and is increased. Their intensity varies with the intensity of grace in a soul.

Whenever the gifts increase, grace increases in equal measure. It is grace that demands and is the measure of the gifts. It is impossible to give or increase the gifts without giving or increasing grace and the virtues. Whatever gives or increases grace, also gives or increases the gifts.[3]

But if the gifts are so closely bound up with sanctifying grace, then the sinner cannot possess them. Indeed, he cannot possess them any more than he possesses the infused virtues (except for faith and hope, provided he has not sinned directly against them).

Does he still receive actual graces? Can he be the subject of the impulsions of the Holy Spirit?

Yes, this is absolutely necessary, otherwise how could he ever emerge from his state of sin, be converted, repent, and be justified? He is not lacking in actual graces, if he takes the means to obtain them. However, it is more difficult for him than for the just man to cooperate with the actual graces he receives. His faculties are less pliable, his will is less docile. There is no oil in his spiritual machine. His soul lacks powerful affinities to divine action. In consequence, God encounters greater recalcitrance and inflexibility in the sinner's faculties, and His action meets greater obstacles to its full efficacy and fruition.

That is why the gifts, even though they are not absolutely necessary, are morally necessary to assure the perfect cooperation of the faculties with grace.

"They [the gifts] may be lacking and yet not stop life or action; but they give life a harmony and an elegance that make the divine simple, lovable, and attractive. They beautify the soul. But they also have an effect upon others. They are a sort of bridge between the very personal infused virtues and the miraculous charisma that are orientated toward the welfare of others" (*Recherches de sc. relig.*, 1920, p. 165).

5. *The value of the gifts.* The gifts are thus the condition of all significant progress in the spiritual life, and one of the most important factors in all types of holiness. No one can practice all the Christian virtues to the point of heroism,

---

[3] Cf. the *Note* at the end of this chapter, which gives one of the consequences of this fact, p. 216 below.

maintaining unfailing control by the soul over the inferior
appetites, and of the will over nature's evil instincts, devote
himself to total and unceasing renunciation, and attain perfection in the gift of self and in dedication to God and neighbor, without the powerful and continuous intervention of
grace (which is a miracle of the moral order), and without
generous, attentive, and persevering cooperation with the
motions of the Holy Spirit. For the Holy Spirit cannot lead
the soul to the heights if it resists His action. The more
necessary and intense God's action, the greater must be the
subject's docility—i.e., the greater must be the influence of
the gifts.

The docility of the saints has always been remarkable.
Many saints never accomplished anything extraordinary, but
we can observe in all of them an extraordinary fidelity to
grace, an extraordinary flexibility to the impulsions of the
Spirit, an extraordinary utilisation of the gifts. It is through
the gifts that they attained to the "passivity" (in the sense
of "docility") that St. John of the Cross considers the indispensable condition of the union of the soul with God and
of its transformation into Him by Him.[4]

This docility is essentially a "gift" of God, but does not
obviate the need of effort. Even with the help of the gifts,
cooperation with the calls of God requires sacrifices which are
always repugnant to nature. With the gifts it is not so hard,
but it will still be hard. It is to avoid hardship that many
ungenerous souls leave these supernatural faculties almost
unused as well as the helps which they bring with them. Such
cowardice and inflexibility cannot fail to grieve the Holy
Spirit and lead Him gradually to diminish His action in the
soul.

We must be careful not to mistakenly conclude that
"docility" tends to lessen the soul's activity, to dispose the
soul to nonchalant acquiescence, and that the gifts are only
principles of passivity. To the contrary! Inertia and non-
chalance consist in not cooperating with the Holy Spirit's

---

[4] Cf. *Le point central de la doctrine de saint Jean de la Croix,* by A.
Philippe ("Doctrine et piété" series, 88 bis, Boulevard de la Tour-Maubourg,
Paris).

invitations, in not entering into His projects, in lazily refusing to cast off lethargy in order to walk, advance, act, and accomplish the good works which He asks. Whatever inclines and inspires us to follow the call of grace, the call to spiritual work, to new acts of virtue, and hence to a more intense exercise of all the powers of the soul, is essentially a source of activity and life.

The sight of the marvels God has placed within us for our perseverance and spiritual progress must inspire us to exploit these riches and to make these precious talents bear fruit.

2. The Gifts in Particular

Having defined the gifts as "supernatural habits that make the faculties of the just man receptive to actual graces," theological writers bring actual graces into the definition of each individual gift. Thus "the gifts become at the same time principles of flexibility and energies, sources of docility and of power that render the soul more passive under the hand of God and at the same time more active in serving Him and in doing His work" (Bishop Gay).

The word "gift" thus has two meanings (and it is easy to turn from one to the other): a *strict* sense, the sense of the general definition which implies receptiveness to graces; and a broad sense, which applies to the individual definitions, implying flexibility and graces, impulsions of the Holy Spirit and docility in following them.

Rigorous logic demands that every definition, whether particular or general, limit itself to the strict sense. In the definitions of each gift, the general definition should refer to the proximate genus, and the second element—the specific difference—should be drawn from the species of motion to which the gift disposes the subject. For example, a correct definition of the gift of *knowledge* should include these two elements: receptiveness to actual graces that help to evaluate created goods from the point of view of faith. In speaking of the gift of *understanding,* we should say: "The gift of understanding is ordered to the graces provided for a better comprehension of revealed truths."

But we shall follow the common practice of using the *broad* sense in what we have still to say about the gifts. The following will be a complement to what has already been said about actual graces and the gifts in the strict sense.

*   *   *

By the gift of *understanding* (intelligence—*intus legere*) the mind penetrates the truths proposed by faith. It understands them quickly, as if by intuition. This is not yet the brilliant light of the intuitive vision. However it is a rapid, transitory, fragmentary (and yet very precious) foretaste of it, a kind of precursive ray of light. It is a communication of God's own light which He mercifully grants to His children.

Every soul, even the least fervent, has at some time benefited from this gift. A certain speculative or practical truth may have remained a tightly closed and obscure book. Preachers and authors had tried in vain to call it to mind and make it come to life. It continued to be without any effect, like the seed thrown by the wayside. The sounds that proclaimed it awakened no echo, projected no light. The soul accepted it out of submission to the authority of the divine Revealer, not perhaps without a certain repugnance deriving from the obscurity of its intellect. It found no food for its devotion in this truth, as if it had been a fruit whose rind could not be broken.

And suddenly after hearing a sermon or reading a page in a book, or even perhaps without any apparent cause, this rind falls away and with lightning rapidity the captive light shines forth radiant and intense. The formerly blinded person cries out with enthusiastic joy: "I have understood! I have understood!" This is the intervention of the gift of *understanding*.

This is the gift that gives the saints, even those without great human means or education, the power to penetrate revealed doctrine and makes them profound theologians capable of insights into the faith that astound geniuses. Such were the Curé of Ars and young Thérèse of the Child Jesus.

But the gift of understanding is not the extraordinary

privilege of miracle-working saints. It belongs to what is known as the ordinary path of holiness. Anyone who earnestly desires it, asks it with faith, and prepares himself to receive it by a spirit of recollection will soon receive it.

On the other hand, we should not depend upon this availability of supernatural light to the point of thinking we are dispensed from making a personal effort in the way of study and research, and of neglecting the natural means of learning from those who have the knowledge and the mission to teach. Here again: "Help yourself and heaven will help you!" The purpose of this gift is only to make up for the deficiencies of courageous and humble souls of good will, to help them nourish their piety with doctrine, which is the only substantial food for a sound devotion.

While this gift is useful and necessary to every soul, it is particularly useful to those who have the difficult responsibility of transmitting divine teachings to others and of making them understand these teachings. How can they acquit themselves of this duty unless they themselves have understood? Students and teachers of theology, seminarians, professors, preachers, catechists, and all members of the teaching Church to whom Christ has said *"Docete*—Teach," must constantly ask the help of the gift of understanding for themselves and for those they teach. And they are wise to begin their studies or their teaching with an appeal to the Holy Spirit: *Veni, Sancte, Spiritus.* . . .

* * *

Wisdom, according to Aristotle, is knowledge through first causes. Since the very first and supreme cause is God, supernatural wisdom consists in explaining everything in terms of God, referring all things back to Him—both the origin of beings and their ultimate end, both the march of peoples under the hidden hand of His Providence and the succession of events in the lives of all of us. God at the beginning and God at the end of all things; God everywhere and in all things; God admirable in all His works and laws, in all His interventions and teachings—this is what a filial heart, helped by the gift of wisdom, discovers and contemplates. With tenderness and rapture, it delights in (*sapere*) everything that the Father does, everything that He says, everything that He is. The gift of wisdom impels the heart to recognize and admire in all things the infallible, magnificent, lovable and loving wisdom of the Father.

Wisdom is a source of light, since it furnishes the supreme explanation of all things and projects its searching light upon their origins and their finality. And above all it is a source of peace and serene trust. For once he is convinced that the very wise love of the Father produces and directs all things, the son puts all things in His hands with filial tranquility: *in pace in idipsum dormiam et requiescam.*

*   *   *

The gift of knowledge [5] relates more to creatures, teaching us to judge them in the light of supernatural principles, from the vantage point of faith and not according to the maxims of the world. Through this gift the Holy Spirit protects us from the snares of creatures and delivers us from their deceitful attractions. He shows them to us in their true light as imperfect, frail transitory goods, powerless to satisfy our hearts. By making us understand that creatures are merely means to lift us up to goods that do not pass and that alone can give happiness, the gift of knowledge keeps us from becoming attached to creatures as our last end and reminds us that this end is God alone.

It is the knowledge of the true value of things that Jesus wanted to teach us when He said: "What does it profit a man, if he gain the whole world, but suffer the loss of his own soul? Or what will a man give in exchange for his soul?" (Mt. 16:26).

The saints have possessed this knowledge in a very high degree. Their unshakable conviction of the nothingness of creatures was one of the chief foundations of their perfection.

Let us ask the Holy Spirit to communicate to us, or to

---

[5] The gift of *knowledge* should not be confused with the extraordinary gift known in mystical theology as "infused knowledge," by which God communicates to the soul in a supernatural way knowledge that it has not learned through natural means.

strengthen within us, this gift which is so precious and so necessary for our spiritual progress (cf. St. Thomas, *Summa*, IIa IIae, q. 9, a. 4).

*   *   *

Understanding, wisdom, and *knowledge* are helps to our faith. Their effect is to assist our knowledge of God, and of creatures in relation to God.

The four following gifts (*counsel, piety, fear,* and *fortitude*) are more concerned with our practice of virtue and make up for our weakness in the fulfillment of the moral law.

The first condition for courageously practicing virtue is to know precisely what it demands of us. As long as the mind has not clearly pointed out what virtue requires, the will hesitates, vacillates, and lacks resolution. We have to be sure of our path to follow it joyfully. We must know our duty in order to accomplish it without faltering. Hence the Church makes us ask the grace "of seeing what we should do" (Prayer over the people, Mass of the Wednesday of the first week in Lent), before asking for the grace of "having the strength to do it." It is often harder to see than to do. In any case, seeing is a necessary condition for doing.

It is often beyond our capacity to discover the will of God for us, our duty, and the best course to follow. We hesitate. Our practical judgment does not dare make a decision. It dreads the consequences of each of the contradictory alternatives between which it must choose. Because of the effects, it fears to pledge itself definitively one way or the other. The conscience remains inhibited, perplexed. And yet a decision must be reached. Sometimes time is short. Circumstances refuse to wait, and drive us toward a decision that is not yet ripe. At such times, we feel an urgent need to cling to the judgment of another who is more prudent or better informed. How satisfying it is, in such troubled moments, to be able to turn to a wise and devoted director, to a friend to whom we can confide everything and of whom we can ask anything! But such a treasure is the greatest rarity, and we cannot always have access to it when we need it.

Fortunate are the children of God! Their own Father offers Himself as their counselor, and through the *gift of counsel* places His luminous perspicacity at their service, tears away the veil of agonizing uncertainty from their eyes, and indicates the course to follow through a supernatural illumination.

He does not even wait until they are reduced to this extreme helplessness to intervene. He helps them in a continuous way to guide their decisions in the direction of the supernatural and of the demands of filial love.

Let us turn to Him before making any serious decision. Let us kneel at the foot of the tabernacle and ask: "Lord, what would You decide if You were in my place? What do You want me to do? In which direction does Your greater glory and the greater good of my soul and of other souls lie? Show me the path to follow: I need Your light. . . ."

Inasmuch as these lights often come to us through intermediaries (especially through priests), we should know how to ask for advice, especially in moments of over-excitement, anger, hatred, fear, vehement desire or passion. For at such times the mind does not see clearly. May the *gift of counsel* inspire us to ask the counsel of God and of His representatives, to make up for the frailty of our own judgment. It is through this gift that we obtain "sound judgment."

Necessary to all in hours of trouble and useful at all times, counsel is indispensable to those whose mission is to govern souls and to lead others. They have special need of this gift, even while taking the human means of enlightenment that both natural and supernatural prudence indicate.

Those under their care are the first to have an interest in asking that this gift be given them so that their advice may be sealed with the mark of divine prudence. Thus the faithful should pray for their priests, penitents for their directors, subordinates for their superiors, and subjects for their rulers.

*   *   *

The virtue of religion, the application of the virtue of justice to the rights of God, tends to make man render to God the worship that is His due as Creator, sovereign Master, and supreme End of all things: adoration, thanksgiving, repentance, and obedience. It tends to make man recognize God's infinite perfection and excellence, and His dominion over all things inasmuch as everything comes from Him, belongs to Him and exists for Him. It impels man to proclaim God as the Author, full of goodness and love, of all the benefits received in the supernatural order; as the Redeemer who merited these benefits; and as the beatifying Object of the eternal vision.

The virtue of religion goes further still. Imbued with charity, it inclines man to honor God as a Father more than a Master. Since God has really become our Father through grace, He wants us to go to Him more as sons than as servants. He does not want our worship to be limited to the cold motive of justice, but He wants it to rise to the level of filial love, and be adorned with tenderness, trust, delicacy, sweetness, and joy. In the Old Law, fear and rigor ruled. In the New Law, taught by His Son, love has become the great moving power. It is above all as a Father that God wants to be adored: "The true worshippers . . . worship the Father" (Jn. 4:23).

But such intimacy and filial sentiments are not natural to us. And if God Himself had not permitted and even asked for them, we would not dare entertain them. And likewise we could not produce such sentiments if He did not help us, if He did not communicate to us the *gift of piety* and the spirit of adoption that makes us cry out: "Father! Father!" This gift is the sweetest, the greatest, and the most important of all; the one that is most closely related to charity, that is most characteristic of our Christian religion; the gift that impels us to treat God as a Father and to honor Him like sons.

* * *

The immediate companion of the gift of piety is the *gift of fear of the Lord* which makes us dread to grieve the Father through sin, to displease Him, to wound His affection, to lose Him forever and at the same time lay ourselves open to the eternal punishments of His outraged love. This fear nurtures a great delicacy of conscience. It tends to deter the soul even from venial sins, from the appearances of sin, from "material" sins, or sins that are not fully deliberate. It makes the soul like an affectionate child who strives to avoid any act, word, or manner that might even slightly displease his father or please him less. What beautiful souls are formed in this way! What purity! These souls must be very dear to the One who adopted them.

This fear also inspires a lively sentiment of their weakness and makes them sense how much such delicacy exceeds their natural strength. Mistrusting themselves, they throw themselves into the arms of their Father who, they know, will surely help. They entrust themselves to Him to defend them against themselves, against their inconstancy, their frivolity, their moral indigence, and the fascination of forbidden goods.

On the other hand they should beware of falling into an exaggerated fear that the Father would certainly condemn, of transforming this delicacy of conscience into anxious scruples, into concern over trifles that embarrasses others and leads to depressing pusillanimity on their own part. Nothing could be less in harmony with the filial spirit. Being sons, they can count upon the all-powerful help of the Father, and should keep their hearts dilated with the love, trust, and joyfulness that are so favorable to spiritual progress. Who has a greater right and duty than they to repeat the words of Psalmist: "Into Thy hands, Lord, I commend my spirit"?

In addition to this filial fear there is also a reverential fear, a sentiment of the infinite grandeur and transcendence of God, a profound respect for His sovereign majesty, which prevents intimacy from degenerating into a heedless familiarity that would make us treat God as an equal [6] and forget that although He is our Father He is also our Master and our Judge.

The gift of piety and the gift of fear are complementary. One imbues adoration with tenderness; the other imbues tenderness with veneration. Through these two gifts, a suit-

---

[6] As too many children nowadays treat their parents.

able mingling, a necessary compenetration of these two sentiments is produced.

Love for the Father must not be limited to sentiments. It must culminate in acts, express itself in devotion, prove itself by meticulous fidelity to all His wishes and by an ardent zeal for His glory. He demands that we immolate our own desires to His, our own interests to His, that we deprive ourselves of all those goods that He forbids and courageously accomplish all that He commands. Does not love mean giving oneself, serving?

Now this constancy in the gift of self, which may at times be heroic, exceeds the capacities of nature. The Holy Spirit provides for it through the *gift of fortitude,* the supernatural help for our weakness.

"It is not only in case of peril of death or even when exceptional heroic acts are called for that the gift of fortitude comes to the rescue. The heroism required by our daily virtues suffices to motivate this intervention by the Holy Spirit whenever our strength for duty and God's service . . . is in danger of reaching its limit, whenever we are worried lest we are not equal to our virtuous tasks. Then our charity instinctively calls for divine help. The Holy Spirit answers our desire by lending us the support of divine fortitude" (Noble, *op. cit.,* Chapter XV).

* * *

Let us conclude this chapter with two remarks:

a. God distributes the gifts (in the broad sense) with a lavishness and diversity that is infinitely superior to the magnificent variety of flowers in June. To some souls, such as the Fathers and Doctors of the Church, a St. Augustine, a St. Thomas, a St. Francis de Sales, eager for divine light and destined to enlighten others, He grants above all the gifts of *understanding, counsel,* and *knowledge.* Others are favored by Him with the gift of *fortitude,* especially in the practice of heroic mortifications, or of *fear,* through their very pronounced sentiment of His Majesty, or of *piety,* in the form of filial trust in Him.

Some souls contemplate Him in Himself, in His perfections, in the Trinity of His Persons, or in His admirable works. Others contemplate Him in their brothers, His sons, whom they serve out of love for Him in many different works of charity: such were St. John of God and St. Vincent de Paul. We could thus differentiate and catalogue the saints according to the gift that is most prominent in their spiritual life. And even so, we could discover and admire many shades of variation in the same gift.

b. As can easily be seen, the gifts can relate to one or another virtue, but they all have a close bond with *charity*. Their principle is God's fatherly love for us, and their purpose is to make us act toward Him like children who love their Father with filial affection. It is because He loves us as sons that God is impelled to succor the weakness of our mind and will. And it is because He wants us to treat Him as a Father that He works to form within us the hearts of sons. He has chosen to teach us Himself: He helps us to penetrate His lessons (*understanding*); to discover in Him the reason for all things, and to see the wisdom of His action in all things (*wisdom*); to thoroughly understand that He alone, and not any creature, is our last end (*knowledge*); to realize wherein the path of duty and goodness lies, that is, wherein His will lies (*counsel*); to express filial sentiments toward Him, especially in the worship that is due Him (*piety*); to nurture within ourselves a filial fear of offending Him (*fear of the Lord*); and, in order to avoid the misfortune of sin, to acquire courage for any sacrifice (*fortitude*).

*   *   *

Note on the interrelationship between the gifts and grace (see p. 205 above):

This is something that we must not forget if we are to clearly understand the definition sometimes given of the sacrament of confirmation: "A sacrament that gives the Holy Spirit with the abundance of His gifts." If these words are taken literally, it might seem that the special effect of this sacrament is to increase the gifts of the Holy Spirit. That would not be correct.

Baptism and penance give the gifts of the Holy Spirit because they give grace; confirmation, the Holy Eucharist, extreme unc-

tion, holy orders, and matrimony increase the gifts because they increase grace. And even so, the Eucharist increases them more
than does confirmation, inasmuch as, everything else being
equal, it brings a greater increase in grace because it unites the
soul intimately with the One who is the Author of grace.

Confirmation *confirms* the baptized Christian, strengthens him
in the faith and in grace: "It gives him the fortitude and courage
to confess the faith of Jesus Christ, and it is through this sacrament that we really become soldiers and champions of Jesus
Christ." This is the definition of confirmation given by Bellarmine's catechism which is accepted by the Church, by the Catechism of the Council of Trent, and equivalently by all manuals
of theology. The special effect of this great sacrament is therefore not to provide the gifts of the Holy Spirit in abundance
but to give the mission and the fortitude to profess and defend
one's faith. This mission and this supernatural fortitude are
evidently gifts of the Holy Spirit, but not in the strict sense in
which we are using the term in this chapter. Cf. *L'Ami du
Clergé*, 1921, p. 347, and the author's work: *Notre Pentecôte*,
p. 140.

"In a note of *Ephemerides Theologiae Lovanienses*, (1924,
p. 515), Father Uniberg admits that Leo XIII and the majority
of theologians consider the gifts to be inseparable from sanctifying grace, but prefers the opinion which he feels is closer to the
teachings of the Fathers, according to which, *saltem ordinarie*,
the gifts would be granted to the soul only at the moment of
confirmation, these gifts being the specific fruit of the sacrament" (*Revue d'Asc. et de Myst.*, 1933, p. 23). Such a view is inadmissible.

THE EFFECTS

OF GRACE

THAT STEM

FROM OUR PRAYERS

AND

GOOD WORKS

THE EFFECTS OF GRACE we have so far studied relate above all to what St. Thomas calls *operating grace:* they are produced in the soul without any intervention on the soul's part. The soul has merely to dispose itself to receive them.

We have still to consider the effects of *cooperating grace,* that is, those effects that the just man, elevated by grace, the gifts, and the virtues to the divine order, is capable of producing himself.

In the case of the first category of effects, he is passive: he receives. In the case of the second, he is more active: he produces with and through the help of grace.

The effects of grace already studied are absolutely inseparable from grace itself: they always follow from it.

The effects we are about to discuss are conditional: they presuppose certain actions on the part of the subject: prayers or good works.

They concern the *influence* of grace upon the efficacy of our prayers and upon the meritorious and satisfactory value of our works.

10 The Power of Glorification and of Impetration

GRACE confers upon the person who possesses it a precious power of glorification and impetration.

Ordinarily, these effects are not discussed.

And yet they are not without significance for the spiritual life, and they help the just to rightly esteem their state.

1. The Power of Glorification

Grace procures this power in two ways: a) by the dispositions that it presupposes or that it implants in the just man; b) and above all by the dignity that it confers upon him.

a. *By the dispositions that grace presupposes.* To receive and preserve grace, a man must have chosen and must continue to will God as his last end; he must recognize Him as being alone capable of terminating, completing the creature, of satisfying its aspirations, of fulfilling its desires for truth, beauty, and happiness. This is a disposition of soul that unquestionably honors God by proclaiming His excellence.

Moreover, the state of grace is a state of obedience to His commandments, of submission to His will, and hence of acceptance of His sovereign dominion, and of more or less implicit affirmation of His rights over every creature.

The just man in the state of grace glorifies God since he affirms equivalently that He is the Creator and the term of all things, the beginning and the end, Alpha and Omega (Apoc. 1:8).

Grace and charity always go together. They are so inseparable that they are often mistaken for one another. Now charity consists in loving God, not only as the cause of goodness, but as Goodness itself, because of His infinite perfections. To love God is to form an intellectual judgment declaring Him better and more perfect than everything else, superior and preferable to everything else; and by an act of the will to esteem Him in actual fact more than everything else, to want Him more than everything else, to be determined to sacrifice everything, even life itself, rather than be separated from Him, to be ready to renounce all things, to suffer martyrdom of heart and body, so as not to lose Him by offending Him. Now, do not all these things glorify God as well, since His glory is defined as: "the affirmation of His excellence, of His perfections, by an intelligent and free creature"?

Nothing gives so much honor as true, disinterested love, made up of admiration, veneration, and profound attachment, a love whose only motive and cause are the perfections of its object. To love someone for his qualities is to recognize, at least equivalently, that he possesses these qualities. To love him above all else is to recognize that because of his qualities he surpasses all things. Is there a more fitting means of giving honor?

Moreover, charity, which grace produces, glorifies God by orientating toward Him as to his last end, all the faculties and the operations of the just man. In the words of St. Thomas: "Charity directs the acts of all the other virtues [that is to say, all good acts] to the last end" (IIa IIae, q. 23, a. 8). Charity makes a person accomplish all these good acts for the glory of God. But this orientation of the just man's actions toward God is itself the affirmation that He is their end, that everything comes from Him, that all things belong to Him, that everything must be subject to Him. This affirmation is the most eloquent homage that can be paid Him, the most striking recognition of His excellence. And so it is that charity, implanted in the heart of the child by grace, is synonymous with dedication to the honor of the Father and fulfills the first and fundamental request of the children of God: "Hallowed by Thy name."

Thus the life of the just man is a continual hymn in honor of the Father. All his actions, providing they conform with the moral law, glorify Him. From each one of them a luminous ray of praise rises up toward Him.

b. *By the dignity that grace confers upon the just.* Grace is a principle of glorification not only because of the dispositions that it presupposes or produces in the soul, but also because of the dignity that it confers.

We draw the reader's attention to this point which is little known and yet of capital importance.

As the adopted son of God, admitted into His family and His close friendship, loaded down with His riches and destined to share His eternal happiness, partaking of His nature and of His divine life, the just man is raised to a dignity that surpasses all natural and human dignity. His is more than princely, or even royal dignity. It is a supernatural dignity, a participation in the dignity of his heavenly Father. He is no longer just a man like every other. He is more than a man, more than the son of a king or an emperor. He is greater than the greatest personages; greater than all those whose genius, works, or exploits have dazzled the world and whose names have the widest renown. He is *a son of God.* This quality raises him to the loftiest heights, and places the noblest crown upon his brow.

But this dignity passes from the person of the just man into his works, conferring upon them a supernatural and divine value. His works are no longer the works of an ordinary man, but of a supernaturalized, divinized man, of a son of God. When he does the will of his Father, when he offers Him worship, when he expresses his sentiments: veneration, trust, tenderness, gratitude, submission; when he proclaims His rights and His excellence, he is not an ordinary man obeying, acting, praying, and praising. He is a member of God's family, he is a son of God.

Now it is an established principle that honor is proportionate to the rank or worth of the person rendering it. If a king's son greets you warmly, shows respect and affection for you, and submits his will to yours, he honors you much more than if he were a poor beggar devoid of respect. It is a dogma in theology that Christ was able to make reparation for the infinite offense made against God by sin because He gave Him infinite glory and thus expiated, satisfied, and merited in an infinite degree through His infinite dignity as God-man.

It should be evident, therefore, that the just man gives much more glory to God than does the sinner by his submission, respect, trust, deep esteem, gratitude, devotion, and supreme love; by all the noble sentiments that he expresses for Him; by the praise he gives Him, by the worship he offers Him, and by the more or less explicit affirmation he makes of His attributes, perfections, His transcendence and His divinity. This glory is of the same nature as the just man's dignity, a glory that is more than human, quasi-divine, much more proportionate to the glory that the infinite Majesty of God deserves.

Grace confers upon the just man a unique power, a supernatural capacity to honor God.[1] Not only does grace honor him by the dignity with which it clothes him, it also permits him to honor his Creator much more efficaciously. While he receives many advantages through grace, he can also, through grace, give much in return. Grace considerably increases the value of his acts and multiplies his power of glorification.

This is one of the foundations of the just man's precious power to merit and make satisfaction (which we shall study later).

Let us point out a few other consequences of the presence of grace in a soul.

Fervent Christians, loving sons of the heavenly Father,

---

[1] What Bossuet says of the saints in heaven can be applied to the just here on earth and expressed in the "present" tense: "God will raise them above anything we can imagine, in order to derive greater glory from their honor. Since the praise of men is of little value, He will make them gods and thereby obligate Himself to pay heed to their praises."

want to prove the authenticity of their love by doing something for Him, and giving Him some good thing in return for all the blessings He has showered upon them. They would like to offer Him the one gift they are able to offer Him and that He asks of them, the gift for which they were created and adopted: His extrinsic glory.

Through grace they can satisfy their need for filial devotion, accomplish their devout intention, and fulfill the desires of their hearts.

If they regret their lack of leisure, strength, and resources to devote to works of zeal, the apostolate, or Catholic Action, because of their physical incapacity perhaps, or because of their obscure and time-consuming tasks, they need not feel discouraged. For they have a means of making up for this lack and of working quite as effectively for the glory of their Father. This means is to increase their grace and thereby increase their supernatural dignity and their power of glorification; to drink deeply from the wellsprings of divine life: the sacraments (especially the Holy Eucharist) and meritorious works. The mere thought of intensifying their power of glorification should lead them as often as possible to the Communion rail and to the confessional, and inspire them to good works.

This thought should also make them turn resolutely away from sin, which not only despoils of supernatural dignity but also deprives man of his capacity to honor God by his sentiments and his acts, thus reducing him to a state of impotence.

Another consequence of grace is this: there is no more urgent, necessary, or important undertaking, or one more pleasing to God than to draw sinners back to the state of grace and to convert infidels so that, once they have become the children of the heavenly Father, they can honor Him through all the actions of their lives. Now, the more just men there are on earth, the more numerous will be those who have the privilege of bringing Him glory.

To make grace increase in those who already possess it is also a powerful means of increasing the glory they give God: "That they may have life, and have it more abundantly"

(Jn. 10:10). Is not this prospect sufficient to sustain and stimulate the zeal of all those who, through Catholic Action or in some other way, strive to exercise the apostolate and to accomplish some good about them? Does it not suffice to inspire priests with a high esteem for their vocation which dedicates them to this sublime task?

Starting from the principle set forth above, it also follows that the prayer of praise of the just man, the worship he renders to God, gives God greater glory and has greater value than that of the sinner. This is not to say that the sinner's prayer and worship are altogether inefficacious and sterile. Indeed every intelligent and free being who recognizes and proclaims the transcendence of God or some of His divine prerogatives thereby honors Him in some way.

If the sinner expressed a supreme preference, a sincere love for God, this act alone would make him pass from the state of sin to the state of grace, that is, it would "justify" him. But there are other less perfect religious sentiments that are not incompatible with attachment to sin and that the sinner can sincerely express to God (for example, adoration, a certain gratitude, faith in His word and in His promises). And these sentiments bring some glory to God. Of course, they bring Him much less glory than if they emanated from the heart of one of His children, one of the "just," than if they were "informed," elevated, completed, and perfected by the movement of a filial tenderness, by "charity."

Therefore, to give prayer and exercises of worship the maximum glorifying power, it is important to be in the state of grace, and as intensely so as possible. This is particularly true for those who are dedicated to these actions by their vocation or mission, for example those who are obligated to recite the Divine Office: "Praise becometh the upright" (Ps. 32:1).

Worship of the Father, "*pietas*," attains its full value, its full efficacy, only when it comes from His children. And just as the prayer of praise (love, adoration, thanksgiving) has greater value on the lips of the just man, so too his prayer of request has greater efficacy.

2. The Power of Impetration

God does not limit Himself to answering the prayers of the just. Even the prayers of sinners find access to His heart. Their requests are also heard. If they were not, what means would sinners have of ever being delivered from their wretched state and of obtaining the helps that are so necessary for their conversion? [2] Our Lord spoke to all men, the just and the sinners as well, when He said: "Ask, and it shall be given you; . . . knock, and it shall be opened to you. For everyone who asks, receives" (Mt. 7:7-8). This is a general promise.

But there may be degrees in the realization of this promise. God may make some wait longer than others, or grant the desires of some more quickly and more fully than those of others.

Do not the saints receive more favors and even miracles from Him? That is why we recommend ourselves to their prayers. The many pilgrims who go to Ars to implore the intercession of St. Jean-Marie Vianney, those who go to the shrine of St. Thérèse of the Child Jesus, and those who come from every corner of the world to beg the help of our Lady of Lourdes, are all convinced of the power of these saintly souls over the heart of God. They are right. For St. Thomas tells us that "the efficacy of prayer is proportionate to the degree of union with God that the one who prays has attained" (IIa IIae, q. 83, a. 11). The more closely united to God we are, the more efficacious are our prayers. As the man born blind told the Pharisees: "We know that God does not hear sinners [by working miracles]; but if anyone is a worshipper of God, and does His will, him He hears" (Jn. 9:31).

God does the will of those who do His will. He fulfills the desires of those who accomplish His wishes. He listens to those who obey Him; He even works wonders for those who answer Him with sacrifices. He is infinitely good for those

---

[2] Tanquerey says that although the state of grace is not necessary in order to pray, it greatly increases the value of our prayers, since it makes us friends of God and living members of Jesus Christ (*Précis de Théologie ascétique et mystique,* No. 648).

who are totally dedicated to Him. In the words of the Psalmist: "The just cried, and the Lord heard them: and delivered
them out of all their troubles" (Ps. 33:18); "He will do the
will of them that fear Him: and He will hear their prayer,
and save them" (Ps. 144:19).

And St. James affirms that "the unceasing prayer of a just
man is of great avail" (Jas. 5:16).

Bossuet explains it this way: "You serve God, and God
serves you. You do His will and He does yours, to teach you
that He is a sincere friend, and that by considering the desires of those who fear Him He allows them to exercise a
sort of dominion over His possessions."

When St. Thérèse of Lisieux was on her death-bed, she
said: "God will be obliged to do my will in heaven, because
I have never done my own will here on earth." But God does
not wait until His friends enter heaven to give them this
power. Already in this world He places His power at their
service.

That is why the Church looks upon miracles as indubitable
signs of holiness, and requires them in cases of beatification
and canonization. Now the just are saints, at least with an
initial holiness (they were called "saints" in the first ages of
the Church). The grace they possess is "sanctifying." They
love God with a love of charity, and through this charity
they are completely united to Him. Their will is one with
His, the supreme rule of all holiness. In return and proportionately, God identifies His will with theirs, in order to
satisfy their desires. Whence the particular efficacy of their
prayers.

Moreover, grace makes a man a son of God. It forms a
filial heart within him, by filling it with charity. It gives his
supplication and his other religious sentiments such appealing accents that the Father cannot resist them. It is the Holy
Spirit Himself who prays in him and for him, who "pleads
for [him] with unutterable groanings" (Rom. 8:26), and
whose prayers are irresistible.[3]

If even selfish and harsh human fathers are moved by their
children's prayers, how much more our loving, generous,

---

[3] Cf. *Messager du Sacré Coeur,* 1934, p. 259.

and merciful Father in heaven! "If one of you asks his father for a loaf, will he hand him a stone? or for a fish, will he hand him a serpent? . . . Therefore, if you, evil as you are, know how to give good gifts to your children, how much more will your heavenly Father give the Good Spirit to those who ask Him!" (Lk. 11:11-13).

Since God has such affection and devotion for His children, how could He remain deaf to their appeals? Since, when they were still in the state of sin and His enemies, He gave them His dearest possession, His own Son, how could He refuse them favors of lesser value but necessary to their perseverance, now that they are members of His family, partakers of His own nature, and destined to share His own happiness? (Cf. Rom. 8:32). Can he who gives a greater gift, refuse a lesser one? It is unthinkable that He should not grant them what they beg of Him with filial trust, now that they have become so dear to His heart. Their community of life with Him implies as a consequence a community of possessions.[4]

That is why the Church addresses her requests to God through the merits of the saints and through their intercession: *Beata Dei Genitrix sanctique omnes intercedant pro nobis ad Dominum*—"May the Blessed Mother of God and all the saints intercede for us before the Lord."

We know what Yahweh declared to Eliphaz, Job's false friend: "My servant Job shall pray for you: his face I will accept, that folly be not imputed to you" (Job 42:8).

Yahweh answered the prayer of the just Abraham and agreed not to inflict terrible punishment upon sinful cities provided he found ten just men within them (Gen. 18:22-23). How, then, could He refuse to hear the prayers of the just under the law of love, begging Him to spare the world whose evil deeds have incurred His anger?

*   *   *

The just should therefore make use of their credit with God to arrest the course of His justice. Let them be bold, and

---

[4] Cf. *Note* at the end of the chapter which contains passages by Father Janvier and Bishop Gay on this subject, p. 230 below.

dare to ask great favors, even miracles, for themselves and for others. Let them beg constantly. They should broaden their desires and multiply their requests, and show themselves insatiable. God's gifts are limited only by their prayers. He has fixed no limits to His mercy except those they place on their own petitions. If He ceases to pour forth His gifts in abundance, it is because they stop asking for them. If He does not grant more favors, it is because they do not ask for more. Through their sonship, they have a claim on His love. Let them take advantage of it and make their fellow-men likewise profit. By making the just participate in the nature of God, grace makes them partake in a certain sense of His omnipotence. It is up to them to make bold use of their power.

They should remember that the favors they ask—if they are true goods useful for their souls—have been merited by Christ, their Brother and Savior. That is to say, He paid for them with His blood. His merits are theirs, and they can rest their prayers upon His merits: *Per Dominum Nostrum Jesum Christum.*

Thus, while the state of grace is not necessary to make our requests efficacious, it increases their efficacy considerably. It makes it much more certain that God will accept them. Hence anyone who wants to ask a favor of God must take the preliminary precaution of being restored to His friendship if he has had the misfortune to lose it through sin. In such case, he must kneel in the confessional before presenting himself at the altar.

Everything that intensifies grace within us increases our credit before the heavenly Father. The value of our suffrages rises with the level of our supernatural life. The more perfectly we become His children, the more powerful we shall be over His heart.

*   *   *

Note on the just man's sharing in God's possessions (see p. 229 above):

Father Janvier says: "Grace works a radical change in us. It brings about a transfiguration of our souls whose sublime reality we cannot understand in this life. Grace deepens the soul, broadens its contours, increases its strength, and elevates all its faculties. At the contact of grace, the mind, the heart, and the will dilate, and the new man of which the sacred books speak shines forth in his grandeur, strength, and beauty. The new man's acts feel the effects of this nobility, their fruitfulness becomes apparent in the measure that the principles from which they stem are more completely immersed in the regenerative waters of grace. As a consequence, the prayer of the saintly soul is far superior in essence to the prayer that proceeds from nature. It finds expression in notes and harmonies of such intensity that our frail constitution is almost shaken by it. It is up to you O Beloved Disciple, and you, Apostle of the Gentiles, and you, Thomas Aquinas, Catherine of Siena, Teresa of Jesus, John of the Cross, and above all, You, O adorable Master, to tell us the power of a prayer that could not pour from You without exhausting You!

"We must go further. Grace is in our souls the equivalent of the blood of God: *semen Dei*. When we are born to the life of grace we are born of God, we partake of His nature, we are members of His race, we become His sons. . . . In the house of God we are neither strangers nor passing guests. When our suppliant voices rise up to God, He hears the cry of His blood and the lament of His posterity. Even a denatured father and mother cannot help being moved by the cry of their own blood. They awaken, they tear themselves from their selfishness, they run, they fly, defying all dangers, to help the child whose heartrending cry they have heard. And why do the joys, fears, sorrows, and hopes of children have such a rapid and violent repercussion on the hearts of their parents? Because the community of blood is like a transmission wire that immediately relays the emotions of children to their parents. The stronger, the more alive, and the closer this connecting link, the greater the unity between them. But God is more intimately attached to the just than parents are to their heirs. A father and mother may forget the fruit of their loins. God does not forget the just. Did not David cry out: 'My father and my mother have left me: but the Lord hath taken me up' (Ps. 26:10)" (*Conférences*, 1919).

Bishop Gay writes: "It is evident that since hope is more justified in the soul in the state of grace, it has incomparably more power. Since Jesus lives within us, He Himself becomes a light for God's eyes. He enables the Father to recognize what we are, to hear what we say, to smile upon our desires, and to place His omnipotence abundantly at our service. This is the significance of our divine Master's consoling words: 'If you abide in Me, and if My words abide in you, ask whatever you will and it shall be done to you' (Jn. 15:7)."

11 The Power to Merit

GRACE gives the just man something more than a special power over his Father's heart. It also furnishes him with the means of acquiring rights over His possessions. Not only does grace clothe the just man's good actions with great efficacy, it also confers upon his good acts a twofold and very precious capacity: the capacity to pay the debts that he may have incurred toward divine justice through his sins; and the capacity to win heaven as a reward. In short, grace gives the just man *the capacity to satisfy* and *the capacity to merit.* We shall discuss the power to merit in this chapter and the next.

Inasmuch as satisfaction requires all the conditions for merit, we shall deal with the latter first. It will then be easier for the reader to understand what we have to say about satisfaction.

A few authors discuss merit in connection with spiritual growth or with the causes of grace, and merit is certainly one of the causes of grace since it is a means of increasing it. However it seems more logical to speak of merit as being an effect of grace, since it is one of its effects before being one of its causes, and since merit presupposes grace whenever it produces higher degrees of grace.[1]

---

[1] This is the opinion of St. Thomas, who deals with merit in connection with the effects of grace. He devotes Question 113 of the Ia IIae to justification, and the ten articles of Question 114 to merit.

The power to merit condignly is a privilege of the children of God, one of the precious consequences of their supernatural dignity, and not the least of the fruits of the divine life in them.

In any case, merit is one of the most effective stimulants to goodness. "Self-interest," even on the supernatural level is legitimate. Is it not one of the powerful levers of human action? Countless souls have bolstered their courage in times of trial by thinking, as did St. Paul, of the "eternal weight of glory that is beyond all measure" (II Cor. 4:17) that would be their reward for valiantly enduring their "present light affliction." How many more have agreed to sacrifice for God the goods of this earth, riches, honor, pleasures; to "lose their life in order to gain it," and thereby receive the treasures of heaven as a hundredfold return. They have chosen to lay up for themselves treasures that neither rust nor moth consumes and that thieves cannot steal (Mt. 6:19), renouncing the easily lost treasures of earth.

The dogma of merit is certainly one of the most powerful principles of holiness in the Catholic Church. By rejecting it, Protestantism [2] has destroyed one of the most powerful resources of the spiritual life. And by thus denying the usefulness of good works, it has dried up one of the most fruitful sources of human energy and of the moral progress of souls.

This false conception of merit is the logical conclusion of the Protestant errors concerning original sin and justification. If the first sin did intrinsically corrupt the nature of man and destroy his freedom; if, in consequence, justification makes no change in this state and is only an external imputation of the merits of Christ, our acts lack three conditions required of them for merit: moral goodness, freedom, and the supernatural dignity of the person. An incomplete notion of Christ's merits and of the gratuitousness of justification completes this heresy. An evil doctrine if ever there were one! If it had triumphed, it would have been the cause of deep degradation for the human race.

---

[2] And certain Orthodox groups as well.

Here again by saving the truth, the Church has saved the world. Her teaching on merit is one of her claims to glory, and the faithful should be devoutly grateful to her for it.

The question of merit is very important because of its moral consequences. We shall therefore examine this matter in some detail.

After a few words on the nature and species of merit, we shall establish its existence and its conditions. We shall then specify the object of merit, namely, what the just man can merit for himself and for others.

1. The Nature of Merit

In everyday language applied to the relations of men among themselves, the word "merit" sometimes signifies fittingness, and sometimes justice in the broad or strict sense. A child has obeyed and we say he deserves a reward. Since he has only done his duty, this is only a matter of fittingness. We say that an earnest student has merited a certain rank in class, and that an invention deserves a prize. These are questions of justice. A crime is punished, and we say: "The criminal deserves his punishment!" This is strict and rigorous justice.

In a very broad and abstract sense, merit would then be the property that makes a human act worthy of reward or punishment.

In a more restricted sense, merit applies only to rewards. The adjective "meritorious" and the verb "to merit" without any direct complement refer only to the earning of rewards. When we say that an action or a life is meritorious, or that a person has merited well of his family, his country, of the human race, we are speaking only of meriting rewards.

We can merit well of men and of God. In the first case we have what might be called human merit; in the second, theological merit.

Theological merit would thus be "the property that makes a human act worthy of a reward from God," or in a more concrete sense: "a human act that is worthy of reward from God."

If the reward is natural, the merit is natural; if the reward is supernatural, then so is the merit. We are going to discuss only supernatural merit.

2. The Species of Merit

When the right to a reward is only one of fittingness, or *de congruo* [3] (from the adjective *congruum*, fitting), there is no necessary equality between the act and its reward. When the right is one in justice, there is a certain equality between the act and the reward, and it is called *condign* merit, *de condigno*. This is merit in the strict sense.

Merit involves two inverse movements, as it were: a going and a coming that re-establish the equilibrium of justice. There is a return that presupposes a receiving.

Merit calls for two persons: one of them owes the other a compensation because the latter has worked for him and has been useful to him in some way.

Merit presupposes that one person gives something useful that he possesses to another, and thus becomes his creditor.

In the case of theological merit, the two involved are God and man: man gives God something and by reason of this fact acquires the right to a reward.

3. The Existence of Merit

We may wonder what anyone can possibly give to God. Does He not have everything, being the sovereign Good and infinite Perfection? What can puny creatures bring Him? Besides, since we have received everything from Him, do we not owe Him everything that we are and everything we have? With regard to our works and our property—our fields, our animals, our lands—we assume we may extract all their fruits without owing them anything. Likewise, if anything of ours can serve God, He has a right to it: He is its author and original owner.

And if this is true in the order of nature, how much more so in the supernatural order which is absolutely gratuitous

---

[3] This division of merit, which was an important contribution of Scholastic philosophy, appeared in the 13th century.

and superior to every natural right. Grace, the principal cause of our supernatural works, is a gift, gratuitous in every respect (as its very name indicates). How then, could grace be the basis for some right to a reward? How could God, supreme Independence, become indebted to His creature?

Certainly God lacks nothing, and no one could add to His intrinsic or essential glory. He knows Himself perfectly, He contemplates Himself with love, and this contemplation and love give Him infinite honor and happiness that cannot be increased.

But God also has a finite glory that comes to Him from finite beings: the knowledge, love, and praise of His perfections by creatures. This is an extrinsic or accidental glory, capable of being procured or not. We can increase it by our good works, or impair it by our sins.[4]

Now, do we not owe God this extrinsic glory, since He who is the principle and end of all things brought us into the world for that very purpose? Is not this extrinsic glory the purpose of all creation and of our whole life?

Yes, and that is why we can never merit in strict justice. For then our works could not to be owed to God in any way, and the principle and condition of these works could not come from Him. In other words, we could merit in strict justice only if God had no dominion over us, only if we were not His creatures and He were not our Creator, that is to say, only if He were not God.

But if God in His wisdom and goodness chooses to help our will to glorify Him by offering it an added compelling motive, does He not have a greater right to reward us for giving Him something that is due Him than do the fathers and masters of earth to reward their children and their subjects? This involves no abdication of His sovereignty, no abasement of His majesty, for He becomes our debtor en-

---

[4] We would like to point out that this concept is vitally important. The foundation, the reason for the merit of our actions is the glory they bring to God. Everything stems from this. Such is the thought of St. Thomas: "God seeks from our goods not profit, but glory, i.e., the manifestation of His goodness. . . . Hence we merit from God, not that by our works anything accrues to Him, but inasmuch as we work for His glory" (Ia IIae, q. 114, a. 1, ad 2).

tirely of His own volition and He is bound only by His own promise (cf. Ia IIae, q. 114, a. 1, ad 3). God owes something because He choses to owe it, and according to St. Augustine, "when He rewards man He rewards only His own gifts." [5]

"How does it happen that God is our debtor?" the holy Doctor asks. "Does He receive something from us? . . . He became a debtor not be receiving but by promising. We cannot say to Him: 'Return what You have received,' but only 'return what You have promised.' " [6]

Thus there could not be any merit in justice, even in the broad sense, except by reason of a promise made by God. Without such a promise, all the qualities of our works would be powerless to establish a right to remuneration.

Now, He has indeed made this promise. But it applies only: a) to works accomplished in the wayfaring state; b) to works that bring Him supernatural glory, that is to say, works that are good morally because they are free and conform to His divine law; and c) to works that are supernatural in their principle through the state of grace, and supernatural also in their motive. These are the conditions of merit which we are about to study.

4. The Conditions of Merit

The conditions of merit may be reduced to six. One condition depends upon God, namely, His promise. Two depend on the work: conformity with the moral law and freedom. Three of these conditions concern man: the wayfaring state, the state of grace, and a supernatural intention.

1. *The condition that depends upon God: the promise*

Did God make such a promise? Since it is absolutely gratuitous, it can only be known through Revelation.

There can be no doubt as to the presence of this promise in Revelation, in view of the clear, explicit, categorical, and repeated testimonies to that effect. The word "merit" is

---

[5] Epist. Sixto, 194,5,19; *P.L.* 33, 880.
[6] *In Psalmos, P. L.,* 37, 1068; Ps. 83:16.

not to be found in Revelation,[7] but the reality to which it refers is expressed in equivalent terms.

Speaking of good works, our Lord says that we must perform them not out of vanity (to be seen by men, as the Pharisees did), but to please God. This is the condition for rewarding these works: ". . . that thy alms may be given in secret; and thy Father, who sees in secret, will reward thee" (Mt. 6:4).

We find the same meaning in the parable of the talents. The servants who made the talents the Master had entrusted to them bear fruit were proportionately rewarded: "Because thou hast been faithful over a few things, I will set thee over many" (Mt. 25:23).

In a hundred other passages Christ establishes a causal connection between our works performed under certain conditions and the happiness of heaven. At the last judgment God Himself will point out the reason for the salvation of the just: "I was hungry and you gave me to eat . . . as long as you did it for . . . the least of My brethren, you did it for Me" (Mt. 25:35-40). "And everyone who has left house . . . for My name's sake, shall receive a hundredfold, and shall possess life everlasting" (Mt. 19:29). "And whoever gives to one of these little ones but a cup of cold water . . . he shall not lose his reward" (Mt. 10:42).

The Epistles of the Apostles contain the same teaching. According to St. Paul, affliction which is only a passing thing will, if endured with courage, prepare "for us an eternal weight of glory that is beyond all measure" (II Cor. 4:17). It is tribulation that prepares this heavenly glory, that is its cause and that merits it. The connection between them is one of cause and effect.

When the Apostle was in prison for the second time in Rome and felt the hour of supreme sacrifice approaching, he wrote these stirring words to his beloved disciple Timothy (then in Ephesus) to console him: *"As for me, I am already being poured out in sacrifice"* (II Tim. 4:6). He spoke of his approaching death as a dissolution, a separation of his

---

[7] We come across it for the first time in Tertullian, one of the Fathers who studied the question of merit most intensively.

soul from his body. Then casting a rapid glance upon his life as an apostle He summed it up in images that were familiar to himself and to his correspondent, the image of the gladiatorial combats and of the races in the arena in which the winner received the prize and the crown. *"I have fought the good fight, I have finished the course, I have kept the faith"* (II Tim. 4:7). He had valiantly fought and run to defend and propagate the faith, that is, the treasure of Christian Revelation entrusted to him by Christ. Having reached the end of the combat and of the race, he bolstered his courage by thinking of the "prize," the "crown" that God was preparing for him: *"For the rest, there is laid up for me a crown of justice, which the Lord, the just Judge, will give to me in that day"* (II Tim. 4:8).

It is a "crown of justice" because it was promised and because it is due to merit. When the supreme Arbiter gives it, He accomplishes a work of equity. He does not award it as He pleases, according to His good pleasure or His preferences, but according to what is due (in conformity with the rules established and the promises made) to those who have won it.

And as if to anticipate the objection that this was a special case and that it would not be the same for other men, the sacred writer adds immediately: *"Yet not to me only, but also to those who love His coming."* That is to say, to all who, like himself, have fought and run for the faith, stirring themselves to self-sacrifice and fidelity through their hope for the crown, for the reward that the sovereign Judge will grant them. Thus there can be no doubt that heaven will be the wages of those who have fought courageously in order to preserve the faith.

If these affirmations do not seem general enough, and seem to apply only to the brave who, after Paul's example, have "fought the good fight," suffice it to remember the declarations Paul had addressed to the Corinthians a few years earlier: "For all of us must be made manifest before the tribunal of Christ, so that each one may receive what he has won through the body, according to his works, whether good or evil" (II Cor. 5:10).

According to these words, our eternal fate will be settled by a judgment, the passing of a sentence. And this sentence will be based on the good or evil we have done during this life: a sentence of condemnation for those who have committed evil, and a sentence of salvation (heaven) for those who have done good. Just as damnation is the result of sin, so too salvation is the result of goodness. Just as damnation is merited by works, so too with salvation. Both of them are
• born of the same principle: *"prout gessit"*—works. Moreover the Apostle adds: "so that each one may receive what he has won . . . according to his works" (II Cor. 5:10).

The Council of Trent was therefore in full conformity with divine teachings when it declared it a heresy to say with the Protestants "that the just man cannot by his good works . . . really merit increases in grace and eternal life" (Session VI, Canon 32, Denz. 842, and Chap. 16, Denz. 809). The Council does not use the expression *"condign merit"* but an equivalent expression that is quite as clear, *vere mereri.* There is question here of true, real merit in the literal and strict sense of the word.

The Protestants object that to admit man's capacity to merit is to diminish the excellence of Christ's merits. If we must still "pay" for heaven and for grace does that not amount to saying that the Redemption was insufficient to this end, since God cannot demand "payment" twice for the same benefits?

We must have a proper understanding of what Christ merited for us. He *totally* merited first grace for us, which we are unable to merit (for to merit grace we would already have to possess it). He merited all other graces for us *radicaliter* in the sense that He obtained for us the power to merit additional degrees of the supernatural life through our good works performed in the state of grace (not to mention the effects of the sacraments). He merited for us God's promise to reward our works. Thus He merited two essential causes of our merit: God's promise and grace. He merited for us the capacity to rise to greater heights.[8]

---

[8] Bellarmine, one of the great theologians of merit says: *"Meruerunt Christi opera apud Deum, non solum ut salutem conqueremur, sed ut eam*

This same doctrine makes it possible for us to answer another difficulty that may present itself to the intellect, and which is this: Justification and salvation are absolutely "gratuitous." That is the great thesis of St. Paul: *"Gratia Dei salvati estis, non ex operibus—* You have been saved by the grace of God, not by works" (cf. Rom. 3:24-28). Now gratuity disappears if we can merit heaven and increases in grace! [9]

We answer that merit does not destroy the gratuitousness of salvation, for:

1. Merit rests, as we have seen, upon a promise by God that is absolutely gratuitous at least in its cause. Christ merited that God should make us this promise; but who merited the promise on which His own merit is founded? Is it not absolutely gratuitous? Are not the Incarnation and the Redemption gratuitous? When God sent His Son to merit for us, was it not a pure effect of His love for us? Therefore the promise, as a principle of merit, is at least radically gratuitous.

2. The first infusion of sanctifying grace, another condition of merit, is also completely gratuitous. We know that this first grace cannot be merited since we must first have grace in order to merit. It is true, of course, that the supernatural dispositions that prepare the way for first grace exert a certain causality upon it. But this is only congruous merit. Moreover, these supernatural dispositions call for grace only because they are supernaturalized by actual graces or their equivalent. Now, could the subject merit this first supernaturalizing principle, since he had nothing supernatural within himself? Certainly not. Thus, justification and salvation are absolutely gratuitous. St. Gregory the Great says: "Our merits are both from God and from us: from God, through grace that must precede them; from us, through the cooperation of our will" (P.L., 76; *Homil. in Ezech.* 9:2).

According to the expression of St. Augustine cited above,

---

per merita propria consequeremur." Suarez shared this opinion, which is the one expressed by the Council of Trent.

[9] Several Fathers of the Church have asked themselves this problem and have clearly solved it. For example St. Augustine, whose doctrine on this point was given the seal of authority by the Council of Orange (529) against the semi-Pelagians (cf. *D.T.C.*, "Mérite," col. 649 ff.).

"when God rewards our merits, He rewards only His own gifts."

But even though our merits come from God, they also come from us, and thus we have the honor to be the artisans of our supernatural elevation and of our eternal happiness. God's pledge to reward good works by the gift of new degrees of participation in His happiness is an effect of His love for His children. It makes them share even now in His own divine life, thus giving them the means of intensifying at will their supernatural life and dignity and their future beatitude. Since this promise is absolutely free and gratuitous on His part, it is one more manifestation of His paternal mercy, and should arouse affectionate gratitude in our hearts.

This is the first and fundamental condition of merit. Other conditions must be added to it, either with regard to the work or on the part of man.

2. *The conditions of merit with regard to the meritorious work.*

One of the essential foundations of merit is the glory that our works bring to God.

Now the only works that bring glory to God are those that are good, virtuous, and that proceed from free choice. Whence come two conditions required for merit: *moral goodness and freedom.*

a. There is moral goodness when there is conformity to divine law. By his obedience to this law man proclaims the supreme dominion of God over him, His supreme authority, His indefectible wisdom, and His perfect holiness. By preferring God to the forbidden goods that temptation suggests to him, he at least implicitly affirms God's transcendent perfection and thereby glorifies Him.

On the contrary, by sinning he dishonors God, insults and offends Him, and in practice denies His excellence, His authority, and His rights over all creatures. Not only does he fail to give God anything good, but he actually harms Him. Justice demands that he be punished, not rewarded. No one can merit in the state of sin or through sin. Only good acts are meritorious.

It suffices that an act be good formally in its *intention*. It may be evil in itself, but if its author thinks it is good it is meritorious. Conversely an act may be good in itself, but if its author thinks it is wrong and performs it anyway then it is a sin. Everything depends on the will's intention. The servant girl, ignorant of ecclesiastical prohibitions to the contrary, who baptized Mortara the little Jewish boy without necessity or his parents' consent, thought she was working for God. Hence her act (forbidden in itself) was meritorious. During the persecutions there were Christians who voluntarily gave themselves up to the executioners or threw themselves at their lashes, thinking they were thereby proving to Christ Jesus a love stronger than death. Their intention made true martyrs of them, and that is why the Church has canonized them (while condemning their conduct). Only the heart's inward intention matters to God, and it alone glorifies God: "The Lord beholdeth the heart" (I Kgs. 16:7).

To be meritorious, an act must be morally good, that is to say, it must be an act of virtue. But inasmuch as virtues are not equal in perfection, they are not equally meritorious. There exists a hierarchy of merit among various acts of virtue. St. Thomas explains: "Just as the architect is better paid than the ordinary laborer even though the latter works harder, so in the supernatural order those who devote themselves to loftier, nobler, more perfect works, such as bishops and doctors, have a right to a greater reward" *(Quodlib.* VI, a. 11; *Comm. in I Cor.,* c. 11, lesson 11). Virtues are more perfect and therefore more meritorious in the measure that they relate more directly to God, the source of all moral perfection. The more divine their object and motive, the more glory they bring to God.

Highest are the "theological" virtues which relate to God, as their name indicates. Faith makes us accept the truths affirmed by God with regard to matters that concern God more or less directly, and to accept them for a wholly divine motive: the infallible knowledge and veracity of God.

Hope makes us desire the beatifying possession of God and the means to attain to it, relying on His faithfulness to His promises.

Charity makes us love God because of His infinite perfections and His paternal affection. Its object is God in Himself with regard to its motive—God not only in one or another of His attributes (as in the case of faith and hope) but in His whole Being. Charity is the virtue that is most divine and most perfectly related to God. It proclaims not only His infallible knowledge and His absolute veracity, but all His perfections. It is therefore the loftiest and the most meritorious of the virtues,[10] the one that we must exercise oftenest and whose acts it is most important to multiply.

Let us not forget that charity toward neighbor, which we have so many opportunities to practice day after day, is simply a practical application of charity toward God, and that it must therefore be placed side by side with it at the top of the scale of virtues and merit.

We should also remember that there is a means of giving the merit of charity to all the acts of the less perfect virtues. This means is to inoculate the motive of charity into them, to perform them out of love of God, *for God* (as we shall explain latter).

If our acts are to glorify God and therefore be meritorious, they must be acts of a virtue and in conformity with divine law.

b. These acts must also be *free*. The Church has defined this doctrine by declaring the Jansenist proposition heretical according to which exterior liberty *(a coactione)* suffices for merit *(Denz. 1093)*.

Ecclesiasticus declares that heavenly beatitude is given to the just man because "he could have transgressed, and hath not transgressed: and could do evil things, and hath not done them" *(Ecclus. 31:10)*. Now as St. Bernard says, "where there is no freedom there is no merit" (Serm. 81 *in Cant.)*.

The reason for this is easy to discover. To merit, we must give God something that we possess, and perform for His glory an act that is good in itself.

Now an act really belongs to its author only if he is responsible for it, only if he initiates it. To be free, an act must

---

[10] There are other reasons for the excellence of charity in terms of merit which we shall discuss later on.

proceed from its author. When an act is imposed by necessity or constraint, it does not proceed from him but from the
cause that forces it upon him.

Besides, what glory can an act give to God if it is forced?
Would anyone feel honored by the mechanical salute of a
dummy or an animal? Honor is given when an intelligent
and free soul affirms its esteem and respect, with a full realization of why it is doing it and with the freedom not to do it.
That is why creatures inferior to man do not in themselves
glorify God. The words "the heavens show forth the glory of
God" (Ps. 18:2) must be understood to mean that they are a
reflection of God's perfections and that we can make use of
them to glorify Him.[11]

A question arises with regard to freedom. It may be asked
whether the merit of a commanded act is inferior to that of
an action freely accomplished. It is generally believed that
commanded actions are inferior[12] inasmuch as the counsels
rank above the commandments and as there is greater love in
giving something we are not obligated to give. This is a
sophism which has distorted the devotion of inadequately
enlightened souls.

Is it true that obligation diminishes freedom? Yes, it does
diminish moral freedom. In fact it eliminates it in the sense
that once a thing is forbidden we no longer have the right to
do it, and once it is commanded we no longer have the right
to omit or cease doing it.

And yet we retain the physical freedom to perform it or
omit it, and this is the freedom required for merit.

However, it may happen that we accomplish a work be-

---

11 Cf. the *Note* at the end of this chapter, containing an explanation of
the consequences of this truth, p. 368 below.

12 However we should not go as far as the Protestant view, which is erroneous. The idea (dear to Protestants) that only works of pure counsel are
meritorious is so alien to the view of Catholic theology that Suarez points
to it as a *quaedam singularis opinio*. He cites in its favor only the authority
of Dionysius the Carthusian, and he himself discards it with the peremptory
verdict: "*Haec sententia non solum temeraria est, sed etiam, ut ego existimo,
erronea. Nam imprimis contrarius est communis consensus theologorum. . . .*
Far from being an obstacle to merit, on the contrary (all things being equal)
command appears to be a circumstance suited to increase it" (Rivière, *D.T.C.*,
art., "Mérite," col. 776).

cause it is commanded, but that we do it grumblingly, with less zeal, love, care, and spontaneity (inasmuch as our pride finds obedience so repugnant). In such a case, our merit would thereby most certainly be lessened. But if we overcome this aversion of our self-love, repress this morbid need for independence, and force ourselves to perform the duty commanded as perfectly as we can, then we shall have triumphed over greater difficulties and thus earned greater merit.

Moreover if the act in question has become obligatory by reason of a vow, there is added to the merit of the virtue proper to the act itself the merit of the virtue of religion, which is precious. This is one of the advantages of the vows.[13]

Frequently there is a twofold merit in accomplishing an act commanded by legitimate authority: the merit of the virtue proper to the act and the merit of the virtue of obedience which is often indistinguishable from the virtue of charity. To obey is to conform, to immolate one's own will to the will of God as expressed by that of one's superior. Is not obedience a higher form of authentic love? Has not our Master declared that obedience to His will is the mark of love? (Cf. Jn. 14:21; 15:10,14).

Anyone who is concerned with his spiritual welfare must not fly from commanded works but on the contrary seek them out and prefer them to those that are free and that he himself chooses. We should have devotion to things that are commanded us. We should place greater value on the obligatory than on the supererogatory. To be pleasing to God, counsel must be added to the commandments, and perfect them.

It is up to us to make our actions as meritorious as possible by performing them with the greatest possible freedom, deliberateness, knowledge, awareness, and attention. To that end, we must be on our guard, watch (*vigilate*), act with de-

---

[13] It is therefore an excellent thing to make vows. But just as there is double merit in the action performed "under vow," so there is a double sin in omitting it. Therefore we must not make vows lightly, without the moral certitude that we shall be faithful to them.

liberation, avoid routine and distraction, which, even though
they do not completely destroy the freedom of our acts, lessen
their freedom and by that very fact diminish the glory they
give to God and the reward they merit. Our purpose should
be to make our acts as human, deliberate, and conscious as
possible, and to this end, live a recollected interior life. We
must want our acts and not merely resign ourselves or submit
to them; accomplish them with conviction, with zeal and a
determined heart, and not only out of routine or impulse,
or through constraint, unwillingly or reluctantly, because we
cannot do otherwise. For all these things are marks of very
reduced volition.[14]

3. *The conditions of merit with respect to man*

Moral goodness and freedom would be required even for
natural merit. Since we are dealing here with supernatural
merit, the glory given to God and the actions that give Him
this glory must be *supernatural in their principle and in their
end*. Merit requires that the subject be supernaturalized by
sanctifying grace and that the motive, the intention, be also
supernatural. But first of all the subject must be in the "wayfaring" state. These are the three conditions required of man.

a. *To merit, man must be in the "wayfaring" state*. There
are two parts to this proposition. One is positive: we can continue to merit until death (this has been established in the
preceding thesis when we proved the authenticity of the
divine promise). The second is negative: it is impossible to
merit after death.

This second truth needs convincing proof in view of the
widespread errors of theosophy and spiritism which are
warmed-over versions of ancient philosophic phantasies concerning successive reincarnations by which all souls can
ultimately be rehabilitated and attain to eternal happiness.

It is almost a tautology to say that man can merit only if
he is in the wayfaring state, for the *status viae* is precisely
the state during which we freely determine our eternal fate
by our merits. The *status viae* is equivalent to the state in

---

14 Cf. the *Note* at the end of this chapter, p. 270 below.

which it is possible for man to merit. We must prove that this wayfaring state, or state of merit, ends with death.[15]

Can this be proved by reason alone, on the basis of the nature of things? That would seem a difficult task. In his *Summa contra Gentiles*,[16] St. Thomas offers reasons that are compelling as reasons of fittingness, but do not seem to have the precision of proofs in the strict sense. Many theologians admit this.

The ultimate reason why merit ends with death is at least that God has decreed this for motives that are supremely wise but not necessarily compelling upon the will, and that do not render a different order of things absolutely impossible. Hence we must establish the *fact* of this divine decree through Revelation, for this is our only means of knowing it.

Writing to the Romans, St. Paul compares the present life to night, and the next life to day: "The night is far advanced; the day is at hand" (Rom. 13:12). Indeed, life is short for every man. "It is now the hour for us to rise from sleep, because now our salvation is nearer than when we came to believe. . . . Let us therefore lay aside the works of darkness, and put on the armor of light" (Rom. 13:11-12). As a stimulant to good works, the Apostle reminds his audience that eternity is approaching. This presupposes that in the next life goodness will not gain merit.

In the Epistle to the Galatians he is more explicit: "And in doing good let us not grow tired; for in due time we shall reap if we do not relax. Therefore, while we have time, let us do good to all men" (Gal. 6:9-10). He says "we shall reap," that is to say, we shall reap the fruit of our acts.

Why hurry if there is an eternity in which to do good? Why "without relaxing," why "while we have time"? Is it not because we shall no longer have time after death? It would be impossible to put it more clearly.

We find the same affirmation in St. Paul's Second Epistle

---

[15] Those who enjoy the beatific vision are no longer in the wayfaring state, but have reached the term and possess their end. They can no longer merit. That is one of the reasons why our Lord, whose soul saw God, could not merit new degrees of grace and glory for Himself.

[16] Book IV, Chapters 93, 94, and 95.

to the Corinthians: "For all of us must be made manifest before the tribunal of Christ, so that each one may receive what he has won through the body, according to his works, whether good or evil" (II Cor. 5:10). This judgment will settle the fate of each one according to his works, whether good or evil. It is a question of justice, and hence of merit. But on what shall we be judged? On works performed before death, before the separation of the soul from the body: "Each one [will] receive what he has won through the body."

Indeed, the Treatise on the Last Ends presents the proof that immediately after death each man will be subjected to a final judgment which will irrevocably fix the fate of his soul with regard to its nature and its degree. But would this judgment be definitive and would it have any reason for being if it were possible to merit afterwards? St. Basil asks: "Tell me, when can we merit a reward? Is it before or after death? What can a dead man do? To which of his works can retribution be due?" (Homily 7, P.G. Vol. 31, p. 301).

That is the measure of the worth of the present life and of the instants that go to make it up. This life is given to us that we may fashion our eternity out of it. Whether we will or not, that is what our life is for. Each of its moments is the seed of something eternal. It slips away, quickly as a cloud, driven by the wind into the sky of our life; but at the same time, it remains with us. It flows by and it stays behind. Something of this moment vanishes like smoke: its physical entity. And yet something subsists forever: its moral worth, its merit or lack of merit. It does not disappear entirely. It has endless repercussions, an echo that continues indefinitely.

Each moment possesses a talent that must bear fruit for heaven, a grace to be used to advantage. We shall be called to account for each one of those moments. Woe to those who let them lie fallow or waste them for the sake of vanity or for evil purposes! We must thank God for each of these moments, since through each one we can increase our eternal happiness. Yes, life is precious; it is good.[17] Longevity is, in itself, a gift of God. But since no one knows if he will receive

---

[17] As Oblé Laprune has demonstrated in *Le prix de la vie*.

this gift or if the end of his life is approaching, he cannot count on hypothetical years in the future to work at increasing his merits. Everyone should strive to gain merits as if the end of the great day were about to toll: that is a matter of elementary prudence.

b. In order to merit, a man must be in the wayfaring state; and he must also be *in the state of grace*. That is easily understood. The man in the state of mortal sin deserves hell (Revelation is categorical on this point, and we must interpret texts by one another). How can he also deserve heaven and the means to attain it? How can he at one and the same time merit to be admitted to glory and to be excluded from it? To possess God and to be separated from Him? As long as he remains enslaved to his sin (and we assume that such is his state), how can he be working for God? (If he is working for God, this intention at least implicitly involves a return of his will toward God, a retraction of his sin, an act of loyalty and love that would justify him.) How can his works be orientated toward God as to their last end if he clings to sin? Hence how can they be meritorious, inasmuch as God rewards only acts performed for Him and makes a return only if we give Him something?

Our Lord's words *"Et Pater tuus . . . . reddet tibi*—and thy Father . . . will reward thee" (Mt. 6:6) do not apply to sinners. God has nothing to reward them for, having received nothing from them. Moreover, He rewards only those whose Father He has become through grace: *"Pater tuus."* This promise (*reddet tibi*) is meant only for the sons of God.

We can readily understand it. A person who needs nothing can be pleased only by gifts that come from friendly hearts and that are marks of sincere affection, loyalty, and submission. What could gifts mean if they came from an enemy known to harbor insulting sentiments? The Lord cannot accept or receive anything from wills that continue to reject Him as their last end, to prefer puny finite goods to Him. And therefore He cannot give them anything in return. He has promised to reward only the works of His children, of those who, by becoming partakers of His nature have become brothers of "the Son in whom He is well pleased," closely incorporated into the Son. "As the branch cannot bear fruit of itself unless it remain on the vine, so neither can you unless you abide in Me" (Jn. 15:4). To "bear fruit" is to perform meritorious acts that are "profitable" to their author. To "abide in Christ" is to receive the supernatural sap, grace. Without grace there can be no fruit, no merit. "Without Me [apart from Me, without My grace] you can do nothing" (Jn. 15:5). That is, we can do nothing useful and profitable from the spiritual point of view: we would be like branches cut off from the trunk, destined to dry up and die, to be sterile and suffer eternal fire.

If grace is necessary simply to have a right to eternal life, it is still more necessary as a means of attaining this life as a glorious reward won by our own labors and due us in justice. If in order to be heirs we must be sons (born of God through grace) as St. Paul teaches (Rom. 8:17; Gal. 4:7), it is even more important that we be sons to possess the heritage as something we have earned.

The same Apostle lays special stress on this necessity in I Cor., Chapter 13. To deter his Christians from vain quarrels concerning charisms or extraordinary gifts, he reminds them that only one thing matters, only one treasure should be the object of all their desires: sanctifying grace. And he designates this treasure by the word "charity" because grace is inseparable from that virtue. "If I distribute all my goods to feed the poor, and if I deliver my body to be burned, yet do not have charity, it profits me nothing [for salvation]" (I. Cor. 13:3), for it is not meritorious. Three times in succession, using solemn words of increasing power, he affirms that everything is useless without grace, even the finest and most heroic actions.

This is also the teaching of the Church.[18]

The Council of Trent declares: "We are said to be justified gratuitously, because none of those things that precede justification, whether faith or works, merits the grace of justification" (Session VI, Chapter 8). Hence, it is impossible to merit *de condigno* before justification and without it. "To those who work well unto the end and trust in God, eternal life

---

18 Cf. the *Note* at the end of this chapter containing the propositions of Baius concerning this subject, condemned by Pius V, p. 270 below.

is to be offered, both as a grace mercifully promised to the sons of God through Christ Jesus, and as a reward promised by God Himself, to be faithfully given to their good works and merits" (Session VI, Chapter 16). We note that this reward is to be granted only to "the sons of God," to those referred to at the beginning of Chapter 16: "to men justified —*justificatis hominibus*," that is to say, to the just.[19]

But why does not actual grace suffice for merit? Why is habitual grace necessary? It is necessary for at least two reasons:

First, because we can have a right to a reward only if we give something that is ours in the strict sense of ownership. If the supernatural dignity of the meritorious act comes only from actual, transitory grace, the subject does not possess the principle of this act or at least he possesses it less completely. It comes almost directly from God. On the other hand, when he possesses sanctifying grace which is in him and belongs to him, he possesses the source of his act. He can therefore make use of it without any new intervention from God; he can accomplish supernatural acts and offer God a glory that comes wholly from himself (not from his nature). The supernatural is *connatural* to him. Thus, by this grace, the honor he gives to God belongs more completely to him.

Moreover, the strict merit in question here presupposes a certain equality in value between the work and its payment, a certain proportion between what is given and what is received. For if we receive something that is superior to what we give, if the wages exceed the value of the labor, this salary is no longer owed in justice, but is a free and gratuitous gift inspired by mercy: it is not due, it is given. Now, since the reward promised for good works is of the divine order (participation in the very nature and happiness of God), the glory that these works give Him must be of the same order,

---

[19] Canon 32 declares it to be heretical to say that the just man does not truly merit through his good works. But to define that the just man merits is not to define expressly that only the just man merits. We can reach this conclusion only by interpreting this definition (as we must) by the Chapters, which are commentaries on the Canons and yet not definitions.

The conclusion that only the just merit must be reached by reasoning from the Council's definition; it is therefore only theologically certain.

offered by divinized beings who partake of the nature of God.

The homage, honor, and glory that the just man gives to God are not the homage, honor and glory of an ordinary man, of a simple creature. They are the homage, honor, and glory of a man who has been raised to a supernatural dignity, of a divinized man, of a son of God. They come from a member of the Father's family, who reproduces His perfections, shares in His nature, enjoys His close friendship, and is the object of His fatherly affection and solicitude. They come from a being destined to share His own happiness and to be united to Him in an ineffable manner. Since honor given is measured by the dignity of the person who gives it, the honor of the just man is divine and therefore equal to the reward received. The labor is equivalent in value to the wages received for it. There is a proportion between what is received and what is given. It follows that there can be *condign* merit in the strict sense.

And since these two conditions are less perfectly fulfilled by actual grace, the merit of the act inspired only by actual grace is less rigorous. It is merit of mere fittingness, and not condign merit in justice. There is condign merit only through sanctifying grace.

It is this supernatural dignity of the person that St. Thomas appeals to in order to establish the proportion between what is received by merit and what is given: "And the worth of the [meritorious] work depends on the dignity of grace, whereby a man, being made a partaker of the Divine Nature, is adopted as a son of God, to whom the inheritance is due by right of adoption, according to Rom. 8:17: 'If sons, heirs also' " (Ia IIae, q. 114, a. 3, c.).

Several consequences flow from the necessity of grace for merit:

1. Grace is not simply a condition for merit; it is also a *cause* of merit in the strict sense. It may even be said that grace is the principal cause of merit. The supernatural value of the glory a human act can give to God stems from grace above all, and consequently it is grace that determines the proportion between merit and the reward received.

In the purely natural order, moral goodness, freedom, the

divine promise, and even purity of intention would have been required for natural merit. The cause that is certainly proper to supernatural merit and that specifies it is grace (together with the supernatural motive).

2. Grace therefore has the greatest possible influence on the value of our works, and exerts profound repercussions on it. Grace is even the chief increaser of the value of our works. The degree and the level of grace correspond exactly with the degree and level of the value of our good works. To quote Father Terrien: "The more perfect sanctifying grace is, the greater the merit of the works and the increase in grace that this merit brings with it. . . . That is the meaning we must see in the following words of the Angelic Doctor: 'The greater the grace that informs an act, the more meritorious is this act.' " (op. cit., Vol. II, Chapter 7).

Thus when we increase grace within our souls, we are proportionately increasing the merit of all our subsequent good works: we are increasing the common and divine multiplier of our activity.

3. Fortunate, therefore, are those who can receive many sacraments, and especially the sacrament that is the easiest and most fruitful source of divine life: the Holy Eucharist! Each Communion brings a considerable increase in grace, in our dignity as sons of God, and hence in the merit of our works. And the supernatural coefficient of our works being thus raised to a higher level, we earn a greater reward. Because in receiving Holy Communion this morning we have raised the level of our grace, the good works we perform today bring God more glory and give us a more intense eternal life than if we had done them yesterday. These works will thus gain more merit than other works, perhaps better in themselves, that we performed earlier with less grace.

Do those Christians who could, with a little effort, receive the Bread of life and do not, realize what they are losing for eternity? What laborious sacrifices it would take to recoup the merits they could so easily have earned through Holy Communion! (Cf. Le Pain Vivant, by the present author.)

4. Every good act of the just man, because it earns an increase in sanctifying grace, makes the next one more

meritorious in a wonderful progression. The man who knows how to take the fullest advantage of the sacraments and to do good works can apply to himself literally the Master's words: "For to everyone who has shall be given, and he shall have abundance" (Mt. 25:29). The more he has, the more he obtains. The more we merit, the more we can merit; the more grace we have, the more grace we can receive.

Since we have so many easy means of increasing the supernatural life within us, it requires culpable sloth and indifference to fail to make this precious talent bear fruit.

The influence of grace upon merit should offer us a powerful motive for doing everything possible to increase grace within us. And if there seems to be too much self-interest in the concern for increasing our merits, let us remember that the measure of our grace is also the measure of the honor we give to God through our works, and that we consequently give more glory to our Father in proportion to our grace. This reason should hold first place in our hearts.

5. What we have just said regarding the role of grace in gaining merit enables us to understand the true foundation of merit. The condignity of merit is not purely extrinsic and arbitrary, resulting from God's promise to reward our good works, as Scotus thought.

Nor does this condignity stem soley from the intrinsic value of our good works, as Vasquez and Bellarmine taught. It comes both from God's promise and from the value of our works. It rests on a twofold foundation.

When our good works are performed in the state of grace and are accompanied by the other conditions for gaining merit, they are not disproportionate to their reward. Because of the supernatural and quasi-divine dignity of their authors, the glory they give to God is in some measure worth what they merit. Our good works are meritorious: their merit is *condign*. Just as the harvest is born of the seed, so the right to supernatural reward is born of the work itself, according to the comparison St. Paul makes. It is the wages of our labor. It is a reward, a remuneration.

But we have said that all glory is due to God, the supreme owner and final end of all things, and that supernatural dignity, which is the principal foundation of merit, is a gratuitous gift of God. Hence our works would have no claims upon Him if He had not previously pledged Himself to reward them. God's promise is necessary. It is one of the foundations of merit. Grace is the other.[20]

All the sinner's actions are not necessarily evil, and Protestants are in error when they claim they are.[21] The sinner can accomplish good works which God may take into account to help him to be converted and to obtain justification. This is particularly true of acts of faith, hope, or contrition, inspired by a supernatural motive. But even if these acts are supernaturalized by actual grace, which is a transitory intervention by God, they remain acts not of a son of the heavenly Father and of a divinized person, but of an agent reduced to the resources of his human nature, to his state of servitude. They are the acts of a man who has fallen from the supernatural order, who has been dethroned from his dignity as a son of God. Consequently they are acts that can give God only human glory, without proportion to an eternal reward, without adequate relation to a supernatural end, and without any direct causal effect upon the attainment of this end.

Thus all the good actions of the man in the state of sin, his efforts, the good things he does and the hardships and sufferings he endures, his sacrifices, his difficult and fatiguing labors to earn his living and that of his family, to fulfill the obligations of his state of life and his duties to his neighbor, his family, or his country—all are lost, lost for eternity. And yet if he were in the state of grace these acts could win him a rich harvest of merits and a magnificent reward. It is true, on the other hand, that psychologically these good works can exercise a salutary effect on his soul, to prepare his conversion and to obtain from heaven the helps necessary for his return to grace.

But the fact remains that God has not promised the sinner any reward, and we know why there can be no question of

---

[20] Cf. the *Note* at the end of the chapter, on the need of actual grace for gaining merit, p. 271 below.

[21] The Church condemned this opinion: Council of Trent, Session VI, Can. 7, Denz. 817.

strict merit in the sinner's case. Therefore if death strikes
the sinner in this state, none of his works or labors can be
remunerated. And if he is given the opportunity to return
to justification, his works and labors will not have merited
this return (with any condign merit). These works will remain eternally unrewarded. They are dead because they were
performed in the state of sin. Unless the branches are united
to the divine vine, they can bear no divine fruit.

Worse still is the fact that in the state of sin all merits
previously acquired in the state of grace are *mortified* together with grace. By condemning the sinner to hell, sin
destroys all his rights to heaven. Like a hurricane that passes
over the countryside, annihilating crops and vines, the
farmers' hope and reward, sin ravages the gains of the past,
it sterilizes the present and jeopardizes the future.

c. To be meritorious every act must be supernatural in its
principle, and come from a supernatural efficient cause or
one supernaturalized by grace and the infused virtues. For
the effect cannot be superior to its cause. There can be no
doubt on this point.

But that does not suffice. A meritorious act must also be
supernatural in its *motive* or *formal object.*

A motive is whatever moves the will to produce an act; it
is the good that attracts and inspires the will, toward which
the will tends, and that the will seeks to obtain either by its
own action or by commanding powers subject to it to act.

Sometimes the motive may be an evil to be avoided. But
since evil is only the privation of a good, to want to avoid
evil is to want to hold fast to the good of which evil is the
absence. Every motive, even when apparently negative, refers
to a good rightly or wrongly presented as a good by the intellect.

If the good is of the natural order, the motive and the act
of the will that strive to attain it are natural. If the good in
question is of the supernatural order, the act of the will is
supernatural in its motive; and this presupposes that this act
is also supernatural with respect to its efficient cause. We
therefore act for a supernatural motive when we seek to at-

tain a supernatural good either directly or by avoiding the
evil that would consist in its loss or absence.

What are the supernatural goods? The first supernatural
good is God, the object of the beatific vision; and then come
all the means that can lead to God and their effects. Supernatural goods, therefore, are: either God Himself considered
as our Father whom we shall some day possess; and the glory,
the knowledge, and the love of Him by His creatures. Or
they are the supernatural goods of man, the possession and
vision of God, that is our supernatural end, and the means
to attain it.

We act for a supernatural motive and to attain a supernatural good when we act to acquire or increase grace and
its precious effects (the virtues and the gifts), to obtain more
abundant actual graces, to accumulate new merits and degrees of glory, to be more perfect objects of God's love and
of His supernatural protection, and even to obtain temporal
goods with a view to using them for our salvation—i.e. to
avoid hell and the privation of the vision of God.

The motive of pure charity that makes us seek God as our
good for His own sake is evidently not the only supernatural
motive. Imperfect love, the motive inspired by the other
virtues, is also supernatural.

Human reason left to its own resources could know
nothing of these supernatural goods of God and man. Since
they are supernatural, reason can know them only through
Revelation. That is why the supernatural motive is often
defined as "the motive proposed by faith" (Marc, *Institutions
morales*, No. 1668), or "the motive provided to us by faith"
as certain catechisms put it.

Are we to conclude that a meritorious act demands a
supernatural motive, superior to that of the corresponding
natural virtues? For example, to be meritorious is it sufficient
for an act of religion to be inspired by justice that commands
us to give God the homage that is His due as the infinitely
perfect Being, the Creator and Master of all things? Or must
this act also be inspired by a sentiment of filial piety toward
God, who has deigned to adopt us as His sons through grace
and become our Father? To be meritorious, does it suffice

that an act of temperance have as its motive the duty indicated by reason to keep the senses under the control of the
soul? Or must this act also stem from the desire to resemble
our Lord? In a word, to be meritorious do the virtues need
to judge the righteousness of their acts insofar as they conform not only with our reasonable animal nature but also
with our supernature as sons of God?

There is some controversy on this point, but the Thomist
opinion, which is the affirmative, seems more probable.[22]

Regardless of the opinion we adopt, we must answer still
another question: *To be meritorious, must an act be moti-
vated by charity?* Does merit require the intervention of
love? Must a motive of charity always inspire meritorious
acts in some way?

A number of Scriptural texts can be pointed to that favor
respectively the affirmative or the negative answer to this
question.

a. On the one hand, it seems incontestable that Scripture
formally affirms the necessity of charity for merit. St. Paul
says that heaven is reserved for those who love God: "Eye has
not seen . . . what things God has prepared for those who love
Him" (I Cor. 2:9). And to paraphrase I Cor. 13:1-3: If I
have not charity, all the works I have just mentioned are
useless for salvation. Even faith, to which Paul attributes
so much efficacy, produces grace only when "it works through
charity" (Gal. 5:6).

According to St. James, God has promised the crown of
life only to those who love Him (Jas. 1:12).

And these Apostles are but the faithful echoes of the
Master.

To whom has He promised a reward from the Father? To
those who have left all things for His name, or offered hospitality to His envoys, or given alms—because of Him and
for His sake. Does this not amount to saying that merit requires the motive of pure charity?

The very nature of merit demands it. No one has a right
to a reward from another unless he has rendered him some

---

[22] Cf. the *Note* at the end of this chapter, setting forth these various opinions,
p. 271 below.

service. No one has a right to a salary unless he has worked for it. Whoever furnishes nothing can expect nothing in return. We can therefore merit something of God only if we have worked for Him, for His glory, for His good—that is to say, only if we have worked out of charity.

This is no doubt the consideration that led a few theologians such as Bannez to allow only accidental merit to acts of the other virtues, even those that are "commanded" by charity.

b. But on the other hand it seems no less certain that in order to stimulate us to virtue and inspire us to good works, our Lord appeals to our supernatural interest by promising us a reward. In the eight Beatitudes, it is with a view of heaven's happiness as a reward that He invites us to poverty, to endure trials and persecutions: "Blessed are the poor in spirit, for theirs is the kingdom of heaven. . . ." (Mt. 5:3-10). If He afterwards advises us not to do our good works to be seen by men, it is so that we may be rewarded by our Father in heaven: "And thy Father, who sees in secret, will reward thee" (Mt. 6:4,6).

In other passages He urges His hearers to believe in His word out of fear of hell and hope of eternal life. "He who believes and is baptized shall be saved, but he who does not believe shall be condemned" (Mk. 16:16).

That is also St. Paul's way: "Whatever you do, work at it from the heart . . . knowing that from the Lord you will receive the inheritance as your reward" (Col. 3:23). God will give to each according to his works; and He will give eternal life to those who seek immortality by persevering in goodness. Paul even stirred himself to patience in tribulations and to self-sacrifice in his apostolate by the thought of his reward.

Now is it probable that the Holy Spirit would urge us to goodness by using this motive of supernatural self-interest, if it were really inadequate? Would not these promises be vain and false, if the practice of virtue, to which we are urged by the lure of eternal happiness, did not in fact give us a right to this happiness?

And why should merit demand a more perfect motive

than does the receiving of grace through a sacrament? In Communion, for example, the interested love of a supernatural good is a sufficient intention.

Beyond all doubt reward is promised not only for acts of pure charity, but also for acts of all the virtues, for obeying the Commandments, for all good works, for courage in trials and persecution, for poverty, meekness, purity of heart, mercy, and alms. To be convinced of this, we need only reread the Beatitudes.

These arguments, and others that we could add, have led a few theologians (Suarez, Pesch) to affirm that the acts of all the infused virtues by the just man are meritorious in themselves, without the direct influence of charity. Since these virtues are supernatural, their specific motive must also be supernatural. And if their motive is supernatural it necessarily relates to the supernatural end that it implies more or less directly. Whoever wills this end, by that very fact wills in a more or less implicit way both the end and the means. Whoever seeks this good, seeks God and glorifies Him.

The above-mentioned texts concerning the necessity of charity are said to refer to habitual charity inasmuch as it is inseparable from grace.

But sound as these reasons are, the reasons that call for the intervention of charity in the gaining of merit retain their value.

What, then, are we to do? We cannot assume contradictions in Scripture. It is not possible that each of these two extreme opinions expressed in Scripture tells the whole truth. Does not the truth lie between the two, in the affirmative portion of each view?

c. This is the opinion of the Thomistic School. The Thomists take from the first view the necessity of charity for merit; but they agree with the second that granted this influence of charity, the acts of the other virtues have their own special merit. Contrary to Bannez, they do not teach that merit is the privilege of charity alone. And contrary to Suarez, they do not believe that the other virtues can merit without the influence of charity. Only those acts are meri-

torious that are "elicited" by charity, or at least "commanded" or accomplished by charity. The motive of charity
is not the only supernatural one. Other motives can also be
supernatural and become principles of merit, but on condition that they are joined to the motive of charity and as it
were fecundated by it. St. Francis de Sales would say that
these motives are like fruits that are inedible by themselves
but which, when preserved in sugar, make a succulent des-
sert. Thus, merit comes in the first place from charity, and
can come secondarily from some other virtue.

But it is not necessary that this orientation by charity be
explicitly renewed for each action. It can be done in advance
and in another act that contains the subsequent action. It
suffices that the motive of charity be *implicit* and *virtual*.

Implicitly, this orientation is actualized by every act of
charity.

To love God with a filial love, for His own sake, disin-
terestedly, is to will His good. For love and benevolence are
synonymous. It is to will His glory, to will to procure it by
our every act, by our whole life, by every means that God
wants us to use, that is, by our whole being. For He created
all things with this end in mind, and He cannot not want
to see it attained.

To love God with a love of charity, that is, with a disinterested love, is to place Him first in our intentions, even
before ourselves. It is to prefer Him to ourselves, to give
ourselves to Him with all our actions. Hence it is to direct
all our present and future actions toward Him as a single
whole.

This total donation, the effect of our orientation by charity, subsists as long as a mortal sin, the opposite of love, has
not made us retract it. When a person has once given himself to God in this way, all his subsequent good acts, even
without his knowing it, are progressively taken up and drawn
toward God by this movement of love of which St. Thomas
speaks (IIa IIae, q. 23, a. 8). That is the virtual intention of
charity.

By a phenomenon analogous to terrestrial magnetism,
charity directs all acts of virtue toward God.

The two last-mentioned opinions thus admit that *all* the good acts of the just man possess an orientation sufficient for gaining merit. There is this divergence, however, in favor of St. Thomas, who holds that all these acts would have two merits: one, the principal merit, coming from the more or less virtual orientation of charity; the other, secondary merit, coming from the virtue to which the act belongs. According to Suarez, on the other hand, good acts would possess this last-named merit only when charity does not intervene to command them; and this intervention would not take place by the very fact of justification. Anyone who wanted to join the merit of charity to the works of his other virtues would have to be sure to do it by an explicit act.

This is a wise precaution to take to make sure we gain this benefit. For while St. Thomas' opinion is the more probable, the other view is not without some plausibility. And it is better to be "tutiorists" [23] if we are concerned about our spiritual interests.

Besides, both views teach that charity can "command" the acts of the other virtues and add its own much more perfect merit to theirs.

The Superiority of Charity. There are at least two reasons for this superiority.[24]

To have a right to remuneration from God, we must give Him something. Our right is all the more rigorous and fruitful in the measure that the donation is more perfect, more total, and that we are seeking His good and His glory: that is to say, in the measure that our motive is more disinterested and our love purer. It is clear that if, instead of working for God, we work for ourselves, even out of spiritual self-interest, we are giving to ourselves rather than to God. We therefore merit less from Him. Now, we really seek God's glory, we act perfectly for Him only through charity. Only charity makes a gift complete and assures the maximum of merit. God in His admirable wisdom has so arranged things that the surest way to work for our own good is to work for

---

[23] That is to say, to follow the surest point of view.
[24] In Chapter 10 above, we indicated a third reason for its superiority.

His good, the best way of loving ourselves is to love Him. Thus we glorify ourselves when we glorify Him.

A second reason stems from the influence of charity upon the intensity of another factor in the gaining of merit, i.e., voluntariness. Charity facilitates and considerably increases voluntariness. What a powerful help charity is when it impels the will toward the object of the virtues and adds its strength to the attraction of this object. Then we are able to do a good work both through love of God and through love of the virtue's own beauty. And how, in consequence, the will's zeal, and hence the intensity of our merit, increase!

St. Thomas says: "It is manifest that what we do out of love we do most willingly. Hence, even inasmuch as merit depends on voluntariness, merit is chiefly attributed to charity" (Ia IIae, q. 114, a. 4).

Let us note besides that by increasing voluntariness charity increases the pleasure of the action (we take pleasure in doing things we love), and consequently impels us to perform more and greater actions with greater zeal, care, perfection, and hence with more merit.

An objection. It may be objected that on the contrary charity, by reducing the difficulty of an act, also lessens merit, as do acquired virtues or habits that make it easier for us to do good. Did not St. Paul say: "Each will receive his own reward according to his labor" (I Cor. 3:8)? And is it not commonly believed that a work is more meritorious in proportion to its difficulty, and less meritorious the easier it is, as Kant taught?

The answer is "No." Merit is not necessarily increased by the difficulty of an act, or decreased by the fact that it is easy. It all depends on the cause of the difficulty or ease, that is, whether we are responsible for it or not. Facility in doing a good work may be voluntary and hence meritorious in its principle, *in causa;* it may come not from nature but from virtue. Such for instance is the facility that the saints have acquired by dint of exercise, struggle, and sacrifice, in overcoming temptation, mastering themselves, and giving themselves. Such is the facility that is the effect of a burning love for God, and that fulfills St. Augustine's words: *"Ubi amatur, non laboratur*—When we love, nothing is hard for us." Such likewise is the facility that results from the voluntary and vigilant flight from the occasions and sources of difficulty in the practice of the virtues, or that comes from an abundance of supernatural helps. Now facility of this sort does not diminish merit, but may on the contrary increase it by making it possible for us to accomplish more difficult works with greater perfection.

Father Terrien says: "Let those souls rejoice who have carried the cross of the Lord Jesus so long that their labors, their penances, and their renouncements have almost become pleasant. The oil that soothes is the oil of love. And this very sweetness is the sign and the cause of a more abundant merit, of a more fruitful penance" (*op. cit.*, Ch. 7).

Likewise, voluntary difficulty does not increase merit. Anyone who exposes himself to the allurements of evil and awakens the sleeping beast within him, who does not take the means (prayers, sacraments, good works) to obtain the graces he needs, who remains with full consent in a state of languishing indifference and has not contracted the habit of conquering his passions, cannot claim to greater merit because of his difficulties. He himself is responsible for them.

But a person may not be responsible for his difficulties. They may stem from a physical state, temperamental or environmental conditions forced upon him by heredity or circumstances. They may result from the fact that the act involved is in itself and objectively speaking more arduous than others (thus martyrdom is unquestionably more difficult than a simple act of love). In such a case, merit would be greater, just as it would be lessened if the act in question were naturally easy.

The fact of the matter is this: granted a person has a certain facility, if he chooses the harder of two acts and performs it as perfectly as he would have performed the other, he will certainly have more merit.

We must meet the objection that merit is measured by the difficulty of the work, with this answer: The objection is valid if the difficulty lies in the work itself,[25] or in the man himself, providing there is no initial responsibility on his part. However it does not hold if his difficulty in performing the work is his own fault. Effort can be the source of virtue, but it is not always the sure sign of it. For example, if it is very hard for you to be patient and meek by reason of your violent and irascible nature, or because your nerves are over-excited as the result of illness, your charity in striving for patience and meekness will be greater before God than if you were endowed with excellent health or with a happy disposition.

If despite your natural crabbedness or your tired nerves, you have succeeded by dint of continued vigilance and persevering efforts to "possess your soul in patience" (Lk. 21:19) and to maintain a serene front, this is authentic virtue and your ease in being meek increases your merits. This is the ideal toward which we must strive with regard to all the virtues: to attain a pleasant facility that makes the practice of virtue agreeable and prompt and that removes all the obstacles to the soul's flight toward goodness.[26]

It is fitting to add that the effort involved in performing a work is not the only or even the principal cause of the degree of merit earned. Merit depends also and above all on the degree: 1) of sanctifying grace; 2) of charity (or purity of intention); and 3) of freedom, attention, and care, on the part of the subject who is acting.

We can thereby understand why the exercise of the virtues by the Blessed Virgin Mary possessed considerable merit, even though the absence of concupiscence made the practice of virtue very easy for her. She brought to her acts of virtue not only a plenitude of grace (*Gratia plena*), but also a superlative degree of love and diligence.

---

[25] "A work can be toilsome and difficult in two ways: first, from the greatness of the work, and thus the greatness of the work pertains to the increase of merit; and thus charity does not lessen the toil—rather, it makes us undertake the greatest toils. . . . Secondly, from the defect of the operator; for what is not done with a ready will is hard and difficult to all of us, and this toil lessens merit and is removed by charity" (Ia IIae, q. 114, a. 5, ad 2).

[26] Cf. the *Note* at the end of this chapter containing a passage of Bishop Vincent on St. Francis de Sales' doctrine on this question, p. 273 below.

No, there is no need to fear that virtue, the habit of doing good, and love of God will diminish the worth of our good works by making them easy. On the contrary, they make possible a considerable increase in merit, and this is especially true of intense love of God.

If we can perform difficult works, heroic acts, that is splendid. We should answer love's impulsion to do these things. But what we must seek after is not so much the difficulty of the work as the perfection of the motive, the intensity of the charity that inspires these works, and care in their execution. It is just as fruitful if not more so to do ordinary actions with a great love of God than to do extraordinary works from a less perfect motive.

The consequence is that small deeds done with great charity are worth more than great deeds done with little charity. It is not within the power of all to perform great works, but great love is within the capacity of everyone. The lowliest works, the most commonplace occupations, the most unpalatable tasks in the eyes of the world can, if done with great love, bring great glory to God and a magnificent reward to their author. That is why God has not demanded great things of everyone, but has commanded that every man love Him with all his heart and all his strength. And that is why, by reason of the love and grace that inform their lives, the last (the lowliest) of this earth may be the first in heaven.[27]

---

[27] St. Francis de Sales explains: "Now I say, Theotime, that a very small virtue may well have more value in a soul in which sacred love rules than even martyrdom in a soul whose love is dormant, feeble, and slow. Thus the smallest virtues of our Lady, St. John, and other great saints were of greater value before God than the loftiest virtues of several other lesser saints, just as many little transports of love on the part of the seraphim are more fiery than the loftiest transports of the angels in the lowest order; and as the song of apprentice nightingales is incomparably more beautiful than the song of the best-trained goldfinches. . . .

"Thus, Theotime, the little absurdities, self-abasements, and humiliations in which the great saints took such great pleasure as means of hiding themselves and sheltering their hearts from vainglory were more pleasing to God than the great or illustrious accomplishments of certain others performed with little charity and devotion, simply because the saints' acts were performed with a high degree of the art and the fire of heavenly love" (Oeuvres, V, 251, 152).

It is important, therefore, particularly with regard to acts commanded by nature (eating, drinking, recreation, rest, satisfying an inclination) that we watch over our intentions and maintain a firm mastery of our hearts, lest pride or some other purely natural motive turn our works away from God. To this end, we must often renew the oblation of our works in express or equivalent terms by acts of love. The Church helps us in this by asking us to repeat many *Glorias* like a sanctifying refrain. Our Lord has given us an inkling of this in the first part of the prayer that He taught us, the *Our Father*. And He has given us the example of His own life, consecrated to the glory of His Father. "For You, my God, for Your glory!" May these easy words rise often from our hearts to our lips, especially in our principal actions, so as to imbue them with as much charity and merit as possible.

Let us keep the treasure of our good works hidden for the sake of charity. Anyone who exposes this treasure to the public eye will soon have it stolen from him, according to St. Gregory (Homil. II).[28]

*   *   *

Note on the necessity of freedom for gaining merit (see p. 245 above):

From the fact that freedom is necessary in order to merit, it does not follow that saints confirmed in grace during their earthly life are incapable of meriting. They enjoy a *de facto* confirmation in grace, or impeccability, which the theologians call *impeccantia:* a preservation from sin as a result of efficacious graces that do not eliminate freedom or the absolute possibility of sinning or of gaining merit. They can sin, but they never sin in fact because God preserves them from it. Such was the case of the Blessed Virgin Mary.

---

[28] "Lay up for yourselves treasures in heaven" (Mt. 6:20). Bourdaloue asks: "And out of what shall we make up this treasure, Lord?" And he answers: "Out of a thousand things you have at hand, and which if they are well managed suffice to enrich you before God. It can be made up of sufferings you endure, occupations you engage in, duties you perform, even the most ordinary actions. Gather them all up, even to the smallest fragments, so that nothing may perish. It may all seem of little value to you, but if you are in grace before God, all of it, sanctified by God's charity, will be of great worth" (Lenten Sermons, Wednesday of the Fifth Week).

There is another kind of impeccability: *de jure* impeccability, which comes not from without but from within, from the very nature of things, and is incompatible with the freedom to sin and hence to merit. That is the impeccability of the blessed in heaven. It is so evident to them that God is the sovereign good, more beautiful than anything else, infinitely perfect, that they cannot be separated from Him or cease to want Him as their end.

How then could our Lord, who enjoyed the beatific vision, merit?

Theologians do not agree in their explanations of this fact. Some answer: God had not given Him a formal command to die for us, but had merely expressed a desire, a counsel.

Others maintain that there was a command involved, but that since the interior portion of Christ's being was not *in statu termini* and did not yet benefit from the effects of glory, He remained free with regard to the precepts even though He already possessed the beatific vision.

Be this as it may, since He merited, He was free.

Note on the extent of freedom and deliberateness in human acts (see p. 248 above):

"How many acts we perform inadvertently each day without even having a chance to reflect, deliberate, or exercise our freedom of choice! But precisely because they are not human they do not merit . . . a reward, they do not count in our life-history. . . . However they halt or interrupt the course of perfection, they prevent our lives from being completely filled, they insert voids into our days. . . .

"The soul of our Lord was always free of any indeliberate act, just as it was never subject to ignorance. . . .

"Without succeeding in eliminating all indeliberate acts, the saints advance in perfection in the measure that they tend to diminish the number of these acts." (P. Hugon, *Vie Spirituelle,* July, 1920, p. 278.)

Note on the condemned propositions of Baius (see p. 252 above):

In his Bull *Ex omnibus afflictionibus* (October, 1567), Pope Pius V condemned, among seventy-nine others, the three following propositions of Baius:

Prop. 2. "Just as the evil act, of its nature, merits eternal death, so the good act, of its nature, merits eternal life" (Denz. 1002).

Of its nature, the good act cannot merit; it requires a super-natural principle: actual or habitual grace. Propositions 12 and 15 will show this.

Prop. 12. "It is a Pelagian error to say: a good work performed without the grace of adoption does not merit the heavenly king-dom" (Denz. 1012). If this is not falling into Pelagius' error, then it is declaring the truth.

Prop. 15. "The reason for merit is not that he who does good possesses the grace of the Holy Spirit within him; but solely that he obeys divine law" (Denz. 1015). The foundation of merit lies in the possession of habitual grace, which implies the in-dwelling of the Holy Spirit.

Note on the Need of Actual Grace for Gaining Merit (see p. 257 above):

After proving the necessity of habitual grace for gaining merit, theological authors usually inquire whether, in order to super-naturalize the meritorious act in its essence, an actual grace is also needed.

Most Thomists (for example, Pesch) answer in the affirma-tive, because sanctifying grace and the infused virtues are *habitus* and no "habitus," no power, even if it is supernatural, can pass from potency to act without an impulsion by the Prime Mover, i.e., a supernatural impulsion. For the object of the movement is a supernatural potency and its effect is a supernatural act.

Other theologians, among them Father Terrien, consider the intervention of actual grace unnecessary for the supernatural acts of the just man. There can be no doubt that the just man needs divine helps in order to do good and avoid evil, and these helps are called medicinal graces. But why insist upon an elevating grace when an act is already supernaturalized by the infused virtues? The just man has no need of it. So runs Father Terrien's argument.

It is certain that the just man needs the impulsion of a Prime Mover in order to exercise his supernatural *habitus.*

The entire controversy thus seems to come down to this: Is the prime impulsion supernatural or not, and should it be called actual grace or not?

Note on the need of supernatural motives for meritorious acts (see p. 260 above):

According to some theologians, "it is not necessary that our actions be specifically inspired by a motive of faith: it suffices that their motive be morally righteous" (Rivière, *D.T.C.*, col. 781). So long as an act proceeds from grace and from a virtue, even if this virtue is merely natural, the act is meritorious. The motive makes no difference, providing it is legitimate. If it is a motive inspired by faith so much the better, for this will only make the merit greater. But this motive of faith is not required. The purely rational motive of the acquired virtues suffices.

Other theologians maintain the contrary view that the act must be directed toward God at least by a natural orientation completed by the impulse of charity that accompanies grace. "Let us admit that meritorious works, those that stem from a motive of faith, come first, but let us not exclude those works of the just man that obey the simple dictates of natural right reason" (cf. Billot, *De Gratia,* Thesis XX:2).

Still another group of theologians, above all among Thomists, hold that an act can be meritorious only if it is totally supernatural, both in its *principle* (grace and the virtues) and in its *motive* or formal object. (Of course the two cannot be separated, and an act cannot be meritorious in its principle without also being meritorious in its motive, at least in an implicit and virtual manner.)

Is it not the formal object or motive that distinguishes and specifies acts and places them in a given order? The logical order is this: supernatural object, supernatural act, supernatural cause. The supernaturality of the subject would be useless and powerless to supernaturalize the act unless the object were also supernatural.

Moreover, God cannot grant a supernatural reward to anyone who does not want one and who does not include this reward among his motives of action. Is not consent indispensable for obtaining our supernatural end and the means to it, namely, the grace that is the object of merit?

These reasons have unquestionable value, and yet we cannot deny that the negative view possesses a certain probability.

In practice, it is prudent to follow the Thomistic view, which is the most demanding of them all. Anyone who wants to assure the fruitfulness of his good works should strive to lift up his sights, elevate his intentions to the supernatural order, and base his motives upon faith. In doing this, he is taking no risks. On the contrary, even if the opposite view is the correct one, he will have considerably increased his merits.

At the same time, the better course should not be presented as the only good one, or the path of the counsels as the absolutely necessary one. "It is good to stimulate the faithful to act as much as possible through motives of pure faith, free of any alloy. It is neither prudent, nor correct, from the point of view of Catholic certitude, to make them think that unless they act with this perfection they are losing their time and their eternal life to boot" (*Ami du Clergé,* p. 395).

Note on the relation between arduousness and merit (see p. 267 above):

This is the doctrine of our Doctor of devotion: "To attain the maximum results with the minimum hardship, such is the ideal of the spiritual life."

"The saint wanted to make us *free,* in the sense given to this word by the liturgy in its beautiful formula: *liberis mentibus serviamus*—i.e., he wanted to provide us with a sort of virtuous automatism by means of habit that overcomes difficulties. He said: 'When the world is dead within you, you will be able to have a little freedom.' He did not think it was indispensable to practice goodness amid tears and suffering. He had understood that to measure merit on arduousness led to strange conclusions, notably the following: that the weak and lazy Christian, whose negligence has rendered the practice of virtue difficult, would have greater merit than the valiant Christian who has made the practice of virtue a second nature by dint of exercise. [St. Francis de Sales] says: 'To be devout we must have, in addition to charity, a great eagerness and promptness in performing charitable acts' (*Introduction,* Part I, Chapter 1). Now this agility, this vivacity, this promptness, are the opposite of arduousness. They are the result of the docility that tends to eliminate suffering, effort in the ordinary sense, from virtuous acts, while preserving their zeal, that is, their loving and voluntary ardor" (M. F. Vincent, *Saint François de Sales, directeur d'âmes,* p. 182 ff.).

12 The Power to Merit— Conclusion

GOD has promised to reward the good works of the just man. But in what does this reward consist? What benefits and what rights does this promise assure him?

We know what he must give to God in order to merit. But what does he receive in return? In other words, what can one merit: 1. *for oneself;* 2. *for others?*

1. For Oneself

1. There are four things that the just man certainly cannot merit for himself.

a. *First grace:* Neither first sanctifying grace nor first actual grace. As we have already seen, to merit he must be in the state of grace; and we are presupposing here that he is not yet in the state of grace (Ia IIae, q. 114, a. 5).

b. But while he is in the state of grace, can he not merit grace for a future contingency when he may lose grace through mortal sin? (This is what theologians, after St. Thomas, call *reparatio post lapsum*—cf. Ia IIae, a. 114, a. 7.) No, he cannot merit that either. Mortal sin mortifies every past right. "It interrupts the movement of grace toward its object," according to the Angelic Doctor. Through sin we merit hell, we cannot merit heaven. Scripture and the

274

Church affirm that all justification, i.e., the passage from sin to the state of grace, is absolutely gratuitous, and hence above any merit in justice. Hence, it is impossible to merit this grace.

Moreover, if we could merit while in the state of grace to return to it after we had lost it through sin, we would infallibly return to the state of grace after each sin. In short, every just man would infallibly be saved. But this is not the case. Regardless of the heights of sanctity he may have reached, every man can still damn himself.

c. Still less can we merit perseverance in the state of grace (Ia IIae, q. 114, a. 9), in other words, impeccability in fact. If we could, then it would suffice to have been just at one time in order to remain just permanently and to be sure of salvation. Alas! Experience proves the contrary to be true. Who fails to realize that he can offend God? And have not souls advanced in holiness, beautiful and sturdy as the "cedars of Lebanon," fallen into sin? In this matter, history agrees with Revelation.

Nowhere in Holy Scripture is the promise of such merit to be found, even implicitly. On the contrary, Scripture often warns the just man to watch and pray lest he succumb to temptation, to save his soul with fear and trembling, to take every precaution not to fall into sin again. This advice has a general application. It presupposes not only that the just man's works cannot merit confirmation in grace, but that no work, excellent as it may be, has this power.

d. For the same reason, no one can merit to die in the state of grace. However this favor—the most important one of all—can be obtained by persevering prayer.

2. Despite these necessary restrictions, the object of merit is still very vast.

a. First, merit means an increase in glory, that is, a right to new degrees of eternal happiness, vision, love, and enjoyment of God. Such is the doctrine taught by our Lord, the Apostles, and the Church.

In the Sermon on the Mount, our Savior promised a reward for each of our works, prayers, alms, done in secret for a supernatural intention: "And thy Father, who sees in

secret, will reward thee" (Mt. 6:4,6,18). Anyone who gives
so much as a glass of water to the lowliest Christian for His
name's sake will not lose his reward (Mt. 10:42). And what
will he receive? "He will receive a hundredfold return . . .
and eternal life." The heavenly treasure that neither rust
nor thieves can harm, the happiness pointed to in the Beatitudes, is unquestionably the glory of heaven. Now if none
of these works save the first merited new degrees of grace,
they would all go unrewarded, since the initial work would
merit as much as all the others and the rest of them would
merit no more than the first.

St. Paul teaches the Corinthians that: "each will receive
his own reward according to his labor" (I Cor. 3:8). And
likewise: "He who sows sparingly will also reap sparingly,
and he who sows bountifully will also reap bountifully" (II
Cor. 9:6).

We find the same metaphor in the Epistle to the Galatians, urging us to do good "while we have time" (Gal. 6:10).
But why should we do much good, if there is no proportionate increase in our reward?

It is amazing to discover that in certain large factories one
man can, by simply turning a switch, set in motion a whole
universe of machines, cogwheels, currents of power, and produce astounding effects. The just man can produce still more
wonderful effects by performing an act that is sometimes just
as easy. He exerts an influence even in heaven and in eternity, raising by several degrees the honor that will be his.

b. And yet is our reward something we can only hope for?
Must we wait until life ends to receive the wages for our efforts? Thank God, we do not. Our merits have immediate
effects. We are more fortunate than the farmer who must
await the results of his plantings during long months of
anguishing uncertainty. We can cull the fruit of our works
almost immediately. Each of our good works wins an increase in supernatural life, an infusion of new degrees of
sanctifying grace (Ia IIae, q. 114, a. 8), of the virtues, the
gifts, and the actual graces.

The Council of Trent defined this truth when it declared
heretical the proposition that "the one justified, by his good

works . . . does not truly merit an increase of grace, . . . and an increase of glory" (Session VI, Can. 32, cf. Denz. 842).

If there is an increase in future glory, there must also be an increase in present grace, which is the means to this glory. Of what use to merit the end, if we do not also merit the indispensable means to enjoy it? Of what use to promise a given amount of money for a certain work, if the means of using the money is not also promised? Since God promises glory in return for our good works, He also quite evidently promises grace, which is the capacity for glory. Each of our meritorious acts confers upon us, together with glory, a right to the corresponding degree of grace.[1]

c. But if sanctifying grace is the indispensable means of obtaining grace, actual grace is the morally necessary means for preserving sanctifying grace, avoiding sin, and overcoming the temptations that would make us lose grace. Anyone who merits sanctifying grace infallibly merits actual graces.

Grace is a principle of life. Now all life is incomplete unless it possesses the necessary helps to defend itself against whatever would destroy it, and also the capacity to grow and to express itself in acts. Progress is a law of life, and exercise is a necessity. Grace brings with it the indispensable energies to attain this result. Anyone who acquires the right to sanctifying grace has the right to actual graces by that very fact.

The sacraments produce actual graces because they produce sanctifying grace. Good works must likewise merit actual graces, inasmuch as they merit sanctifying grace.

These helps are measured out, with regard to their number and power, in proportion to the intensity of one's merit.

Every good work wins some of these helps for its author. They are always offered to him. He is free to resist them or to accept them. If he accepts them, they become efficacious.

It is probable that some works merit efficacious graces. What are these works? We cannot answer with certainty. But if prayer can obtain such helps, should not the same be true of good works to which Scripture attributes so much

---

[1] This raises a question which we shall discuss in the *Note* on p. 286 below, so as not to interrupt the continuity of the text.

power before God? As the angel told Tobias: "Alms . . . maketh to find mercy and life everlasting" (Tob. 12:9).

Since the just man's good works, in proportion to their value and their number, merit actual graces for him, it follows that here again he will be better protected than the sinner against temptation and trial, stronger in the face of duty, and better prepared to make the renunciations and sacrifices that virtue demands.

If he takes advantage of these helps to accomplish new, more perfect, and more numerous acts of virtue, he will receive new, more numerous, and more perfect helps. And if, persevering in his good will, he continues to join his efforts to God's he will rise from degree to degree, from peak to peak toward the radiant summits of perfection. His life will be a continual ascent toward God.

This is the secret of all holiness: to respond loyally to inspirations, giving more as we receive more so that our talents of grace may bear fruit. This fidelity and progress should be the law of every Christian life. Grace is somewhat like money. Those who already possess the largest assets receive greater interest, undertake more lucrative ventures, and make their fortune more quickly. But there is this consoling difference between grace and money: while access to financial wealth is closed to many, everyone can acquire spiritual riches, namely holiness, by living in the state of grace and by responding through good works to the helps offered.

The helps that the just man's good works merit are not all necessarily spiritual in themselves. They may be *material or temporal* in the broad sense. But we must agree on what these benefits are.

d. God wills to give only real rewards to our works that glorify Him, and these rewards are not always the ones we expect. In God's eyes and in very truth "man's only real good is his last end and whatever leads him to it" (Ia IIae, q. 114, a. 10). If He foresees that temporal goods such as wealth, honors, health, talents, and success will serve for His glory and the salvation of souls, and be means to sanctification and not obstacles, He may grant them as graces.

Alas! Too often such is not the use made of God's tem-

poral gifts. For many, these advantages are occasions of sin
and become real evils, whereas suffering and trials are salutary by taming their pride, making them stop to think, de-
taching them from creatures and from the world. Their
Father, who knows this, will therefore sometimes visit
troubles upon them (always in proportion to their strength)
as rewards for their virtues and for their ultimate good.

More usually God's love wisely measures out for His children a series of successes and failures, joys and sorrows, that
complement one another in their spiritual effects and keep
the soul alert, in moral balance, and constantly forging
ahead (cf. *L'Enfant de Dieu*, Chapter 11).

Under the blows of tribulation, the just are sometimes
tempted to cry out against harshness and injustice, and to
sulk at God. They ask themselves "what they have done" to
arouse His anger. They cannot believe that they have
merited such treatment by reason of their sins. Indeed, they
have merited it not by their sins (although it would be foolish pride on their part to claim to be perfectly free of sin),
but by their good works. And they are wrong in attributing
to His anger something that is an effect of His love. They
are in error when they consider as a punishment something
that is a precious reward, and when they judge as an evil
something that is really a good.

The error is frequent even among believers. What incom-
prehension of spiritual things! What ingratitude toward
their Father! However our Lord has taken the trouble to instruct us on this point: "I am the true vine, and My Father
is the vine-dresser. Every branch . . . that bears fruit He will
cleanse, that it may bear more fruit" (Jn. 15:1-2). Could He
have shown more clearly that the trials, renunciations, and
sacrifices that God sometimes imposes upon the just are
veritable graces, the effects of merits acquired, and destined
to help them acquire still greater merits? We must not take
as a flogging what is really a caress from the Father, and as
a punishment something that is only an affectionate remedy.
St. Thomas tells us so: "Temporal evils are imposed as a
punishment on the wicked, inasmuch as they are not thereby
helped to reach life everlasting. But to the just who are

aided by these evils, they are not punishments but medicines" (Ia IIae, q. 114, a. 10 ad 3).

If God sometimes allows the just man to suffer trials despite the scandal it causes to many (as in the case of the holy Job), if He does not exempt the just man from suffering or protect him against misfortune, and even seems to abandon him to the blows of adversity, the explanation for this behavior, so astonishing at first glance, is to be sought in the capacity of the just man through grace to merit and to make satisfaction for himself and for the world. We must ascend to this supernatural summit of grace to pass sound judgment on blessings and evils, and to grasp the real value of things.

2. For Others

The just man can merit for others: 1) *not* by condign merit; 2) but *by congruous merit.*

1. No one can pass on to others merit in the strict sense. It is an indisputable fact that merit is personal and inalienable. The divine promise is one of the foundations of this merit, and God has not promised anyone the favor of giving to others the reward of his good deeds. On the contrary He has affirmed that this cannot be done and that Christ is the only Redeemer in the strict sense, the only Pontiff, the one intermediary between Himself and men, the one Head in whom all things must be "recapitulated." For "No one comes to the Father but through [Christ]" (Jn. 14:6); "neither is there salvation in any other" (Acts 4:12). "From the justice of the one [Jesus] the result is unto justification of life to all men" (Rom. 5:18); and "by the obedience of the one the many will be constituted just" (Rom. 5:19). Now none of these words would be true if we could merit for others in the strict sense, as Christ did, for then we would be saviors as well as He.

God decreed that His Christ was to be the only one to receive this mission and this power. To Christ alone did He give what the theologians call *capital grace.* Because of the infinite dignity of His person, Christ alone can give the Father infinite glory, and only His actions could have an infinite value of satisfaction and merit. We might mention in passing that Christ could not merit for Himself since together with His human life, He had received the maximum of grace that God has ever decreed to give. Since Christ already possessed the beatific vision, He was not in the "wayfaring state," which is necessary for personal merit.

Similarly, when anyone entrusts all his merits into the hands of the Blessed Virgin Mary, so that she may dispose of them as she pleases, there is no question of condign merit in the strict sense, for this is incommunicable. There is question only of the satisfactory value of good works, or congruous merit.

Likewise, Mary was not a "Redemptrix," in the same way as our Lord. She gave us our Redeemer by becoming His Mother. She united her own sacrifice to His, thus uniting her expiations to His and offering them up for us, together with her incomparably precious congruous merits. She is the dispenser of the Savior's merits. But she was no more able than we to merit for others by condign merit. Her merits, like our own, were personal. They won for her a continuous and prodigious ascent in the spiritual life, the acquisition of a maximum of grace and glory, inferior to Christ's but far superior to that which any other creature ever has or ever will attain.

We still profit by it in a certain manner, indirectly. By increasing her sanctifying grace, Mary's merits increased the satisfactory value of all her works which she offered for us, as well as her congruous merits and her power of intercession which are entirely at our service.

No one but our Lord was able to merit for all men in the strict sense of the word, since His merits are of infinite value. He merited glory for us, as well as grace and the means to obtain it, and forgiveness of our sins. He merited that we might be able to merit for ourselves. This power is His alone.

2. However, we can participate in this power of Christ's in a certain manner through *congruous merit,* which is founded not on God's promise [2] but on a certain fittingness; not on

---

[2] Hence our merit differs from Christ's in several respects:
a. By reason of its *cause.* The dignity of Christ's acts did not come, as

justice but solely on divine liberality, on the friendship that
sanctifying grace establishes between the just and God, on
the union that it effects between their wills and hearts. The
just man, being God's child, makes God's interests his own,
loves what He loves, wants what He wants. Likewise, God,
being the just man's Father, wills what the just man wants
up to a certain point and loves those whom he loves. St.
Thomas says: "Because the just man does God's will, God
does the will of the just man and fulfills his desires with regard to the salvation of others" (Ia IIae, q. 114, a. 6).

It is fitting that this touching and generous intention,
inspired by the charity of Christ, to provide for the spiritual
needs of others and to give the Father new sons or to make
the sons He already has more loving, be realized. Can anyone who knows the Father's heart imagine that He would fail
to encourage a desire that is so close to His own? Christians
must resemble and associate themselves with Christ in His
work of saving the world, and those whom He has incorporated to Himself need the opportunity to cooperate in the
development of His Mystical Body. It is fitting that the
Father encourage a certain communication of spiritual goods,
a mutual exchange of benefactions, a fraternal exercise of
charity among His children, and even among those who have
not yet become His children.

The Church has always believed and taught this. In the
words of her divine Founder: "Unless the grain of wheat falls
into the ground and dies, it remains alone" (Jn. 12:24), she
has read the general law of every apostolate: the necessity
and fruitfulness of good works and sacrifice in order to do
good to souls. In the Church's eyes, the Apostle's surprising

---

the dignity of ours does, chiefly from grace even though He possessed grace in
the maximum degree. It was rooted in the hypostatic union with the divine
Word.

b. Whence a difference in value: His merit was literally infinite, whereas
ours is not.

c. There is a difference in *subject*. Our merit is personal, Christ's was for
all men. He merited for Himself only the glorification of His body and of
His name.

d. Christ's merit was intended for others, but it could have its full effect
upon them only by their free consent. It was a radical merit that presupposed their cooperation.

words to the Gentiles: "What is lacking of the sufferings of Christ I fill up in my flesh for His body, which is the Church" (Col. 1:24), apply to all who want to collaborate in the salvation of their brothers. And it is through immolation and renunciation that they must obtain the graces that enlighten, stimulate, stir, and convert. No one can be a savior unless he is a redeemer in some way. No one can sanctify others unless he sacrifices himself.

The Church has seen the seed of Christians in the blood of her martyrs; and she has looked upon the sufferings of her first missionaries as the source of the conversions they brought about. And the trials endured by the founders of religious orders, directors of good works, and fervent priests have seemed to her the reason for the efficacy of their ministry. Did she not proclaim St. Thérèse of Lisieux the secondary patroness of the Missions because she felt her sufferings and prayers contributed powerfully to the conversion of infidels? And do we not have proof that, in consideration of the virtue of the just, God shows mercy even to sinners? He would have saved the wicked cities of Sodom and Gomorrha if even ten just men had been found in them. And surely it was through his good works and mortifications that the Curé of Ars obtained the sanctification of his parish. We know that the saintly pastor once answered one of his colleagues who was discouraged because of his failures: "You say you have done everything you could? Have you fasted? Have you given alms? Have you prayed?"

It is commonly believed that St. Stephen merited the conversion of St. Paul by his own martyrdom.

In Corneille's famous play, Pauline attributes her conversion to Polyeucte's martyrdom.[3]

This power is the glorious privilege of the just man. The reasons on which it is based do not hold for the sinner. The sinner's need to receive is too great. What could he do for others? Fallen from his supernatural greatness, what glory can he give to God? How could he appease His justice

---

[3] Cf. the *Note* containing the passage from Corneille referred to above, and lines from Claudel's *L'Annonce faite à Marie*, p. 289 below.

toward others when he continues to arouse His anger by his own offensive dispositions?

The just man, on the other hand, has the means of influencing God. Whoever he may be and whatever his condition and his occupations, he can contribute to the salvation of his fellows. Without leaving his home, while remaining wherever Providence is holding him, while carrying out the duties of his state of life, he can be a missionary and exercise apostolic action! From all his good works sanctifying emanations spring forth (which God directs as He pleases toward other men). By lifting himself up, he lifts other souls up with him. It does not matter if he is an invalid, sick, physically helpless, stretched out on a bed, nailed to a cross, tied down to some daily work, obliged to earn his own livelihood and that of his family by unpleasant toil, burdened with heavy responsibilities, reduced to poverty, prevented by necessity from participating in good works, forced to stay at home, in the workshop, in the fields, or in the factory. As long as he remains in the state of grace, he retains, through his merit (in the broad sense) and his good actions and sacrifices (and his prayers) the capacity of cooperating efficaciously in the sanctification of the human race. For he can still work or suffer. Suffering is the best form of action. When did Christ exercise the most intense and fruitful influence? Was it not during His Passion?

From what we have said, it follows that the first condition to be fulfilled by those who want to take a useful part in Catholic Action or in the apostolate is to return or to remain in the state of grace. And we might mention in passing that every baptized Christian should want to exercise apostolic action, as the Sovereign Pontiffs constantly remind us. Without the state of grace, they cannot expect to obtain God's help. If they do not possess supernatural life, how could they expect to transmit it to others? Thus we see that through sin many precious contributions are lost for the conversion of the world and for the triumph of the Church. (Cf. *L'Enfant de Dieu,* Chapter 18).

It follows that the just must take cognizance of this privilege which imposes responsibilities upon them. They must make the fullest possible use of it. The thought not only of their own welfare but that of their brothers as well should inspire them to multiply their meritorious works that are profitable to themselves through condign merit and to others through congruous merit.

Can the just man merit (*de congruo*) first grace for sinners? St. Thomas (cf. Ia IIae, q. 114, a. 4) and most theologians answer in the affirmative.

When others are concerned, the question of the impossibility of meriting for oneself does not arise.

Nor is the absolute gratuity of justification an argument against this. For in following through from cause to cause, we must necessarily arrive at a first grace merited by no one but Christ. In any case, the subject will not have merited this grace himself, and it is absolutely gratuitous as far as he is concerned.

Conclusions. All our morally good acts without exception —provided they are freely performed and that we are in the state of grace—are meritorious. This is true even of our most commonplace acts, those which humiliate us perhaps because they belong to an inferior order, even those that cost us no effort because our bodies and our faculties find satisfaction in them (e.g., resting, eating, taking care of our bodies, our attire, recreation, proper diversions and pastimes). Everything we do to provide for our own subsistence and that of our families, to improve our situation by legitimate means, to cultivate and develop our faculties, all the lowly labors of each day, all our little troubles and annoyances, all that we do and endure, everything that involves an act of the will, even the most interior and imperceptible act, has been promised a reward by the Father.

Each of these acts will have endless repercussions in heaven, and win for us added degrees of vision, possession, and delight in God's infinite beauty. It will bring an intensification of our eternal activity, tighten the bonds that unite us to our supernatural end, and increase our aptitude and right to possess this end. Our Lord has told us that even the giving of a glass of water will not be unrewarded (cf. Mt. 10:42).

We may despise these acts and accomplish them indifferently, without zeal or pleasure. But God does not have such a low opinion of them since He rewards them by giving us new participations in His divine life here on earth, and, later on, in His divine happiness. Through grace, these acts are all great and fruitful, they are all divine and rich in their effects. Suffering and acting will pass, but the fact that we have suffered and acted will remain eternally. Our sufferings and actions will follow us to the great beyond by winning greater happiness for us: *"Et opera eorum sequuntur illos."*

It is a very precious thing to be able to merit. How grateful we should be to God for having willed to help us in our weakness by promising to repay us for doing what we already owe Him on so many counts; for having added to our eternal happiness the honor of making it our own achievement in a certain respect; for having given our earthly existence meaning and importance, and for giving an almost infinite value to our smallest efforts, labors, and difficulties; for having so greatly magnified our human activity, and giving us the faculty of amassing great treasures. Surely we should thank Him for these favors every day.

But let us remember that love is proved by acts. We cannot express our gratitude for His gifts more opportunely than by striving to make the best use of them, to make them bear fruit, to multiply our good works, and to intensify the causes that increase our merit.

In His mercy, the Father, who knows our laziness, our cowardice, our fear of effort and sacrifice, helps us wisely by a fruitful process of pruning through trials and crosses (always proportioned to our strength) that give us an opportunity to make acts of patience and renunciation. Let us cooperate with His action.

*   *   *

Note on the right to new degrees of grace won by meritorious acts (see p. 277 above):

When does this right come to fulfillment? Are these degrees of grace given for each meritorious action? Would it not suffice if they were given us when we enter heaven, inasmuch as the means is absolutely necessary only at the moment the end is to be obtained? That is what Scotus thought.

The Scotist opinion has some important consequences. If it is true, then our merits do not at present help to increase grace within us. We are thus deprived of the precious effects of this increase here on earth.

a. But this view does not square with the doctrine of the Council of Trent, notably Canon 24 of the 6th Session, which declares it heretical to declare "that the justice received is not preserved and also increased before God through good works, but that those works are merely the fruits and signs of justification obtained, but not the cause of its increase." In Chapter 10 of the same Session, we read: "Having, therefore, been thus justified and made the friends and domestics of God, advancing from virtue to virtue, they are renewed . . . and are further justified." This refers to the just in this life. It is in this life and not upon entering heaven that they receive the grace merited by their works.

Such is the general opinion of the theologians. Since glory is not to begin until after the periods of trial and of expiation, there are good reasons for deferring it. The same is not true of grace. Glory is the reward of the final state, grace is the reward of the wayfaring state.

Since we can receive grace through the sacraments here on earth, why can we not receive it through our merits? If the demands of the sacraments are immediately satisfied, why not those of merit? If the principle of vision is given to us even in this life, why should it not be given to us in its various degrees?

Yes, the grace that our works merit for us is given to us during our earthly life.

b. Is grace given to us *immediately,* as soon as we perform a meritorious act? This is the only point of controversy at the present time between the school of Suarez (Suarez, lib. IX, No. 232) and the Nominalists on the one hand and the school of St. Thomas on the other.

The former answer this question in the affirmative. Each of our good acts, feeble as it may be, immediately produces its fruits of grace, according to the Suarezian school.

St. Thomas declares that the meritorious act must be more fervent, more perfect, and involve better dispositions on the part of the subject than the preceding act, otherwise the right to grace will remain in abeyance until this condition is realized by a later act. "Just as eternal life is not given at once, but in its own time, so neither is grace increased at once, but in its own time, viz., when a man is sufficiently disposed for the increase of grace" (Ia IIae, q. 114, a. 8, ad 3).

The reason is that grace is always given according to the subject's dispositions. If the fervor of the dispositions implicit in a good act does not exceed the fervor of preceding acts, the soul's capacity for grace is not increased by that act. Hence it cannot receive more grace.

Another argument is drawn from the analogy that must exist between infused habits and acquired habits. The latter increase in perfection only by progressively more difficult or perfect acts. The same is true of infused habits.

The partisans of the Suarezian view answer that these arguments are not apodictic, and that the argument of the analogy between habits of different orders should not be pressed lest inadmissible conclusions be reached. They also claim that the Thomistic explanation does not square with the declarations of the Council of Trent. For the Council does not place these restrictions on the fruitfulness of merit. It sees only one thing as preventing the just man from receiving eternal life corresponding to the life of grace, as a reward for his good works: to die in the state of mortal sin. Likewise, it sets only one condition for the definitive possession of this increase, namely, to die in the state of grace (cf. Can. 32, Session VI).

Now according to the Thomistic view, another condition would be added: that one have performed, before dying, an act of charity more fervent than the preceding ones.

And if this more fervent act of charity is not performed, what happens to the merit that has thus far remained in abeyance? If the grace that this merit calls for is produced anyway, the principle of the necessary dispositions does not apply. If it is not produced, then, despite Christ's promises, a good work goes unrewarded, for the degree of glory that has been merited cannot be obtained for lack of corresponding grace.

But these reasons are not unanswerable either. In practice, the Thomistic opinion retains its probability. Therefore in order to be more certain of collecting all the merits of our actions, we should strive to bring more and more fervent dispositions to our works, more ardent charity, greater attention, and strive to perform increasingly difficult acts.

We have nothing to lose and everything to gain by putting this opinion into practice.

Note on conversions won through the merits of others (see p. 283 above):

Quotation from Corneille's *Polyeucte:*

"His blood, with which the executioners have just covered me,
Has unsealed my eyes and opened them.
I see, I know, I believe, I am undeceived:
You see me baptized with this blessed blood. . . ."

And Felix, who had commanded his execution:

"I have made a martyr of him, his death makes a Christian of me."

This is one of the great ideas that Claudel teaches in his *Annonce faite à Marie:*

"God is a miser and never permits a creature to be kindled
Without consuming a bit of impurity,
Either its own or the impurity that surrounds it, like
the coals of the lighted censer! . . .
Suffering is powerful when it is as willful as sin! (Act II, Scene 3).

"My daughter is dead, the holy Pucelle
Has been burned and thrown to the winds, not one of
her bones remains upon earth.
But the King and the Pope have been restored
to France and to the Universe.
The schism is coming to a close, and once more
the Throne rises up above all men" (Act IV, Scene 5).

We find the same teaching in Ghéon's *Le Pauvre sous l'escalier.*

13 The Power to Make Satisfaction

GRACE gives the just man the capacity to become God's creditor through his merits.

It does still more.

Since the just man remains God's more or less insolvent debtor by reason of the reparation he owes for his offenses, grace provides him the means of "liberating" himself by conferring upon him the power to make satisfaction.

This effect of grace is not usually discussed. Merit receives all the attention. Merit may in certain instances even be confused with grace. This is a serious mistake, for while the effects of merit and grace are alike in several respects, they are essentially distinct.

We shall show that grace confers the power to make satisfaction: 1. for ourselves; 2. for others.

1. For Ourselves

We know that after the remission of sin there may remain a debt of temporal punishment to pay. The Council of Trent has declared heretical the propositions that "God always pardons the whole penalty together with the guilt" (Canon 12, Session XIV), and that "it is a fiction that there often remains a temporal punishment to be discharged after the

eternal punishment has been removed by virtue of the keys"
(Canon 15 and Chapter 8, Session XIV). (Cf. *Dans les bras du
Père*, Chapter 4.)

It is a debt to be paid in this world or in the next. Anyone who has neglected to do it before his death will have to
acquit himself of it amid the purifying torments of purgatory.

It will be much harder in purgatory. The time for mercy
having passed, justice will reclaim its rights and exact its
full due (cf. Mt. 5:26).

Moreover, there will no longer be access to the expiatory
procedures (indulgences, Mass, etc.) which act *ex opere operato,* or nearly so, here on earth, and which are far more
efficacious in the matter of satisfaction than is the human act.
There will only remain personal suffering. And even this
will have a lesser satisfactory value than it did in the present
life, for it will no longer be free. The debt will then have to
be paid to the last farthing, and the means of paying will be
fewer. It is therefore most important to pay our debts here
and now, and as quickly and completely as possible.

Habitual grace provides us with the means of paying our
debts, and this is not one of its less significant effects. To be
more exact, grace makes it possible for us to use the means
instituted for this purpose, None of them would be usable
without grace. It is grace that gives them their value.

These means are of two sorts.

Some of them act *ex opere operato,* or almost so. Their
effect is greater than the value of the subject's action, and
has a different source. These means are: sacramental penance,
Mass, the indulgences.

The other means act *ex opere operantis.* That is to say,
they derive all their value from the subject. These means are
arduous good works.

The satisfactory efficacy of the latter has been defined,
against the Protestants, by the Council of Trent when it
declared: "The liberality of the divine munificence is so
great that we are able through Jesus Christ to make satisfaction to God the Father not only by punishments voluntarily
undertaken by ourselves to atone for sins, or by those imposed
by the judgment of the priest according to the measure of

our offense, but also, and this is the greatest proof of love, by the temporal afflictions imposed by God and borne patiently by us" (Session XIV, Chapter IX). We find almost the same words used in Canon 13 of the same Session, which declares the opposite view heretical.

St. Thomas says: "The trials of this life purify us of sin and are also satisfactory" (*Suppl.*, q. 15, a. 2).

1. But none of these sources of satisfaction is open *without sanctifying grace,* and only the just can draw from them. Most theologians admit that while sacramental penance received in the state of mortal sin is valid, it remains in abeyance until the return to the state of grace, as do the fruits of a "formless" sacrament. In dealing with sacramental penance St. Thomas does not admit such a possibility. He maintains that this would require God to accept payment from the sinner and would presuppose a relation of friendship between them: "In satisfaction made to God, . . . although the offense be already removed by previous contrition, the works of satisfaction must be acceptable to God, and for this they are dependent on charity" (*Suppl.*, q. 14, a. 2). In the following article, he denies that good works performed in the state of mortal sin can "revive" with regard to their statisfactory value any more than to their meritorious value.

Likewise, according to the more common view (St. Alphonsus, I, VI), even though the penitent in the state of mortal sin can fulfill his obligation to perform his penance for previous sins, it is considered an impropriety, and probably a sinful one, on his part to have neglected to acquit himself of this obligation sooner. This amounts to setting up an "obex" or obstacle to a portion of the efficacy of the sacrament of penance previously received.

Grace is also necessary to gain *indulgences* for oneself. The Church has formally declared this in her Code (Can. 925). Grace is necessary at least when performing the last act prescribed for gaining an indulgence. Hence the expression used in the granting of certain indulgences: "To those who are sincerely contrite and have confessed their sins . . . ." This means they must be in the state of grace. The gaining of indulgences is a work of satisfaction, that is, a work that

serves to pay the debt of temporal punishment for sins already forgiven. The reason for this is that in addition to its
ordinary satisfactory value as an arduous work performed in
the state of grace is added a much greater value that comes
from the Church's power of the keys, somewhat like the
power of sacramental penance.

The sinner has no part in the very abundant satisfaction
produced by the Mass that he celebrates or attends, or that
is said for him. No one can benefit from satisfaction, whatever its source, unless he is in the state of grace. Satisfaction,
whatever its origin, can profit only the just man.

To make satisfaction is to make or complete reparation for
an offense against God. It is to give Him glory in compensation
for the glory which He has been robbed of by sin. How can
glory be restored to Him if one persists in stealing it from
Him? How can reparation be made for an offense that continues in the form of attachment to sin, to the forbidden
good, and in a disposition of will that has not—through contrition and justification—stopped preferring creatures to God
and restored Him to His place as its last end? Can justice be
"satisfied" as long as these offensive dispositions subsist? In
the words of St. Thomas, "it is impossible for a man to make
satisfaction for one sin while holding to another; even as
neither would a man make satisfaction to another for a blow,
if . . . he were to give him another" (*Suppl.*, q. 14, a. 1). Satisfaction must remove the offense and restore friendship. Sin,
by preventing friendship with God, makes all satisfaction
impossible.

There can be no satisfaction unless God accepts it. Now
God does not accept satisfaction from anyone who remains
his enemy by persisting in sin. He receives only the reparation of his children, the just, who are united to Him by the
bonds of charity. Thus it is impossible for someone who has
fallen back into sin to make satisfaction by his good works
for sins previously forgiven.[1]

---

[1] The reason Daniel advised Nabuchodonosor to redeem his sins by alms
(Dan. 4:24), was not so that he might expiate them but so that through his
liberality he might obtain forgiveness by meriting the means of expiation
de congruo.

2. Together with the state of grace, satisfaction also demands the wayfaring state, *"status viae."*

However satisfaction differs from merit on this point. After death, it is absolutely impossible to merit, whereas it is still possible to expiate in purgatory. That is why St. Thomas says that the souls in purgatory are, from that point of view, still in the wayfaring state (cf. *Suppl.,* q. 14, a. 2). But even though they lovingly accept the satisfaction imposed on them, this satisfaction is no longer free and hence has less value. The theologians say it would be more exact to call it "satis-passion," or imposed satisfaction.

We can therefore see that while freedom increases the value of satisfaction, it is not an indispensable condition for it. If we prefer, we can say that freedom is indispensable to satisfaction as God accepts it here on earth, and not to the satisfaction that He imposes in the life beyond the grave.

3. The conditions for making satisfaction are the same as for merit (the divine promise, the wayfaring state, moral goodness, freedom, a supernatural motive and subject), plus the condition of *penality*. An action can be expiatory only if it is painful, if it involves a renunciation, a sacrifice, a constraint. St. Thomas says: "Satisfaction regards both the past offense, for which compensation is made by its means, and also future sin wherefrom we are preserved thereby: and in both respects satisfaction needs to be made by means of penal works. . . . For although nothing can be taken away from God, so far as He is concerned, yet the sinner, for his part, deprives Him of something by sinning" (*Suppl.,* q. 15, a. 1).

The sinner takes exterior glory from God, by refusing to affirm His sovereign rights and His infinite perfection, in order to enjoy an illicit pleasure or to avoid an obligatory sacrifice. He unjustly takes something away from God in order to give it to himself. Order and justice demand that in return something be taken away from him, that a punishment be imposed upon him. To quote St. Thomas again: "Now a good work, as such, does not deprive the agent of anything, but perfects him [naturally, by means of the facility it creates in him, and supernaturally through merit]: so that the deprivation cannot be effected by a good work unless it be penal" (*Suppl.*, ibid.). In order to make satisfaction we must carry our cross, as our Savior did, and die to something.

Granted equally good dispositions, the work that has the greatest satisfactory value is the one that is most painful. But what we have already said about merit (cf. pp. 265 and 266 above) also applies here. If the lessening of the difficulty or painfulness results from greater charity or from a freely acquired habit, it does not diminish the degree of satisfaction. On the contrary, facility may increase satisfaction by increasing the voluntariness of the subject, the perfection of the act, or the purity of the intention. Most good works or good actions are painful for the most part. In order to make up our minds to do them and to accomplish them perfectly without haste and without sloth, in the moderation of order and with an attitude inspired by faith, an effort of the will is always necessary. This is true even of actions called for by strong natural needs: eating, drinking, being hungry and thirsty, relaxation after a long effort at concentration, rest after a tiresome day.

We can therefore say that all or almost all of the just man's works have a satisfactory value, whose degree depends on the degree of glory they give to God. Therefore this degree is measured by the degree of arduousness, freedom, nobility of motive, perfection in virtue, and above all, charity and grace with which they are performed.

And we must include among good actions not only those in which we are active, but also and above all those in which we seem to be passive, such as: acceptance of death, endurance of suffering, patience in disappointments and trials, resignation in the face of the various crosses that each day weigh down on our shoulders, for they require no less energy, activity, and love. To suffer, to remain calm, "to possess one's soul in patience," not to revolt—all these are powerful actions. To endure is to bear something. Since these crosses are imposed upon us, contrary to the more hidden and lowly desires of our being, they are more painful and hence have greater power of satisfaction than great and brilliant actions.

The same is usually true of actions that are commanded.

Thus the good works of the just man have a twofold value

in relation to the degree of his grace: a value of merit, and a value of satisfaction. Through each of them, he pays his debts and he earns. He settles his debt and he increases his credit. He stops being a debtor and becomes a creditor in relation to God. He reduces his purgatory and increases his heavenly happiness.

And he can also make satisfaction for others.

2. For Others

This is a very considerable privilege. The just man can pay not only for himself but also for *other just men*.[2] A transfusion of satisfaction among the just is possible.

There are indulgences that can be gained only for oneself: for example, the plenary indulgence at the hour of death.

Others can be gained only for others: the indulgence of the privileged altar, and the jubilee indulgence that is reserved for the deceased.

According to a very commonly held opinion, the very special fruit of the Mass, the fruit that accrues to the celebrant in his satisfactory role, is inalienable.

The same is true of sacramental penance. Being an act of the penitent, that is, an integral part of the matter which the subject alone can posit, it can benefit no one but him (at least in its medicinal effect).

The other satisfactions of the first type (indulgences and the satisfactory fruit of the Mass) are transmissible.

The satisfactions of the second type (good works) are also transmissible. It goes without saying that this does not include the medicinal effect, which is to preserve us from future sins. St. Thomas says: "One man's fast does not serve to conquer the flesh of another, . . . any more than the good acts of one man make another acquire the habit of these acts" (except accidentally by meriting for the other helps that will help him to win these victories). This effect belongs to the subject.

---

[2] Cf. the *Note* at the end of this chapter, in which the answer to the following question is given: Is the state of grace required for gaining indulgences for others? (p. 301 below).

The second effect (the payment of the debt of temporal punishment due for sins already forgiven) can be transmitted to others. One man can "pay up another's debt provided he is in the state of grace and that his works have satisfactory value . . . . It is Catholic doctrine that the just man can make satisfaction in the strict sense for others, with regard to the debt of punishment, provided he is in the state of grace" (cf. *La Vie Spirituelle*, 1926, p. 640).

The reason for this is evident. Charity has greater power with God than with men. For God is charity, He is goodness, and nothing is more pleasing to Him than the translation of love by benefactions, as is the case of His own love. And so if human creditors agree to accept the payment of debts by others than those who owe them, how much more true is this of God! Did not St. Paul counsel us to bear one another's burdens? (Gal. 6:2).

Moreover, satisfaction for others is more efficacious because of the charity it presupposes and the renunciation it involves. A lesser punishment pays as much for another as a greater punishment suffered for oneself.

On the contrary the merit of justice, as we have already said, is absolutely inalienable. In this respect it is basically different from satisfaction. This stems from the will of God and the nature of these things. Being a physical reality,[3] grace and its attendant capacity for the beatific vision cannot increase in an adult without also perfecting his moral dispositions. Now it is precisely the meritorious act itself that works this perfecting: it merits because it makes its subject more perfect; it draws down more grace because it expands the soul's capacity. To merit for another would produce an increase in grace in one and the perfecting of dispositions in another. It would be doubly monstrous if these two interrelated realities did not coexist.

Through a special permission of God, Christ was able to merit for us. But even so we must merit His merits in a concrete way. That is to say, the adult must dispose himself to receive the grace merited by Christ in proportion to the degree of this grace.

---

[3] This is St. Thomas' explanation (*Suppl.*, q. 13, a. 2, ad 1).

Satisfaction requires the presence of grace in the agent and in the subject; but satisfaction does not produce or increase grace. It is not a physical reality produced in the soul, but the payment of a moral debt, a reality of the intentional order, such as rights and duties. It is possible to benefit from satisfaction without any perfecting of dispositions or increase in capacity. "The temporal punishment due to sin after the guilt has been forgiven is not measured according to the disposition of the man to whom it is due" (*Suppl.*, q. 13, a. 1 ad 1). The proof of this is that a person can have greater perfection and more grace, and still owe a greater debt of punishment.

Thus the just man, animated by charity, can pay his neighbor's debts.

How does this substitution come about?

Through the intention of the one who makes satisfaction. God certainly respects his generous wishes, unless His sovereign wisdom has good reasons for disposing of them in a different manner.

Those who make the total consecration to the Blessed Virgin Mary (according to St. Louis-Mary de Montfort) entrust all their satisfactions to her and give her the right to distribute them in any way she pleases.

If no recipient of another's satisfactions is designated, or if the person designated is incapable of receiving them, either because his debts are all paid or because he is not in the state of grace, then the satisfactions remain the property of their owner to wipe out his own debt of sin.

If the person making satisfaction no longer has any debts to pay, then his satisfactions are placed in the Church's treasury. It is even more probable that God applies these satisfactions to the just who are united to their possessor by certain legitimate bonds, whether natural or supernatural (relatives, friends, brothers through grace), in proportion to their degree of grace. Since this transferability of spiritual goods, or communion of saints, is founded on grace, it must be measured by the intensity of grace, and the larger share accrues to those who have the greater grace.

And so it is that the just who still need to make satisfaction participate in the satisfactions of other just men who have already paid their own debts. They share in the satisfaction of the saints who are always plentiful in the Church; in the satisfactions of victim souls who are increasing in number all over the world, and who dedicate themselves to making reparation to the Sacred Heart for the sins of men. They also share in the satisfactions of the Blessed Virgin Mary, which were very intense, like her charity, her grace, and her sufferings, and were never applied to her since she was without sin. It is indeed the intention of Mary Co-Redemptrix and of all the saints that the fruit of their works benefit their neighbor according to God's own plans.

By the very fact that the just man possesses grace and in the measure that he possesses it, he receives a large share in the satisfactions of his brothers. The sinner, on the other hand, receives none.

The just man has his share of the general fruit of satisfaction of all the Masses that are celebrated all over the world; and if he participates in the Holy Sacrifice himself he receives another special share. The sinner receives none.

If Mass is offered up for the just man, he receives all its fruits of satisfaction; the sinner would receive none.

The just man gains all the indulgences attached to the good works he performs: recitation of the Angelus, the Rosary, ejaculations, the Way of the Cross, participation in various services, ceremonies, or pilgrimages, participation in certain works of charity or in the apostolate. He does not need to specifically think about it, providing he has once had the implicit intention of gaining these indulgences. For the sinner, all these treasures are lost forever.

Without doing anything more, by virtue simply of his state of grace, the just man pays a part of his debt to divine justice and shortens his purgatory by each of his good actions, by each of his sufferings, by each of his trials. These brief sufferings spare him long and severe punishments in the life beyond. And far more important (for this negative aspect contains something positive), by reducing the duration of his expiatory torments, he increases the duration of his eternal happiness.

The sinner has no such benefits. His greatest sacrifices, his heaviest crosses, his most arduous efforts are forever lost from this point of view, as well as from the point of view of merit. Not only are his good works mortified with regard to their meritorious and satisfactory effects, as is the case of those that preceded mortal sin. They are actually *dead*, powerless, without effect or value from this twofold point of view. They are absolutely sterile. And yet, if they had been accompanied by grace, they could have been so fruitful, so precious. But lacking the sap of divine life they cannot produce supernatural fruit. Regardless of his good works, the sinner's debt remains undiminished, as do the claims of divine justice against him.

This is an immense and irreparable loss for him and for others! He is actually lying if he says he still loves his deceased relatives and friends and yet refuses to return to the state of grace. For he thus remains helpless to help open the gates of heaven for them. He is heartless.

Nor does he understand his own best interests. By prolonging his state of sin he voluntarily prolongs the length of his punishment. By remaining in sin he agrees to remain forever in the flames of expiatory fire in the event he dies without recovering grace.

The just man is much the wiser.

To live in the state of grace is to draw more freely from the Church's treasure of satisfaction, it is to share more abundantly in the fruits of Christ's sacrifice, to win for one's own works their full harvest of spiritual benefits, and give inestimable value to one's life. By living in the state of grace we spare ourselves rigorous expiations after death and reach heaven more quickly; we can if we wish procure the same advantages to many souls, truly become their liberators, earn their eternal gratitude, and acquire a special right to their friendship and to God's friendship as well. For by our help we make it possible for God to receive into His happiness some of His children who had until then been kept away by their unpaid debts.

Through their satisfaction as well as through their prayers and merits, the just are therefore great benefactors of hu-

manity. Even their most insignificant works in human terms
have considerable value and the most salutary repercussions.
Through grace they exercise an extraordinary influence over
the world of spirits. They share in a certain respect in the
outpouring goodness and power of God. They cooperate in
a real way in the redemptive work of expiation and merit.
Their sufferings purify and liberate others.

How precious every loving soul must hold this capacity to
make satisfaction for its own sins and those of others, this
faculty for exercising charity toward its brothers by paying
their expiatory debts, and toward the Father by making
reparation for the sins committed against Him and offering
Him the honor of which others rob Him.

A truly sublime intention, very close to Christ's intention
in His Passion.

We should therefore look upon the trials and crosses that
befall us with an eye to the satisfaction and merit they can
bring us and others. In God's loving and wise plans these
hardships are meant to be for us an occasion not only for
increasing our eternal happiness by our merits but also of
shortening our purgatory and that of others, as well as of
glorifying our Father and more closely resembling our Lord.

Through this power to make satisfaction, grace unites us to
Christ, the restorer of God's glory and the Redeemer of men.
It associates us in His great priestly mission; it makes of
every life a long Mass.

God has truly "made [the just man] honorable in his
labors, and accomplished his labors" (Wisd. 10:10).

*   *   *

*Note on the necessity of being in the state of grace for gaining
indulgences for others (see p. 296 above):*

Is the state of grace necessary for gaining indulgences for
others?

a. Certainly not, in the case of the privileged altar, whether
personal or real; or in the case of the apostolic indulgence to
members of Third Orders or to those in danger of death, conferred by the priest in virtue of special powers granted to him.
Here, as in the sacraments, the minister's holiness is not required

for assuring the effects. Strictly speaking, the minister does not gain an indulgence but administers it.

b. With regard to other indulgences there is a controversy. Those who favor the negative view say that the indulgence does not come from the dignity of the man but from a concession by the Church using her power of the keys. It is as a subject and not as a cause that the sinner cannot gain any indulgence for himself. He can gain indulgences but he cannot receive any.

It might be pointed out that in this case sin would be only an obstacle to gaining the indulgence for oneself, and that when this obstacle disappeared the indulgence would revive and profit the subject, as with grace in "formless" sacraments. This gain would be valid even for the sinner, although unfruitful. Such a position is untenable.

The partisans of the affirmative say that in order to give, one must possess. No one can pass on to others something to which he has no right for himself. Anyone who cannot gain indulgences for himself cannot gain any for others. The reason a priest can, through the sacraments, produce effects in others which he himself is incapable of receiving is because he is a minister acting by virtue of God and in the name of the Church.

The same is not true of ordinary indulgences. The person who gains them is not a minister. His act, to which they are attached, is neither the act of the Church or of God. It does not produce its effect *ex opere operato* in the strict sense. It is therefore probable that without grace no one can gain indulgences for others.

c. The same answer must be given to the question whether the sinner can make someone else benefit from the satisfactory fruit that would accrue to him, if he were in the state of grace, from his attendance at the Holy Sacrifice of the Mass. By offering the sacrifice in union with the priest and with Christ, he does co-offer in a certain respect, but he is not a priest in the sense of being a minister of the Church. He acts in his own name only. That is why, although even the unworthy celebrant can apply to those for whom he celebrates the special fruit of satisfaction, it does not follow that the layman's attendance at Mass can have the same satisfactory effects, nor even that the unworthy priest can pass on the satisfactory effect of the Mass that applies to him in particular. As in the case of indulgences, it remains at least probable that a person who is not in the state of grace cannot pass on to others the satisfactory effects of the Mass since he cannot acquire them for himself.

14 A Supernatural Life

As WE have seen, grace is the seed of glory for the soul and of immortality for the body.

It is a participation in the nature of God that makes the soul resplendent with beauty and like God.

It is a divine adoption that makes us brothers of Christ and of all other just men, and assures us of God's fatherly love.

It brings justification, rectification, and sanctification of the soul.

It makes the soul the intimate dwelling of God.

It brings the infused virtues, actual graces, and the gifts of the Holy Spirit.

It gives a supernatural power of glorification and prayer, and enables us to merit and make satisfaction for ourselves and for others.

It follows that: 1. grace is *a life;* 2. *an intense life;* 3. *a precious life.*

We shall consider this life in our final chapter, which is as it were the direct consequence of the preceding ones.

1. Grace Is a Life

Our Lord has given grace the name of *life* (Jn. 10:10), or *birth,* which amounts to the same thing (Jn. 3:3). Having

303

come to bring us grace, He says that He came "to give us life": *"Veni ut vitam habeant, et abundantius habeant."*

He calls the Eucharist—the source of grace—"the bread of life" (Jn. 6:35, 51, 52). He compares grace to the sap that flows from the vinestock into the branches (Jn. 15:1). And John, who has the deepest insight into His thought, speaks of it only as *life* or *birth.*

While St. Paul also uses the word "life," he speaks more often of "grace," and seems to have been the first to use this term. The experience of his own justification impressed upon him the gratuitousness and supernaturalness of this gift. Moreover, he was constantly called upon to defend the doctrine of grace against the naturalistic errors of the Judaizers.

In many passages Paul not only calls loss of grace through sin *death* (which presupposes that grace is a life), but he also uses the word *death* expressly and constantly in this connection. For example, in Chapter V of his Epistle to the Romans, in which he attributes to Adam's sin (contracted by all men) both death of the body and death of the soul, he says: "For if by reason of the one man's [Adam's] offense death reigned . . . much more will they who receive the abundance of the grace and the gift of justice [which is equivalent] reign in life through the one Jesus Christ. Therefore as from the offense of the one man the result was unto condemnation to all men, so from the justice of the one the result is unto justification of life to all men" (Rom. 5:17-18).

Christ made abundant reparation for the ravages caused by sin; He restored life abundantly to those in whom sin had produced death. Adam was an agent of death, Christ is the source of life through justification. In Chapter VI, St. Paul shows how, when we receive grace through baptism, we receive a new life, the life that comes from Christ, through which we live with Him. "But if we have died [to sin] with Christ, we believe that we shall also live together with Christ. . . . Thus do you consider youselves also as dead to sin, but alive to God in Christ Jesus. . . . For the wages of sin is death, but the gift of God is life everlasting in Christ Jesus our Lord" (Rom. 6:8,11,23).

To the Ephesians he says: "Even when we were dead by

reason of our sins, [God] brought us to life together with Christ (by grace you have been saved)" (Eph. 2:5).

According to nature, we have three lives: the vegetable life of plants; the sensitive life of animals; and an intellectual life like that of the angels and of God. Grace brings us a fourth and much more precious mode of life: the supernatural life.

What is life? We must not confuse life with existence, for it is possible to exist without living. The minerals exist but they do not live. Life is a principle of spontaneous action. The living being moves itself, acts under its own impulsion, is the cause of its actions. This is not to say that it never needs the stimulus of an exterior agent, but that its acts go beyond this stimulus and are not wholly caused by it.

Life presupposes an intimate and permanent force that nourishes the being's activity, enables it to react to its states of rest or movement, to modify them, to give and to produce more than it receives, to initiate action and movement and not simply transmit it. To live is to create. You meet a friend, his body causes a reaction in your eye. The organ of sight aroused, the sense reacts and sees. An image is formed that gives rise to others. The intellect is set into motion: a thousand thoughts crowd in upon you, a thousand memories revive; the heart is stirred, sentiments are aroused. The will is awakened and commands your body to approach, your hand to shake your friend's hand, your tongue to speak and express your joy and affection. Thus there has come into being a long and perhaps intense series of actions, without proportion to the insignificant impression upon the retina that provoked them, of which you are almost the sole and total author. These actions are born of your own resources for activity, of your own life.

Life is that by which a being acts of itself, by which it does not receive all its actions from outside and does not depend totally on outside influences, but enjoys a certain spontaneity or independence.

The plant nourishes itself, draws, transforms, and assimilates life-giving sap, grows, and multiplies.

Through its own powers, the animal perceives bodies,

knows what they mean for it, flees from them or seeks them out, and performs its actions according to its image or sensible picture of these bodies. The animal has spontaneity and independence, and hence a higher degree of life.

Man knows why he acts. He knows his goal, and orders his actions with reference to it. He also has a higher degree of spontaneity and independence, and hence an added degree of life.

Life is a principle of spontaneous activity. It is a principle, something permanent that existed before the act and continues to exist after the act. It is something over which the subject has some control, from which he has only to draw in order to act, without having to seek the entire causality of his operations from the outside. We are not constantly performing acts of the sensible or intellectual life. But even when we abstain from such actions, we retain the principle of action that produces them and from which we can draw when we please without the additional intervention of an exterior agent.

This, then, is life, *the permanent principle of independence in action.* Independence and spontaneity are the consequences of the permanence of this principle. A being is not independent or self-sufficient in its action if it must receive each of its actions from the outside.

That is precisely what happens in the case of actual grace unaccompanied by sanctifying grace. As its name indicates, actual grace is directed only to the act. It begins and ends with the act, and does not remain afterwards. God is obliged to intervene each time. The soul does not bear within itself the wherewithal to act supernaturally. According to St. Thomas, the principle of the supernaturality of its acts is not connatural to it, does not belong to it and is not permanently retained. The soul that depends solely on actual graces lacks the independence and spontaneity essential to life. It does not possess supernatural life.

The case of the soul possessing sanctifying grace, and the accompanying virtues, gifts, and other supernatural helps, is altogether different. These supernatural realities dwell in the soul, and if left to themselves would remain there always unless sin forced them out.

They are the property of the soul, and it makes use of them as it pleases. Through them the soul possesses all it needs to accomplish supernatural acts as coming from its own capacities. Through them the soul is self-sufficient in its actions. It possesses supernatural spontaneity, supernatural life.

But is not life something substantial? Are not our vegetative, sensible, and intellectual life part of our very substance? How can grace, which is an accident, be a form of life? True, the principle of our natural life is substantial. It is also true that the subject of a life must be a substance.

But it is not essential to life that it be a substance. What is essential to life is that it be a principle of spontaneity in action. All the rest (whether it be substance or accident) does not enter into its concept. Now grace fully realizes this condition, as we have seen.

The possession of sanctifying grace is a *state* (we speak of being in the state of grace). But this word must suggest the idea of a stable mode and not of something immobile or inert. For if it is a state, it is also and above all an *activity*, a principle of action, *a life*.

Let us indicate two practical consequences of this fact.

1. If grace is a life, the sin that destroys it makes one die in the literal sense. To die is to lose life. (The body dies when the vegetable and sensible life cease within it.)

Since the soul is immortal in its essence, it cannot lose its natural life. But it unfortunately has the capacity to lose its supernatural life, which is not essential to it. Even one serious sin will destroy this life. In all truth, therefore, such a sin is "mortal," it is spiritual suicide. Corporeal death, the effect and punishment of sin, is also the symbol of the more disastrous death that sin inflicts upon the soul. St. Paul teaches that those who become slaves to sin by committing it find spiritual death. *Servi . . . peccati ad mortem* (cf. Rom. 6:6).

All the dead are not in their graves! There are healthy and elegantly clothed bodies, whited sepulchers, dragging around

the cadavers of souls that the sword of Satan, the murderer
(as St. John calls him) has stricken down. They are branches
cut off from the divine vine, and no longer receive its life-
giving grace. They are dried up and marked for the fire
of hell.

How important, therefore, is the avoidance of sin!

2. If grace is a life, and if every life is the principle of
action, it is all the more desirable that this action be exercised in the measure that this life is nobler, more perfect,
and more precious. Must we not, therefore, make the grace
within us pass into act as much as possible, and make our
activities participate in its value? According to the comparison our Lord has suggested (cf. Mt. 13:33), just as the
leaven mixes in with the whole mass of the dough, raises
it, warms it, transforms it and quickens it, so the divine life
within our souls must not remain an inert dignity. It must
progressively penetrate our whole being and its every activity
—to improve it, divinize it, and assimilate it to God's action,
of which grace is a participation. Divine life calls for divine
action.

The Holy Spirit is constantly working to this end in our
souls: "The Spirit also helps our weakness" (Rom. 8:26).

2. An Intense Life

The Father kindles filial love in the hearts of His adopted
children and helps them to cooperate with His action by His
actual graces and His "gifts." By these means He stimulates
their souls to an increasingly generous, more perfect, and
more fervent practice of all the virtues. Through appropriate helps, He makes the practice of the virtues more accessible and easier. He inspires them to put to use all the virtualities, all the principles of natural and supernatural action
that they possess. He invites them to a more intense activity,
a more intense life.

He continues His own interior life within their souls: His
contemplation and love, His delight in the wonders of His
own Being, the incessant relations between the Three Persons which constitute an infinitely intense activity. Within

their souls He continues to be in pure and limitless act, that is, to act with a power that surpasses anything we can conceive.

He wants to associate us to His own power of perception, love, and joy,[1] and to make us participate in it in the measure that it is compatible with our present condition. He invites us to follow His example and to plunge into this ocean of life. His presence within us is translated by an incessant call to the eternal and unceasing feast of the Three Persons in the bosom of the Trinity, to the divine banquet of the Bridegroom's wedding. And His graces draw us to it. If we were more docile to the action of grace within us, if we answered its invitations more eagerly, we could attain a most ardent spiritual life, a high degree of devotion, and fruitful activity. We need only look through the biographies of the saints to realize this, for they are incomparable in the variety and beneficence of their works, the extent of their influence, and the fullness of their interior and exterior life.

In heaven, grace will be the principle of unexcelled activity since it will be the principle of the beatific vision in which all our powers will be unceasingly in act. That is to say, all our natural and supernatural powers of action, knowledge, love, and enjoyment; all the powers of the soul, and after the resurrection, all the powers of the body. It will be an activity of which we have no idea here on earth, a participation in the infinite activity of God.

The future efficacy of grace gives us some idea of what it is already accomplishing, and what power of action, what perfection of life it gives us here and now.

---

[1] Through grace God raises His intellectual creatures up to His own level, He calls them to His eternal life of knowledge and love. "God wants the spirits He has created in His omnipotence to share in the eternal exchange of fruitful knowledge and mutual love among the divine Persons. By this very fact He makes them participate in His eternity. For eternal life is to know the Father, and the Son whom He has sent. Through this knowledge divine life is communicated to them. From that moment they participate in the very act of the Three. . . . Through the Son they can receive real, personal Love, divine Love subsisting in an absolute life. This eternal, living, and life-giving Love gives itself to creatures. It is the love of the Father for the Son, the love of the Son answering the Father's, and the mutual love of the Father and the Son. And all Three Persons love the soul in which they dwell" (Bishop Gay, *op. cit.*).

Even now grace enables us to perform actions of which no natural life is capable, actions above the strength of all creatures and that truly belong only to God. The power of this supernatural life, whose principle is grace, by far surpasses the power of every other form of life. If the just man overcomes his evil instincts, if he imposes renunciations and sacrifices upon himself, if he restrains and constrains his lower life in some measure, it is only in order to give a greater and more complete development to his superior life, the life of grace. "Every branch that bears fruit [the Father] will cleanse, that it may bear more fruit" (Jn. 15:2). He mortifies only in order to give life.

Grace, therefore, is the influx of life into our soul, a supernatural force of renewal, of spiritual growth. Like a strong plant, it tends to spread and bear fruit in acts, to form more and more perfectly within us the replica of the Only-Begotten Son.

3. A Precious Life

The life that is constituted by grace is infinitely precious, far superior to every form of natural life, and above all to the life of the body.

Plants and animals possess the life of the body, and in possessing it we do not rise above them. The life of grace makes us rise to the top of the scale of beings in another order, the divine order. Grace raises us up to God.

Do what we may, the life of the body must some day come to an end. True, this will be only for a time, but corporeal life will not be restored to us until the general resurrection. The life of grace, if we so will, will last as long as our soul—forever. It is *eternal life*. Whatever we do to nurture our life of grace has unlimited repercussions, unending effects.

The chief superiority of the life of grace is that it is the principle of incomparable happiness. We can do without our bodies. We can live without them. The possession or privation of our bodies has no essential influence on our eternal fate. Even without a body, we can—providing we have grace—enjoy the essential happiness of heaven. Without grace, on the other hand, even if we have our bodies there is only hell.

The life of grace is the most perfect that a creature can possess, the most intense, the loftiest, the most honorable, the most magnificent. It is life par excellence, life pure and simple as the Gospel calls it: *Vita.*

We must therefore prize the life of our soul more than that of our body, and fear losing it more than life of the body. And yet to what lengths we go to preserve our bodily life! What efforts, and care! The reason man works, finds lodging, clothes himself, and eats, is to prevent death. The reason he takes precautions against accidents and dangers, that he takes such pains to get well when he is sick, even when it involves great expense and heavy sacrifices, is to avoid death. It is death he dreads in the murderous implements of war, in the serpent's venom, in the assassin's dagger, in thunderbolts. He lives only in order not to die, he lives only in order to live. To live! To live! That is his unceasing quest.

Logically, should we not first strive to possess supernatural life? Should we not dread sin, that makes us lose this life, more than we fear death (for sin is more deadly), and consider sin as the greatest misfortune? When there is a conflict between the two lives, and one of them must be sacrificed, should we not prefer the life of the soul as the martyrs did? Indeed, it is never permitted to avoid temporal suffering or misfortune, or even to save one's own life or that of others, by committing a sin.

To save our lives, we sometimes resign ourselves to painful operations, or even agree to the amputation of a limb. To acquire or preserve grace, we must have the courage to demand of ourselves indispensable sacrifices, separations, and renunciations, in accordance with our Master's pressing advice: "If thy right eye is an occasion of sin to thee, pluck it out and cast it from thee; for it is better for thee that one of thy members should perish than that thy whole body should be thrown into hell. And if thy right hand is an occasion of sin to thee, cut it off. . . . (Mt. 5:29-30).

To save our lives we submit to the humiliation of revealing to a physician our own and our families' defects, we show our wounds, and confess even our most shameful weaknesses. To acquire and preserve grace, should we not be willing to confess our sins and our evil tendencies to the physician of souls, the priest?

It is up to our practical faith to orientate our urge to live toward the true life, the life that does not pass away and that makes us divine.

With every fiber of our beings, we aspire to life. There is no more fundamental, pressing, or irresistible drive. The deepest, most vehement, and most persistent of our desires is *to live,* and to live as intensely as possible.

It is through grace that we are given the power to satisfy this desire most easily and fully. Those who possess grace are more alive than others, since they possess an additional and superior life. Although there may be no outward signs of this fact, its reality is guaranteed by faith.

Dear readers, all of you—and especially those of you who are young—love life. Like young plants basking in the June sun, you sense an unknown sap boiling up within you. Your youthful faculties, your eagerness to act, your fresh young souls resemble an underground spring that seeks an outlet in order to pour itself out and do fruitful work. Or again they are like buds breaking open in the hope of producing succulent fruit. A secret instinct warns you that you have not reached maturity, that you are like seeds that have just begun to grow. You realize that vast developments are possible within you and that you are called to great progress, that you have still much to learn. An irresistible drive makes you hold your arms out to life, to a higher and more perfect life.

Many do not know how to satisfy these aspirations or are grossly mistaken as to the means to use, too often choosing only immoderate and vicious ones that lead to death. And so their souls are brought to debasement and servitude, and their bodies to usury and corruption.

But you who have the faith know where *the true life* is to be found—the incomparable supernatural life that is superior to all your desires, your hopes, and your aspirations. You know that this is the life of eternal springtime whose intense activity magnificently surpasses anything that can be observed in nature. It is the life that produces only heavenly flowers and divine fruits, the life that God Himself engrafts upon the poor wild stock of your imperfect human nature and that makes you share in His own life. You know that this life is *the life of grace*.

Epilogue and Conclusions

THE wonderful effects of sanctifying grace have many consequences which it is salutary for the soul to know and to meditate upon.

We have already pointed out several of these consequences at the end of earlier chapters.

There are still other and very important consequences.

In order not to make the present work too lengthy, we have discussed these consequences in two works which are sequels to the present study. One, *Notre trésor: La Grâce,* deals with the consequences that concern grace itself. The other volume, *L'Enfant de Dieu,* deals with the consequences that relate to the Father, whose sons we become through grace.

We shall limit ourselves to explaining two of these consequences by way of an epilogue and conclusion. The first consequence, which is more dogmatic, deals with the *nature* and the definition of habitual grace. The second, which is more mystical, concerns the incomparable *value* of habitual grace and the *high esteem* we should have for it.

1. The Nature of Grace

In the sciences, "a tree is judged by its fruit," beings by their acts. The procedure is to go from the exterior to the in-

314

terior, from operations to properties and faculties, and from these latter to nature. We know causes by their effects. That is the logical procedure.

Now that we have studied the *effects* of grace, it is possible for us to indicate its principal characteristics and to conclude to its nature, in short to propose a definition of grace.

As we have already said, the principal and fundamental effect of grace is to make us capable of seeing God face to face and of possessing Him directly. Through this effect of grace we shall be able to perceive Him as He perceives Himself, intuitively, and no longer as we perceive Him here on earth *"per speculum et in aenigmate—*through a mirror in an obscure manner"* (I Cor. 13:12). Thus grace is the principle within us of supernatural faculties of vision, love, and possession.

We are the ones who shall see God and possess Him. This action will be ours; it will proceed from us; it will belong to us as does its effect. We shall be the authors and beneficiaries of this action, just as we are of the immanent acts of our intellect and will. Several consequences flow from this fact, of which we shall enumerate the principal ones.

Grace is a *spiritual* reality. The faculty, the act, and the object of the act are necessarily of the same nature. The effect (the act) cannot be superior to its cause (the faculty); and the faculties (as well as their acts) are specified by their object.

Since God is pure Spirit, our vision will likewise be spiritual; and grace, the principle of this vision, must also be spiritual as are the soul and the faculty that it elevates to the capacity for this vision.

It follows that only intellectual creatures capable of spiritual acts (the angels and men) can be adorned with grace. Animals, plants, and minerals are incapable of it.

Grace is necessarily a *physical* reality,[1] and not merely a

---

[1] It should be noted that *physical* is not synonymous with *material*. The word "physical" is not here opposed to spiritual, but to "moral." The intellect, the will, the soul are physical as well as spiritual realities. The same is true of grace.

reality of the moral order as in the Protestants' concept that grace is an imputation of Christ's merits. If grace changed nothing within the soul, if it deposited in it no new principle of action, how could we become capable of the act of vision which, being both physical and supernatural, presupposes a physical and supernatural faculty (the mere imputation of merits adds nothing to the soul and confers no new capacity upon it)?

Grace must also be something *intrinsic* to the soul, deeply implanted within it (although distinct from it), forming in union with the soul a single principle of operations, belonging to it completely, stemming from the same person, and "inherent" to its substance.

If grace were purely extrinsic and came only from God— as in the case of the Protestant "imputation"—we would not be the ones who saw and possessed God, but on the contrary He would see and delight in Himself. Such a conception amounts to denying that the just have the power to go to heaven.

This would also seem to be the consequence of the view held by certain theologians (including Peter Lombard) who identify grace with the Holy Spirit. If this were the case, God would see and enjoy Himself, but we would not see and enjoy Him. The act of vision and enjoyment would not be ours. But St. Paul assures us that *we* shall see and know Him: "We see now through a mirror in an obscure manner, but then face to face. Now I know in part, but then I shall know even as I have been known" (I Cor. 13:12). Therefore grace deposits within us a faculty of vision that is truly our own; it is intrinsic to the soul.

Grace also has a third characteristic: *it is distinct from God*. Certainly it attracts God to us, it is something of Him, a participation in His nature. But it is not God Himself. This truth is theologically certain, the conclusion of the teachings of the Council of Trent: "The single formal cause [of justification] is the justice [the grace] of God, not that by which He Himself is just, but that by which He makes us just" (Session VI, Chapter 7). Consequently, it is distinct from Him inasmuch as it is distinct from His own justice, that is, from Himself.

Moreover, this same Council has defined that grace can increase. But how could it increase if it were God Himself? For He is absolutely immutable: *Immotus in te permanens.*

We have seen that the sacred writers call grace a seed, a birth, a new life received from God. But is not seed, the life received, always distinct from the one who gives it? To be born of God and to become His children we must either possess His divine nature in common with Him as the Son possesses the divine nature in common with the Father (but this is impossible for us), or we must receive from Him a reproduction of His nature, distinct from it. Grace is such a reproduction.

Between Creator and creature, there is no middle ground. Everything that is not God is a creature. Therefore grace is something created (in the sense that we shall explain later).

Distinct from God, grace is also distinct from the soul and its faculties (by virtue of a real distinction). The very obvious reason for this is that the soul can subsist without possessing grace (as is the case before baptism or after sin has destroyed grace), without undergoing any change in its nature or ceasing to exist.

If grace and the soul were identified, they would be absolutely inseparable. We would receive grace with life and we could never lose it. It would belong to the very substance of the soul, which, being simple and indivisible, cannot be deprived of one of its elements without ceasing to exist.

It would also follow that both the soul and grace would be of the same order. Either they would both be supernatural (and the soul cannot be supernatural in itself), or they would both be natural (and this, grace is not).

That is also why grace cannot be *a substance.* It cannot be a complete substance (i.e., one that does not enter into composition with any other and that constitutes a distinct and independent person). Such a supernatural being would be identical with God. Grace is added to our substance, stems from our personality, and constitutes a single principle of action in union with the soul.

Nor can grace be an incomplete substance, that is, an element of the substance of the soul. Since the soul is simple in itself, it cannot be composed of substantial elements.

Besides, the soul could not exist without grace if grace were one of its constituent elements. And we know that such is not the case.

Since grace is not a substance, it is an *accident* in the scholastic sense of the word: something that is joined to, added to, that supervenes (*accidit*) within a subject, within a substance, and thereby modifies it. A being must of necessity be either a substance or an accident. The Council of Trent explicitly declares that grace "inheres in the soul"— *gratia animae inherens.* This is evident inasmuch as grace "supervenes" in a soul after its essence has already been constituted and after it has begun to exist.

To what "category of accidents" does grace belong? Does it belong among the accidents that matter presupposes: quantity, time, place, and location? No, for grace is spiritual. Does it belong to the category of transitory things: action or passion? Again, no. Grace is a permanent principle, it is "habitual." Nor does it belong to the category of "relations," which are moral and not absolute physical realities like itself.

There is still the category of *quality* to consider. Among the qualities, grace comes closest to the species known as *habitus,* without adequately fulfilling the definition of a *habitus.* Actually the *habitus* modifies a being *"in accordance with its nature—secundum propriam naturam,"* whereas grace raises man above his nature. Hence grace is a *quality* only in an incomplete, analogical sense. There is nothing quite like it in created nature: it is unique in its genus.

Now we have said that grace is a *permanent* "accident." It remains in the soul as long as sin has not driven it out. It is not transitory like actual grace, which is given for a specific act and ends with it. That is what we mean when we say that sanctifying grace is *"habitual."*

We know that Scripture considers grace as the effect of a birth, a regeneration, and as it were a life, the source of a divine sonship and divine likeness; and all these notions express permanence, stability, duration.

The Council of Trent teaches that grace can increase, and this presupposes that it remains within us.

If grace were only a transitory act, children incapable of spiritual acts could not receive it, and yet they do receive grace in baptism.

And above all grace is something *supernatural,* that is, something that is above "the nature, the strength, and the demands of all created beings." It is the pure effect of God's love. As we have already seen, the definition of man includes the intellect and the will as essential components of man, but it does not include grace. One can be a man without grace—before receiving it and after losing it. The catechumen is a man before his baptism; the sinner is a man, too, after his sin. Grace can be added to or it can be lacking to a human being without essentially modifying his nature. It does not enter into the constituent and necessary elements of his essence as a man.

Grace is above nature; it raises it to a superior order without robbing it of any of its natural perfections. It is supernatural, since it renders human nature capable of an operation—the beatific vision—which is natural only to God.

Grace is purely gratuitous. It is a gift, as its name—chosen by the Holy Spirit—indicates: *gratia.* This is the great idea that St. Paul stresses in all his teaching, and in a special way in his Epistles to the Romans and to the Galatians against the Judaizers who attributed salvation and justification to the works of the Mosaic Law. He vigorously affirms that justice (grace) does not come from our works, that is, from ourselves, but from Christ alone, providing we have faith in Him: "[We] are justified freely by His grace through the redemption which is in Christ Jesus" (Rom. 3:24). "And if out of grace, then not in virtue of works; otherwise grace is no longer grace" (Rom. 11:6). Its very name—gratuitous gift —indicates it.

Like St. John (cf. I Jn. 3), St. Paul sees in the gift of grace, and in salvation or vision of which grace is the principle, the effect of God's great mercy and admirable love for us: "But

God, who is rich in mercy, by reason of His very great love
wherewith He has loved us even when we were dead by
reason of our sins, brought us to life together with Christ
(by grace you have been saved) . . . that He might show in
the ages to come the overflowing riches of His grace in kind-
ness towards us in Christ Jesus. For by grace you have been
saved through faith; and that not from yourselves, for it is
the gift of God; nor as the outcome of works, lest anyone
may boast. For His workmanship we are, created in Christ
Jesus" (Eph. 2:4-10). Each sentence here is an affirmation
of the supernatural gratuitousness of grace.

Being supernatural, and hence above the powers of all
created beings—for whatever is above a nature is also above
its powers: *operari sequitur esse*—grace must necessarily be
produced in its entirety by *God*. It cannot be drawn from
pre-existing matter, since it is immaterial.[2]

Sanctifying grace is a spiritual, physical, intrinsic principle, distinct from God and from the soul, an accident of
the genus quality, permanent and supernatural in its essence and in its cause.

It might be defined as follows:

*Sanctifying grace is a supernatural life that makes us heirs
of heaven, partakers of the nature of God and sons of God,
temples of the Blessed Trinity, capable of performing supernatural and meritorious acts.*

This definition calls to mind the principal effects of grace
(that we have studied and to which the others are related),

---

[2] Can it be said that grace is created? For a thing to be defined as "created"
in the strict sense of the word, three conditions are required:

(1) It must be produced by God, at least as its principal efficient cause;

(2) it must be produced in its entirety, without being drawn from any
pre-existing matter: it must be produced from nothing—*ex nihilo sui;*

(3) it must be produced *ex nihilo subjecti,* that is, without having to be
received in a subject, and hence it cannot be an "accident."

The production of grace realizes the first two conditions: its author is
God, and it is not the terminus of a change in pre-existing matter. However
it lacks the third condition: *ex nihilo subjecti,* for grace is not a substance.

However the presence of the first two conditions—which are the most important ones—makes it permissible to say that grace is a creature, as Scripture
does: *nova creatura;* and also to call the Holy Spirit who produces grace
Creator Spiritus—Creator-Spirit.

and implies those of its characteristics that we have just enumerated.

We say that grace is *a life that makes us heirs of heaven* or of the beatific vision. Therefore it is something spiritual, physical, intrinsic, and permanent.

It is a *supernatural* life. Therefore it "supervenes" in the soul after its human essence has been constituted. It is added to the soul's natural life, and therefore is an accident.

It is a *supernatural* life, including everything necessary to produce supernatural acts (faculties of the supernatural order, the infused virtues), and also to defend itself and to grow (actual graces and gifts). And supernatural acts are those that give glory to God and that win from Him a reward of the same order.

This entire work has been the elaboration of the above definition.

2. The Value of Grace

The value of grace is made evident: a) by its effects; b) by the esteem that Christ, the Blessed Virgin, and the Church have for it.

Grace occupies the highest place among all created values, and is far superior to them. There is in grace, and hence in the just man, more perfection, more being, more genuine riches, more real goodness, than in all the rest of the universe.

Here are some of the things that grace can win for us: grace gives us access to heaven; it is the principle of our eternal happiness; it is the seed of glory; it unites us to God even now in an ineffable manner, and later on it will unite us to Him face to face. Grace is worth as much to us as the precious effects it produces in our souls and the incomparable riches it brings us.

Grace places the just man far above his fellows who are in the state of sin. It raises him up to a superior order, the divine order. It confers a divine dignity upon him.

Through grace, the just man possesses a new life, infinitely more perfect than any natural life, a participation in the life of God Himself, and supernatural faculties that are the principles of supernatural operations.

The just man can do great things of which others are incapable. In the next life he will be able to see God intuitively, as He sees Himself, and enjoy Him proportionately. Here on earth, he can glorify Him and exert great power over His heart. He can depend on God's paternal presence, tenderness, and solicitude. He can make satisfaction and gain merit. That is to say, he can give to even his most commonplace actions a superhuman grandeur and fruitfulness. Through grace he can rise as high as he wants among created beings. He can ennoble, enrich, and develop his being, and constantly add new perfections to it. Through grace, his field of action is vast. Great as his ambitions may be, he will never reach their limits.

The Psalmist has compared the just man to a palm tree and to a cedar: "The just shall flourish like the palm tree: he shall grow up like the cedar of Libanus" (Ps. 91:13). These are the two most beautiful trees of the East. The palm tree, with its powerful trunk that seems to have sprung up all at once, its abundant flowers and fruits, its fronds that are always green, contrasts with the burning sands of the desert where it grows and offers the weary traveler its beneficent shade. The cedar, the giant of the mountains, defies hurricanes and spreads out its strong branches against the wind.

The trees that had been planted within the enclosure of the Temple received a sort of veneration. They were given every care and surpassed all other trees in vigor, luxuriance, and fertility. These were the trees to which the inspired poet compared men in the state of grace:

> Planted in the house of the Lord
>   they flourish in the courts of our God:
> In old age they shall still be fruitful,
>   green-growing, full of vigor.
>   (Ps. 91:14-15.)

Likewise the passing of the years, far from weakening the fruitfulness of the soul in the state of grace, merely increases it. Such a soul knows neither decline nor old age. Its life is an uninterrupted and prodigious growth until it reaches its full bloom in glory and the blessed possession of God.

That is the wonderful efficacy of grace.

And Christ paid His Father a high price to acquire it for us. In the words of St. Paul, "you have been bought at a great price" (I Cor. 6:20). And St. Peter continues: "You were redeemed . . . not . . . with silver or gold, but with the precious blood of Christ, as of a lamb without blemish and without spot" (I Pet. 1:18-19). Christ paid for grace with His life. Life is worth more than all the goods of this earth. This is even truer of the life of a God-Man, of a being who possesses knowledge, holiness, genius, mercy—in fact every perfection—in an eminent degree. Even though His life was beyond price, He deemed it of less worth than grace since He was willing to die in order to win grace for us. And what a death He died!

Grace is worth the blood of a God.

And not only did He unhesitatingly pay for grace with His life, but He looked upon grace as the goal of every instant that made up His life, the goal of His Incarnation, of His apostolate among us, of all the institutions that He left behind.

He came to give the life of grace to those who did not have it, and to give it more abundantly to those who already had it (cf. Jn. 10:10).

The effect of the sacraments that He instituted is to confer grace. Baptism gives grace, Penance restores it; the Eucharist in particular increases it; Holy Orders communicates it. And all the sacraments safeguard it.

Such is also the purpose of the Church that He instituted and endowed with supernatural prerogatives to this end; the purpose of the revealed doctrine and moral teaching that He left us. The conferring of grace is the purpose of His unceasing action within souls and in the world. It is the stakes of the gigantic battle that He and His Church have been waging through the ages against the powers of evil that are relentlessly striving to destroy grace. The history of religion, and in the last analysis all history, is nothing but the history of God's action on behalf of grace.

This does not surprise us when we know what grace brings us.

No, it is not surprising that grace is the greatest good that Christ could, and willed to, offer to His Mother, to the creature chosen among all His favored creatures, to the one who was destined to form His body. Inasmuch as the inferiority of a mother reflects upon her son, filial love and concern for His dignity demanded that He give her in abundance His greatest riches, all that He knew was best and most precious. Now what did He give His Mother? Wealth? She was born poor and remained poor all her life, a woman of the people, obliged to work for a living. Did He give her honors? Until her death, hers was the most hidden, the humblest life. Did He give her pleasures? We cannot so much as speak of them with reference to the one who is rightly called the Queen of martyrs, the Mother of Sorrows, and whose whole life was a long immolation.

These passing goods do not count in God's eyes. He recognizes only one good, infinitely superior to all others, one good that is proportionate to His filial love, one good whose eminent dignity He had decreed to bestow upon Mary: *sanctifying grace*. He chose to bestow it upon her from the moment of her conception, from the first instant of her life, so that she received it together with life and was never one moment without possessing it. He conferred grace upon her in a degree that placed her above all other creatures (except her own Son), and that made her *"full of grace."* This is the privilege of her Immaculate Conception considered in its positive aspect. This is the greatest and best gift that His infinite power and His loving desire to give her the fullest measure of all good things were able to discover. This is the most precious gift, the highest honor, the most outstanding favor He chose to bestow upon her. This, then, is how He esteems *grace*. And we should esteem it no less than He.

The Church has made Christ's high regard for grace her own. She considers the Blessed Virgin's singular privilege one of her most magnificent titles to glory. Through the solemn definition of Pope Pius IX on December 8, 1854, she took the trouble to affirm this truth. To celebrate the anniversary of this proclamation, she instituted a feast of the first class and composed in its honor an office overflowing with affectionate enthusiasm.

And this gesture proved so pleasing to the One whom it honored that she approved and confirmed it, so to speak, by calling herself *"the Immaculate Conception"* at Lourdes. For the past century she has continued to answer to this name by a series of miraculous favors that seem to be unabated. This is an incontestable sign of the joy it brings her to see her earthly children recognize this glorious prerogative, and of the high value she places on grace.

If it had been necessary, she could have understood the value of grace by the words and gestures of the Angel of the Annunciation. For the first time in Scripture, a heavenly spirit humbled himself before a human creature. The Angel Gabriel greeted her first and with deepest respect: *Ave!* (cf. Lk. 1:28).

Why? What was there about Mary to inspire so much veneration from such a lofty personage? He himself gave the answer: *Gratia plena* (full of grace). She possessed the fullness of grace in time, for she had possessed it from the beginning of her existence and preserved it without interruption. She possessed the fullness of grace with regard to its intensity. She has a maximum of grace that men will never attain. Full of grace! God's messenger could find no more glorious title for the future Mother of the Word.

The Church, like her Founder, concentrates her efforts upon grace. To procure grace to those who do not have it, to help those who possess it to preserve and increase it within them, to make known the necessity and the splendors of grace: this is the principal purpose of all her actions, and especially of her sacraments and of her teaching. Her dream is to keep all her members in the state of grace and to perfect them in it, meanwhile drawing others toward grace. She can say with our Savior: "I came that they may have life, and have it more abundantly" (Jn. 10:10).

Through the powerful voices of her bells, the Church

sings out her delight when she has just conferred grace upon someone through the sacrament of regeneration. Christians should join in her joy, and celebrate the anniversary of their baptism as the principal and happiest event of their lives.

After the example of Christ, the Blessed Virgin, and the Church, they should have the highest esteem for grace. For grace is by far their most precious possession. Whoever possesses it is richer than the world's richest men. A single degree of grace is worth more than all the gold in the universe.[3] This is the treasure that our Lord speaks of, that we must amass eagerly and cling to with our hearts, that neither worms nor rust can destroy nor thieves steal. To acquire and preserve it, we must be willing to sell and sacrifice all the rest if that is necessary (cf. Mt. 6:10,21; 13:44).

*   *   *

During World War I, the French troops in certain sectors of Alsace had to be revictualled by means of aerial transports somewhat like Alpine cable cars. Baskets were carried along a steel cable held up by iron posts. These baskets, spaced a few meters apart, were filled with provisions: coal, wheat, meat, munitions, etc. When they had climbed over the Vosges Mountains and down the other side, they would drop their precious cargoes near the lines, one after the other.

That is a picture of life. Our days are carried along on the chain of time which marches on irresistibly. They come to our souls to be filled, and return to the granaries of heaven to unload their supernatural riches and stock up our eternity.

We should take the greatest care to fill our heavenly bins to overflowing through meritorious works (and the reception of the sacraments, especially the Holy Eucharist), accom-

---

[3] We all know the following famous passage from Pascal's *Pensées:* "All bodies, the firmament, the stars, the earth and all its kingdoms are not worth the least of the spirits. All bodies and spirits and all their works are not worth the slightest movement of charity. From all bodies no one could succeed in expressing the smallest idea, that is impossible and belongs to another order. From all bodies and spirits no one could draw a movement of true charity, that is impossible and of another, the supernatural order." (Editions Brunschvieg, p. 697).

Charity and grace go together, and here they are used interchangeably.

plished with the best possible dispositions. We should gather up while there is time, for life is short.

Pour forth, we beseech Thee, O Lord, Thy grace into our hearts, that we . . . may be brought to the glory of . . . resurrection. (Prayer of the Angelus).